THE WORKS OF
ALEXANDRE DUMAS
IN THIRTY VOLUMES

❧

THE PAGE OF THE DUKE OF SAVOY
VOLUME ONE

❧

ILLUSTRATED WITH DRAWINGS ON WOOD BY
EMINENT FRENCH AND AMERICAN ARTISTS

Copyright © 2013 Read Books Ltd.
This book is copyright and may not be
reproduced or copied in any way without
the express permission of the publisher in writing

British Library Cataloguing-in-Publication Data
A catalogue record for this book is available from the
British Library

Alexandre Dumas

Alexandre Dumas was born in Villers-Cotterêts, France in 1802. His parents were poor, but their heritage and good reputation – Alexandre's father had been a general in Napoleon's army – provided Alexandre with opportunities for good employment. In 1822, Dumas moved to Paris to work for future king Louis Philippe I in the Palais Royal. It was here that he began to write for magazines and the theatre.

In 1829 and 1830 respectively, Dumas produced the plays *Henry III and His Court* and *Christine,* both of which met with critical acclaim and financial success. As a result, he was able to commit himself full-time to writing. Despite the turbulent economic times which followed the Revolution of 1830, Dumas turned out to have something of an entrepreneurial streak, and did well for himself in this decade. He founded a production studio that turned out hundreds of stories under his creative direction, and began to produce serialised novels for newspapers which were widely read by the French public. It was over the next two decades, as a now famous and much loved author of romantic and adventuring sagas, that Dumas produced his best-known works – the D'Artagnan romances, including *The Three Musketeers,* in 1844, and *The Count of Monte Cristo,* in 1846.

Dumas made a lot of money from his writing, but

he was almost constantly penniless as a result of his extravagant lifestyle and love of women. In 1851 he fled his creditors to Belgium, and then Russia, and then Italy, not returning to Paris until 1864. Dumas died in Puys, France, in 1870, at the age of 68. He is now enshrined in the Panthéon of Paris alongside fellow authors Victor Hugo and Emile Zola. Since his death, his fiction has been translated into almost a hundred languages, and has formed the basis for more than 200 motion pictures.

CONTENTS

FIRST PART

	PAGE
I. WHAT A MAN, IF PLACED ON THE HIGHEST TOWER OF HESDIN-FERT, MIGHT HAVE SEEN ON THE 5TH OF MAY, 1555, AT ABOUT TWO O'CLOCK IN THE AFTERNOON	5
II. THE ADVENTURERS	12
III. IN WHICH THE READER MAKES THE MOST AMPLE ACQUAINTANCE WITH THE HEROES WE HAVE INTRODUCED TO HIM	24
IV. THE DEED OF PARTNERSHIP	34
V. COUNT WALDECK	45
VI. THE JUSTICIARY	54
VII. HISTORY AND ROMANCE	66
VIII. SQUIRE AND PAGE	81
IX. LEONE-LEONA	90
X. THE THREE MESSAGES	104
XI. ODOARDO MARAVIGLIA	119
XII. WHAT PASSED IN THE DUNGEON OF THE FORTRESS OF MILAN ON THE NIGHT OF THE 14TH AND 15TH OF NOVEMBER, 1534	129
XIII. THE DEMON OF THE SOUTH	143
XIV. IN WHICH CHARLES V. KEEPS THE PROMISE MADE TO HIS SON DON PHILIP	155
XV. AFTER THE ABDICATION	182

CONTENTS

SECOND PART

		PAGE
I.	The Court of France	195
II.	The King's Hunt	209
III.	Constable and Cardinal	224
IV.	War	238
V.	In which the Reader finds himself again in a Country he knows something of	255
VI.	Saint-Quentin	264
VII.	The Admiral keeps his Word	278
VIII.	The Tent of the Adventurers	288
IX.	A Fight	296
X.	M. de Théligny	307
XI.	The Awaking of M. le Connétable	316
XII.	The Escalade	324

THE
PAGE OF THE DUKE OF SAVOY

FIRST PART

I

WHAT A MAN, IF PLACED ON THE HIGHEST TOWER OF HESDIN-FERT, MIGHT HAVE SEEN ON THE 5TH OF MAY, 1555, AT ABOUT TWO O'CLOCK IN THE AFTERNOON

LET us at once transport, without further preface or preamble, those of our readers who do not fear to take a leap of three centuries across the past in our company, into the presence of men we would have them know, and into the midst of events we would have them witness.

The time is the 5th of May, of the year 1555. Henry II. is reigning over France; Mary Tudor over England; Charles V. over Spain, Germany, Flanders, Italy, and the two Indies —that is to say, over a sixth part of the world.

The scene opens in the neighborhood of the little town of Hesdin-Fert, which Emmanuel Philibert, Prince of Piedmont, has lately rebuilt, intending it to take the place of Hesdin-la-Vieux, captured by him last year, and razed to the ground. So you see we are travelling in that part of old France which was then called Artois, and which is known to-day as the department of the Pas-de-Calais.

We say of old France, because Artois did actually become a portion of the patrimony of our kings under Philippe-Auguste, the conqueror of Saint-Jean-d'Acre and Bouvines; but, though it formed a part of France in

1180, and was given by Saint Louis to his younger brother, Robert, in 1237, it afterward lapsed, somehow or other, into the hands of three women—Mahaud, Jeanne I., and Jeanne II.—thus falling under the control of three different houses. Then, with Marguerite, sister of Jeanne II. and daughter of Jeanne I., it passed to Comte Louis de Mâle, whose daughter brought it, together with the counties of Flanders and Nevers, into the house of the Dukes of Burgundy.

Finally, after the death of Charles the Bold, Mary of Burgundy, the last heiress of the gigantic name and immense possessions of her father, made, on the day she married Maximilian, son of the Emperor Frederick III., both name and possessions part and parcel of the domains of the house of Austria, in which they were swallowed up, as a river is swallowed up in the ocean.

It was a great loss for France, for Artois is a fine and rich province. Consequently, for three years, with varying fortunes and unforeseen results, Henry II. and Charles V. have been struggling face to face, and foot to foot, the one to regain, the other to keep it.

During the furious war in which the son encountered the old enemy of the father, and, like the father, was to have his Marignano and Pavia, each had his good and bad days, his victories and defeats. France had seen the army of Charles V. driven in disorder from the siege of Metz, and had taken Marienbourg, Bouvines and Dinant; the Empire, on the other hand, had stormed Thérouanne and Hesdin, and, furious at its defeat before Metz, had burned the one, and levelled the other to the ground.

We have compared Metz to Marignano, and the comparison is not exaggerated. An army of fifty thousand infantry and fourteen thousand cavalry, decimated by cold and disease, had vanished like a mist, leaving as the sole trace of its existence ten thousand dead, two thousand tents and a hundred and twenty cannon!

So great was the demoralization that the fugitives did

not even try to defend themselves. Charles of Bourbon was pursuing a body of Spanish cavalry; the captain who commanded it halted and rode straight up to the hostile leader.

"Prince, duke, or simple gentleman," he said, "or whatever else you be, if you are fighting for glory, seek it elsewhere; for to-day you are butchering men too feeble to fly, even, far less to resist you."

Charles of Bourbon sheathed his sword, and ordered his men to do the same; and the Spanish captain and his troop continued their retreat without being further troubled by them.

Charles V. was very far from imitating such clemency. When Thérouanne was taken, he ordered it to be delivered up to pillage and razed to the ground. Not only were the private houses destroyed, but even the churches, monasteries, and hospitals; not a vestige of a wall was left standing, and that there might not be one stone left on another, the inhabitants of Flanders and Artois were called in to scatter all that remained.

The summons was eagerly obeyed. The garrison of Thérouanne had been a thorn in the side of the people around, and they flocked to it, armed with spades, hammers and pickaxes, which they plied with such goodwill that the city disappeared like Saguntum under the feet of Hannibal, or Carthage before the breath of Scipio.

Hesdin was treated in the same way as Thérouanne.

But, in the meanwhile, Emmanuel Philibert had been named commander-in-chief of the troops of the Empire in the Low Countries, and, if he could not save Thérouanne, he was at least able to rebuild Hesdin.

He had accomplished this immense work in a few months, and a new city sprang up as if by enchantment, a quarter of a league from the old. This new city, planted in the middle of the swamps of the Mesnil, on the banks of the Canche, was so well fortified that it excited the admiration of Vauban a hundred and fifty years after, although, during the course of these one hundred and fifty years the system of fortification had entirely changed.

Its founder called it Hesdin-*Fert;* that is to say, he had joined, in order to compel the new city to remember its origin, these four letters to its name, F. E. R. T., given with the white cross by the Emperor of Germany, after the siege of Rhodes, to Amadeus the Great, thirteenth count of Savoy; they signified: *Fortitudo ejus Rhodum tenuit,* which means, "His valor saved Rhodes."

But this was not the only miracle wrought by the promotion of the young general to whom Charles V. had just confided his army. Thanks to the rigid discipline which he established, the unhappy country, which for four years had been the theatre of war, was beginning to breathe; the severest orders were given to prevent pillaging and marauding; every officer guilty of disobedience was disarmed and imprisoned in his tent for a longer or shorter period, in sight of the whole army, and every private, taken in the act, was hanged.

The result was that, as hostilities had very nearly ceased on both sides, during the winter of 1554 and 1555, the last four or five months seemed to the inhabitants of Artois, when compared with the years that had elapsed between the siege of Metz and the reconstruction of Hesdin, something like a golden age.

There was still, now and then, some castle burned here and there, some farm pillaged, or house plundered, either by the French, who held Abbeville, Doullens and Montreuil-sur-Mer, and who ventured on excursions into the enemy's territory, or by the incorrigible marauders, reiters and gypsies who hovered on the outskirts of the imperial army; but Emmanuel Philibert was so successful in clearing the country of the French, and dealt such rough justice to his own soldiers that these catastrophies were becoming daily more rare. Such, then, was the condition of the province of Artois, and especially in the neighborhood of Hesdin-Fert, on the day when our story opens; that is to say, the 5th of May, 1555.

But after giving our readers a rapid sketch of the moral and political state of the country, it remains for us, in order to complete the picture, to give them an idea of its material aspect—an aspect that has totally changed since that period, thanks to the invasions of manufactures and the improvements in agriculture.

In order to accomplish this difficult task, and revive a past that has almost vanished, let us try to depict the scene which would meet the gaze of a spectator standing with his back to the sea on the loftiest tower of Hesdin, and having under his eyes the horizon, extending in a semicircle from the northern extremity of the little chain of hills which hides Béthune, to the last southern bluffs of the same chain at the foot of which Doullens rises.

He would have first, in front of him, advancing in a point toward the banks of the Canche, the thick and gloomy forest of Saint-Pol-sur-Ternoise, whose vast green foliage, spread like a mantle over the shoulders of the hills, continued until its borders were dipped in the sources of the Scarpe, which is to the Scheldt what the Moselle is to the Rhine.

To the right of this forest, and, as a consequence, to the left of the observer we are imagining placed on the loftiest tower of Hesdin, at the back of the plain, sheltered by the same hills that bound the horizon, the villages of Enchin and Fruges indicated, by the bluish clouds of smoke which enveloped them like a transparent mist or translucent veil, that the chilly natives of these northern provinces had not yet bid adieu, in spite of the appearance of the first days of spring, to their kitchen fires, those jovial and comforting friends of the days of winter.

In front of these two villages, and not unlike a half-distrustful sentinel, who, though he has ventured to leave the forest, still thinks it better to keep close to its border, rose a pretty little dwelling, half chateau and half farm, called the Parcq.

A road, which shimmered like a gold ribbon on the green robe of the plain, might be seen stretching for some distance from the entrance to the farm, and then dividing into two branches, the one running straight to Hesdin, the other skirting the forest and connecting the dwellers in the Parcq with the villages of Frévent, Auxy-le-Chateau, and Nouvion in Ponthieu.

The plain, extending from these three places to Hesdin, formed the basin opposite the one we have just described; that is to say, it was situated to the left of the basin of the forest of Saint-Pol, and, consequently, to the right of the imaginary spectator who has been our cicerone so far.

It was the most remarkable part of the landscape, not by any means on account of the natural features of the ground, but because of the fortuitous circumstances that gave it animation at the present moment.

In truth, while the opposite plain was covered with ripening harvests, this was almost entirely hidden by the camp of the Emperor Charles V.

This camp, surrounded by ditches, and hemmed in by palisades, included an entire city, not of houses, but of tents.

From the centre of these tents rose the imperial pavilion of Charles V., like Notre Dame de Paris in the Cité, like the palace of the popes in Avignon, or like a three-decker in the midst of the crested waves of the ocean. At its four corners floated four standards, one of which ought to have sufficed human ambition: the standard of the Empire, the standard of Spain, the standard of Rome, and the standard of Lombardy; for this hero, this conqueror, this victor, as he was called, had been crowned four times—at Toledo, with the crown of diamonds, as King of Spain and the Indies; at Aix-la-Chapelle, with the crown of silver, as Emperor of Germany; and, in fine, at Bologna, with the golden crown, as King of the Romans, and the iron crown, as King of the Lombards. And when an attempt was made to have his coronation take place at Rome and Milan instead of Bologna, when it was shown to him that the brief of Pope Stephen forbade the golden crown to be taken from the Vatican, and the decree of the Emperor Charlemagne prohibited the iron crown from leaving Monza, the haughty reply of this conqueror of François I. and Luther and Soliman was that it was his custom not to run after crowns, but to have crowns run after him.

And note well that these four standards were surmounted by his own standard, which pictured the Pillars of Hercules no longer as the limits of the Old World, but as the gateway of the New, and flung forth to all the winds of heaven this ambitious device, grown more portentously large by its very mutilation, *Plus ultra!*

At about fifty yards from the emperor's pavilion stood the tent of the commander-in-chief, Emmanuel Philibert, not distinguishable from those of the other captains, except that it bore two standards: one bearing the arms of Savoy—a silver cross on a ground *gules*, with these four letters, whose meaning we have already explained, F. E. R. T.; and the other, his own private arms, representing a hand raising to heaven a trophy composed of lances, swords and pistols, with this device, *Spoliatis arma supersunt;* that is to say, "Arms are still left to the despoiled."

The camp, which these two tents overlooked, was divided into four quarters, in the midst of which crept the river, crossed by three bridges. The first quarter was intended for the Germans; the second for the Spaniards; the third for the English. The fourth contained the park of artillery, entirely renewed since the defeat of Metz, and raised to the number of a hundred and twenty cannons and fifteen bombards, by the addition of the pieces taken from the French at Thérouanne and Hesdin.

On the breech of those taken from the French, the emperor had engraved his two favorite words, *Plus ultra!* Behind the cannons and bombards were ranged, in three lines, the caissons and wagons containing the military stores; sentinels with drawn swords, but without arquebuse or pistol, were there to see that no one approached these volcanoes, which a single spark would make burst forth in flame.

Other sentinels were stationed outside the inclosure.

In the streets of the camp, regulated like those of a city, thousands of men were moving about with military activity, tempered, nevertheless, by German gravity, Spanish pride, and English moroseness.

The sun was glinting on all these arms, which sent back his rays in flashes; the wind played with all these standards and banners and pennons, furling and unfurling their silky folds and brilliant colors at its own sweet will.

This activity and noise, which always ruffle the surface of multitudes and of oceans, formed a striking contrast to the silence and solitude on the other side of the plain, where the sun only lighted up the shifting mosaic of the harvests, then at different stages of maturity, and where the wind stirred those rustic flowers which young girls delight to weave into purple and azure garlands wherewith to adorn themselves on Sundays.

And now that we have devoted the first chapter of our book to a description of what would have met the eyes of an observer stationed on the highest tower of Hesdin-Fert at any time during the 5th of May, 1555, let us devote the second chapter to certain things that would have escaped his eyes, however piercing they might be.

II

THE ADVENTURERS

THE things that would have escaped his eyes, however piercing they might be, were taking place in the thickest, and consequently gloomiest spot in the forest of Saint-Pol-sur-Ternoise, at the back of a grotto which the trees enveloped with their shade and the ivy with its network; while for the greater security of the present occupants of this grotto, a sentinel, hidden in the brushwood, lying flat on his stomach, and as motionless as one of the trunks on the ground around him, was watching to see that no profane eye disturbed the important conventicle, to which, however, we, in our capacity of romancer—that is to say, magician before whom all doors are thrown open— propose introducing our readers.

Let us take advantage of the moment when the sentinel, who has not seen us, but whom we have discovered, turns his eyes in the direction of the noise made by a frightened goat bounding through a brake, to glide, unperceived, into the grotto, and follow in its slightest details the incident occurring there, sheltered, as we are, behind a rocky projection.

This grotto is occupied by eight men, differing in face, costume, and temper, although, from the arms they bear, or which lie on the ground within reach of their hands, it is clear they have adopted the same calling.

One of them, with ink-stained fingers and a sly, crafty countenance, is dipping his pen—with the nib of which he smooths out one of those hairs to be found on the surface of badly made paper—in an inkhorn such as law-clerks, ushers, and copyists then wore at the girdle, and is writing on a makeshift stone table propped on two massive supports; while another, holding a burning pine branch, is illuminating not only the writer, table, and paper, but also himself and his six other companions with more or less brilliancy, according to their proximity or remoteness.

Undoubtedly the document in question must be interesting to the company at large, seeing the ardor with which they severally take part in its concoction.

Three of them, however, seem less taken up than the others with this purely material concern.

The first is a handsome young man, about twenty-four or twenty-five years old, elegantly clad in a cuirass of buffalo-hide, proof against sword and dagger surely, if not against a bullet. A maroon velvet jacket, a little faded undoubtedly, but still very presentable, after disclosing, at the shoulder, a sleeve cut after the Spanish style—that is to say, after the latest fashion—fell about the length of four fingers below the jerkin, falling in ample folds over breeches of green cloth, also of the newest mode, and lost in a pair of boots high enough to protect the thighs on horseback, and soft and pliant enough to sink down below the knees when the wearer is on foot.

He is humming a rondeau of Clément Marot, all the time twisting his black silky mustache with one hand, and combing, with the other, his hair, which he wears a little longer than was fashionable at the period, evidently with the object of turning to the best account the soft wavy locks with which Nature had endowed him.

The second is a man scarcely thirty-six years old; only he has a face so scarred and furrowed by wounds that it is impossible to assign him any age. His arm and a portion of his chest are bare; and on whatever part of his body happens to be exposed to view, a series of scars may be observed, quite as numerous as those that adorn his visage. He is engaged in attending to a wound which has denuded a part of the biceps; luckily, the wound is in the left arm, and therefore the consequences will not be so grave as if it had affected the right. He is holding between his teeth the end of a linen bandage, which he is binding tightly round a handful of lint applied to the cut, first having steeped the said lint in a certain balm prepared according to the prescription of a gypsy, and believed by him to be infallible. For that matter, not a word of complaint issues from his lips, and he appears as insensible to pain as if the member he is trying to heal was made of pine or of oak.

The third is a man of forty, tall and thin, with pale features, and the lineaments of an ascetic. He is on his knees in a corner, slipping a chaplet of beads between his fingers, and, with a volubility that belongs only to him, is hurrying through a dozen *Paters* and a dozen *Aves*. From time to time his right hand drops the chaplet, and resounds on his breast with the reverberation of a cooper's mallet on an empty cask. But after he has pronounced a *mea culpa* two or three times in a loud voice, he returns to his beads, and runs them as rapidly through his fingers as a monk does his rosary, or a dervish his *combolio*.

The three personages we have still to describe have a character, heavens be praised! not less marked than the five we have already had the honor of passing in review under the eyes of our readers.

One of these has his two hands pressed on the very table on which the writer is performing his task; he follows, without missing a single stroke, all the turns and twists of the pen. It is he that has the most observations to make on the document in question; and it must be admitted that his observations, although tinctured with egotism, are always full of artfulness, and, strange to say, so much do the two things seem opposed, of sound sense also. He is forty-five, has cunning eyes, small and deep-set, under fair, bushy eyebrows.

Another of them is lying flat on the ground; he has found a stone good for giving a sharp edge to swords and a keen point to daggers. He is turning the discovery to account, and, by repeated rubbings on this stone, accompanied by an abundant expenditure of saliva, he is gradually restoring the point of his poniard, which had become blunted, to its usual sharpness. His tongue, which sticks out between his teeth from a corner of his mouth, is itself a witness to all the attention and, we may add, all the interest excited in him by his present occupation. However, this attention is not so absolute as to hinder him from lending an ear to the discussion. If the clauses of the instrument meet his approval, he simply gives a nod of satisfaction; if, on the contrary, it wounds his moral sense or sets his calculations at defiance, he rises, approaches the scribe, places the point of his dagger on the paper, with these four words, "Pardon; you are saying?" and does not raise his dagger until he is perfectly satisfied with the explanation—a satisfaction expressed by a still more abundant salivation and more furious rubbing of his dagger on the stone, thanks to which the weapon promises soon to resume its pristine keenness.

The last, and here we must begin by acknowledging the wrong we have done in ranking him among those occupied with such purely material interests as are for the nonce engrossing the scribe and his assistants; the last, with his back supported by one of the walls of the grotto, his hands hanging by his side, and his eyes raised to heaven, or rather to the damp, gloomy vault on which, like will-o'-the-wisps, the flickering rays of the pine torch are playing—the last, we say again, is at once a dreamer and a poet. What is he searching for at the present moment? Is it the solution of some problem such as were lately resolved by Christopher Columbus or Galileo? Is it the form of one of those tercets constructed by Dante, or one of those octaves chanted by Tasso? Only the demon that keeps watch and ward within him could give us an answer; and he concerns himself so little with material questions—being entirely absorbed in the contemplation of abstractions—that he has allowed all the clothing of the worthy poet, which is not steel or copper or iron, to fall into rags.

And now that we have so far sketched the portraits as well as we could, it is right to give a name to each of them.

The individual holding the pen is called Procope; he is a Norman by birth, and almost a jurist by education; he lards his conversation with axioms drawn from the Roman law and aphorisms borrowed from the Capitularies of Charlemagne. Any one who is a party to an interchange of documents with him may count on a lawsuit following close on the transaction. It is true that whoever will rest satisfied with his word shall find his word golden; only his manner of keeping it does not always square with morality, at least as that virtue is apprehended by the vulgar. We shall quote only a single example of this—an example, also, which accounts for the adventurous career he has adopted at the time we meet him. A noble lord of the court of François I. came, one day, to propose an affair to him and three of his companions. The royal treasurer was to bring, that very evening, a sum of a thousand gold crowns from the Arsenal to the Louvre; the proposal was to stop the treasurer at the corner of the Rue Saint-Pol, take the thousand crowns from him, and share them as follows: five hundred with the great lord, who would wait in the Place Royale until the job was done, and who, as a tribute to his rank, demanded half; the other half between Procope and his three companions, who would thus each receive one hundred and twenty-five crowns. The word was pledged on both sides, and the matter was finished according to agreement; only when the treasurer had been duly robbed, murdered, and flung into the river, the three companions of Procope ventured the proposal to slope toward Notre Dame instead of keeping the appointment at the Place Royale, and so save the whole thousand crowns, instead of remitting five hundred of them to the noble lord. Whereat Procope reminded them of their pledged word.

"Gentlemen," he said gravely, "you forget that this would be to violate a treaty, to deceive a client!—No, our loyalty must be beyond reproach. We shall remit to the duke" (the great lord was a duke) "the five hundred gold crowns that belong to him, every one of them. But," he continued, seeing that the proposal excited some murmurs, "*distinguimus:* when he has pocketed them, and is forced to confess that we are honest men, nothing will prevent us from forming an ambuscade at the cemetery of Saint-Jean, by which I know he must pass; it is a deserted spot, and quite the place for an ambuscade. We shall treat the duke as we did the treasurer; and, as the cemetery of Saint-Jean is quite close to the river, both will be found, to-morrow, in the nets of Saint-Cloud. So, instead of one hundred and twenty-five crowns, we shall have two hundred and fifty each, which two hundred and fifty we may enjoy and dispose of without remorse, seeing we have kept our word faithfully to this good duke!"

The proposal was accepted with enthusiasm, and the plan

carried out accordingly. Unfortunately, in their eagerness to throw the duke into the river, the four partners did not perceive that the duke was still breathing. The coolness of the water revived him, and, instead of going to Saint-Cloud, as Procope expected, he landed on the Quai de Gèvres, pushed on to the Chatelet, and gave the provost of Paris, who at that time happened to be M. d'Estourville, such an accurate description of the four bandits that they judged it prudent to quit Paris the morrow after, being apprehensive of certain legal proceedings, at the end of which, notwithstanding Procope's weighty knowledge of the law, they might have been forced to abandon a thing valued more or less by even the deepest philosophers; that it to say, life.

Our four rascals, then, had left Paris, each making for one of the four cardinal points. It was the lot of Procope to seek the north. Hence it is we have the pleasure of meeting him again, with pen in hand, in the grotto of Saint-Pol-sur-Ternoise, selected by his new companions on account of his singular merit to draw up the important instrument we shall deal with in a moment.

He who is holding a light for Procope is named Heinrich Scharfenstein. This unworthy follower of Luther, whom Charles V.'s ill-treatment of the Huguenots has driven into the ranks of the French army, along with his nephew, Franz Scharfenstein, at the present moment acting as sentinel outside, is of gigantic stature. Indeed, uncle and nephew are both colossuses, and are animated by the same soul and moved by the same spirit. Many pretend that this single spirit is not enough for two bodies each six feet high; but they are not of this opinion themselves, and are certain that things are quite right as they are. In ordinary life they rarely condescend to have recourse to any auxiliary whatever, be it man, or tool, or machine, in order to attain the end before them. If this end is to move some enormous mass, instead of investigating, like our modern scientists, the nature of the machines that enabled Cleopatra to transport her ships from the Mediterranean to the Red Sea, or of the engines by means of which Titus raised the gigantic blocks of the Flavian circus, they bravely encircle the objects to be displaced with their four arms, knot a chain with their fingers of steel, incapable of being broken, make one simultaneous effort with the regularity that. distinguishes all their movements, and the object leaves the place it has for the place it is intended to have. If the thing aimed at is to scale a wall or to reach a window, instead of embarrassing themselves, like their companions, with a heavy ladder, which hinders their march when the expedition succeeds, and must be abandoned when the enterprise fails, they go unencumbered to the scene of their operations. One of them—it doesn't matter which—braces himself against the wall; the other mounts on his shoulders, or, if necessary, stands on his hands raised above his head. With the help of his own arms, the second attains an altitude of eighteen or twenty feet—an elevation almost always sufficient to gain the crest of a wall or the balcony of a window. In battle it is always the same system of physical association: they march side by side, keeping the same step; but there is this difference—while the one is striking, the other is plundering. When the striker is tired of striking, he passes his sword, or battle-axe, or club to his companion, just saying these words, "Your turn now!" Then there is a change of characters: the striker plunders, and the plunderer strikes. Moreover, their mode of striking is very well known and highly appreciated; but, as we have said, in a general way, there is more esteem felt for their arms than for their brains, for their strength than for their understanding. And now you know why one of them has been stationed as a sentinel outside, and the other is acting as a candlestick within.

As to the young man with black mustaches and curly hair, who is crisping his mustaches and combing his hair, he is named Yvonnet; Paris is his birthplace, and his heart is true to France. Besides the physical advantages we have mentioned, it ought to be added that he has the hands and feet of a woman. In peace he is always lamenting, like the

Sybarite of old; a crumpled roseleaf wounds him; if marching is in order, he is exhausted; and he becomes dizzy if any one hints at climbing. When he is asked to think, he grows hysterical. He is as nervous and impressionable as a young girl, and this sensibility of his must be managed with the greatest care. In daylight he has a horror of spiders, and at night the sight of a toad will drive him out of his wits; while a mouse throws him into a fainting-fit. Darkness is equally repugnant to him, and only a great passion can enable him to get the better of this antipathy. However, we must render him this justice, he has always some great passion on hand; but he almost always arrives near his mistress, if the rendezvous is during the night, quite scared and trembling; and, in order to recover his composure, he requires as many reassuring words and attentions and caresses as were lavished by Hero on Leander when he entered her tower all dripping from the waters of the Dardanelles. It is true that as soon as he hears the trumpet, it is true that as soon as he smells the powder, it is true that as soon as he sees the standards pass, Yvonnet is no longer the same man: there is a complete transformation in him; there is no more languor, or dizziness, or hysterics. The young girl becomes a ferocious soldier; it is all cut and thrust then, and he is a regular lion, with claws of iron and teeth of steel. He who shrank from mounting a staircase to reach the bedchamber of a pretty woman, clambers up a ladder, hangs by a cord, clutches at a thread in order to be the first to reach the wall. The combat over, he washes, with the greatest care, his face and hands, changes his clothes and linen, then gradually becomes the man we are now looking at, curling his mustaches, combing his hair, and flipping, with the end of his fingers, the impertinent dust that has fastened on his garments.

The man binding up the wound he has received in the biceps of his left arm, is called Malemort. He is a sombre and melancholy character, who has but one passion, but one love, but one joy--war! an unfortunate passion, a love badly rewarded, a joy short and fatal; for scarcely has he had a taste of carnage than, thanks to the blind and furious ardor with which he throws himself into the *mêlée*, and to the little care he takes when striking others not to be stricken himself, he is sure to catch some terrible pike-thrust, or some awful present in the shape of a musket-ball; and then he groans lamentably, not at the pain of the wound, but at the sorrow he experiences at seeing others keep up the dance without him. Fortunately, his flesh heals easily, and his bones knit together with a speed that is marvellous. At the present moment he can reckon up twenty-five wounds— three more than Cæsar! and he has a sound expectation, if the war continues, of receiving twenty-five new ones before that stroke which will put an end to his glorious and painful career.

The lean personage praying in a corner, and telling his beads on his knees, is styled Lactance. He is an ardent Catholic, and is afflicted by the neighborhood of the two Scharfensteins; he is afraid their heresy may sully him. Obliged by his profession to fight against his brothers in Jesus Christ, and to kill as many of them as he can, there is no austerity he does not practice to counterbalance this stern necessity. The cloth robe he is wearing at present, like a kind of shirt, next the skin, is lined with a coat of mail; that is, except we regard the coat of mail as the stuff and the cloth as the lining. However this may be, in battle the coat of mail is on the outside, and so becomes a cuirass; when the battle is over, the coat of mail is on the inside, and becomes a hair-shirt. And, for that matter, it is surely a satisfaction to die by his hand; for the person killed by this holy man is sure, at least, of not wanting prayers. In the last engagement he slew two Spaniards and one Englishman; and, as he is in debt to them, particularly on account of the heresy of the Englishman, who cannot be satisfied by an ordinary *De Profundis*, he is crowding *Pater* and *Ave* on *Pater* and *Ave*, leaving to his companions the care of the purely temporal concerns they are absorbed in at the present moment. When he has settled his account with heaven, he will descend to earth and sign the document, not without the erasure and addition of some clauses rendered necessary by his tardy intervention.

The man resting his two hands on the table, and watching with an attention that never wanders—being, in this respect, the exact opposite of Lactance—every penstroke of Procope, is called Maldent. He was born at Noyon, his father being of Le Mans and his mother of Picardy. He has been foolish and prodigal in his young days; and so, now that he has attained an age of sobriety and wisdom, he will make up for lost time, and manage his affairs prudently. He has had a multitude of adventures, which he recounts with a simplicity that is not without its charm. But it has to be admitted that this simplicity disappears entirely when he and Procope debate some point of law. Then they realize the legend of the two Gaspards—the one of Le Mans, the other Norman—a legend of which they are perhaps the real heroes. However, Maldent gives and receives a sword-thrust bravely; and, although he has not the strength of Heinrich or Franz Scharfenstein, the courage of Yvonnet, or the impetuosity of Malemort, he is at need a comrade that may be relied on, and will not desert a friend in trouble.

The grinder sharpening the dagger, and trying the point of it on his nail, answers to the name of Pilletrousse. He is a thoroughbred freebooter. He has, turn about, served Spaniards and Englishmen. But the English are too great hands at a bargain, and the Spaniards are not the best of pay; so he has decided to work on his own account. Pilletrousse prowls about the highways; during the night, especially, the highways are full of pillagers of all nations. Pilletrousse pillages the pillagers; only he respects the French, who are almost his fellow-countrymen. Pilletrousse is a Provençal; Pilletrousse is even good-hearted. If they are poor, he helps them along; if they are weak, he protects them; if they are sick, he nurses them; but, if he meet a real fellow-countryman—that is to say, a man born between Mount Viso and the mouths of the Rhone, between the Comtat and Fréjus—the latter can dispose of Pilletrousse body and soul, money and blood; *trou de laire!* you would think Pilletrousse was the obliged party!

In fine, the ninth and last, he with his back to the wall, and his arms moving this way and that, and his eyes raised to heaven, is named Fracasso. He is, as we have stated, a poet and a dreamer: very far from resembling Yvonnet, whom the darkness frightens, he loves those fine nights lighted by the stars alone; he loves the craggy banks of rivers; he loves the resounding shores of the sea. Unfortunately, as he is forced to follow the French army wherever it goes—for, although an Italian, he has pledged his sword to the cause of Henry II.—he is not free to wander according to his inclination; but what does it matter? To the poet everything serves for inspiration; to the dreamer everything supplies material for his dreams; only, distraction is a necessity for dreamers and poets, and distraction is rendered almost impossible in the career adopted by Fracasso. Thus often, in the middle of the fight, Frascasso stops suddenly to listen to the notes of a clarion, to view a passing cloud, to admire some fine feat of arms performed before his eyes. Then the foeman in front of Fracasso profits by this distraction to deal some terrible blow that awakes the dreamer from his dreams, the poet from his ecstasy. But woe to that foeman if, despite the advantage given him, he has taken his measures badly, and has not at once stunned our Fracasso! Fracasso is sure to exact vengeance, not for the blow received, but to punish the ill-bred person who has brought him down from the seventh heaven, where he was floating, upborne by the multi-colored pinions of imagination and fancy.

And now that we have, after the manner of the blind old bard divine, made the catalogue of our adventurers— some of whom cannot be quite unknown to such of our friends as have read "Ascanio" and "The Two Dianas"—

we must recount the cause of their meeting in this grotto, and the nature of the mysterious document they are so anxiously engaged on.

III.

IN WHICH THE READER MAKES THE MOST AMPLE ACQUAINTANCE WITH THE HEROES WE HAVE INTRODUCED TO HIM

ON the morning of this same day, the 5th of May, 1555, a little troop of four men, who seemed to form a part of the garrison of Doullens, had left that city by slipping out of the Arras gate, as soon as this gate had been, we will not say open, but half-open.

These four men, muffled up in long cloaks, equally serviceable for concealing their weapons and guarding them from the stiff morning breeze, followed, with all sorts of precautions, the banks of the little river Authie, until they reached its source. From thence they diverged in the direction of the little chain of hills we have already so often mentioned, continued their course, always with the same precautions, along its western slope, and, after a two hours' journey, at last arrived at the outskirts of the forest of Saint-Pol-sur-Ternoise. There, one of them, who appeared more familiar than the others with the locality, took command of the little band, and, guiding himself at one time by a tree more leafy or more devoid of branches than its fellows, at another, renewing his acquaintance with a rock or a sheet of water, he at length reached the grotto to which we ourselves conducted the reader in the beginning of the preceding chapter.

Then he made a sign to his companions to wait a moment, looked with a certain anxiety at some grass that seemed freshly trampled on, at some branches that seemed recently broken, and, throwing himself flat on his stomach, and crawling like a snake, disappeared within the cavern.

His comrades, who stayed outside, heard the echo of his voice; but the tones denoted nothing alarming. He was interrogating the recesses of the grotto; and as these recesses answered him only by silence and solitude, as the triple echo of his voice was the only sound he heard in response to his triple call, he soon reappeared at the entrance and made a sign to his comrades to follow him.

The three comrades did so, and, after some obstacles that were easily overcome, found themselves in the interior of the cave.

"Ah!" murmured the one who had so skilfully conducted them, with a sigh of heartfelt satisfaction, "*tandem ad terminum eamus!*"

"Which means?" asked one of the three adventurers, in a very pronounced Picard accent.

"Which means, my dear Maldent, that we are approaching, or have approached, the term of our expedition."

"Pardon, Monsieur Procope," said another adventurer, in a strong Teutonic accent, "but I don't very well understand. Do you, Heinrich?"

"No, I don't understand either."

"And why the devil should you want to understand?" replied Procope—for the reader has already guessed that the person addressed by Franz Scharfenstein was our legist Procope, or *Brogobe*, as we should have to write, if we proposed reproducing the impossible *patois* of our two Germans. "If I and Maldent understand, what else is required?"

"Ya," replied the two Germans, philosophically; "that's all that's required."

"Well, then," said Procope, "let us sit down and eat a bite and drain a glass, to pass away the time; and while we are doing so, I'll explain everything."

"Ya, ya!" said Franz Scharfenstein; "let us eat a bite and drain a glass, and while we are doing so he'll explain everything."

The adventurers looked round them, and, thanks to the fact that their eyes were growing accustomed to the darkness, which, besides, was less great at the entrance to the grotto than in its depths, they perceived three stones, which they drew close together, in order to be able to talk more confidentially.

As a fourth one could not be found, Heinrich Scharfenstein politely offered his to Procope, who was without a seat; but Procope thanked him with the same courtesy, stretched his cloak on the ground, and lay down on it.

Then bread, cold meat, and wine were taken from the wallets carried by the two giants; the whole was placed in the centre of the semicircle, of which the three adventurers formed the arc, and Procope, lying at full length, the chord; after this they attacked their improvised breakfast with a fury that showed their morning promenade had not been without its effect on the appetite of the feasters.

For nearly ten minutes nothing was heard but the sound of jaws grinding, with a regularity that would have done honor to machines, bread and meat, and even the very bones of the fowls borrowed from the neighboring farmyards, and composing the most delicate part of the repast.

Maldent was the first to find his tongue.

"You were saying, my dear Procope, that, while eating a bite, you would explain your plan. The eating is more than half over—at least, as far as I am concerned. Begin, then, your explanation. I am listening."

"Ya!" said Franz, with his mouth full; "we are listening."

"Well?"

"Well, it is thus—*Ecce res judicanda*, as they say in the law courts."

"Silence, you Scharfensteins!" exclaimed Maldent.

"Why, I haven't said one word," replied Franz.

"Neither have I," continued Heinrich.

"Ah! I thought I had heard—"

"And I, too," said Procope.

"All right; some fox we have disturbed in his hole. Go on, Procope, go on!"

"Well, then, you'll have it in a nutshell. About a quarter of a league from here there is a pretty little farmhouse—"

"Why, you promised us a chateau!" observed Maldent.

"Goodness gracious! aren't you particular, now?" said Procope. "Well, then, agreed, I apologize. About a quarter of a league from here there is a pretty little chateau—"

"Farmhouse or chateau doesn't matter," said Heinrich Scharfenstein; "the thing that does, is the booty we are likely to get there!"

"Bravo, Heinrich! that's the way to talk! But this infernal scamp Maldent quibbles like an attorney. I will continue."

"Ay, continue."

"About a quarter of a league from here, then, there is a charming country-house, inhabited only by the proprietors and one male and one female servant— It is true the farmer and his workmen are living at some distance."

"How many do they all number?" asked Heinrich.

"Ten, or thereabout," replied Procope.

"My nephew and myself will give a good account of the ten. Eh, nephew Franz?"

"Ya, mein uncle," replied Franz, with the laconism of a Spartan.

"Well," continued Procope, "the affair is settled; we'll spend the time till nightfall drinking and eating and telling stories—"

"Drinking and eating, particularly," said Franz.

"Then at nightfall," continued Procope, "we leave here just as noiselessly as we came; we gain the border of the wood, and creep along a sunken road, which I know well, up to the foot of the wall. There Franz will mount on his uncle's shoulders, or Heinrich on his nephew's; the one on the shoulders of the other will climb over the wall and open the gate. The gate open—you understand, Maldent? the gate open—you understand, you, Scharfenstein?—the gate open, we enter."

"Not without us, I venture to hope," said a voice two steps behind the adventurers—a voice so strongly accentuated that it not only made Procope and Maldent start, but even the two colossuses.

"Treason!" cried Procope, bounding on his feet, and taking a step backward.

"Treason!" shouted Maldent, trying to penetrate the darkness with his eyes, but not stirring from his place.

"Treason!" cried the two Scharfensteins together, drawing their swords, and making a step forward.

"Ah! a fight. You want a fight? Well, I'm not disagreeable. Here, Lactance! here, Fracasso! here, Malemort!"

A triple howl resounded from the back of the cavern, indicating that those appealed to were perfectly willing to respond.

"A moment! a moment, Pilletrousse!" said Procope, who had recognized the fourth adventurer by his voice; "what the devil! we are not Turks or gypsies, to cut one another's throats in the middle of the night without trying to come to an understanding first. Let us have a light, so that we can see each other's faces, and so know with whom we have to do. Then let us arrange matters, if possible; if not, why, we can fight!"

"Let us have the fighting first," said a gloomy voice, which issued from the depths of the grotto, but really seemed to issue from the depths of hell.

"Silence, Malemort!" said Pilletrousse; "in my opinion, Procope's proposal is most acceptable. What do you say, Lactance? and you, Fracasso?"

"I say," replied Lactance, "that if this proposal may save the life of one of our brothers, I accept it."

"And yet there would have been something so poetic in fighting in a grotto, where the dead might also be entombed! but as we must not sacrifice material interests even to poetry," said Fracasso, dolefully, "I subscribe to the opinion of Pilletrousse and Lactance."

"But I insist we have a fight for it!" growled Malemort.

"Now look here, you attend to your arm, and don't bother us," said Pilletrousse; "we are three against you, and Procope, who is a lawyer, will tell you that when three are against one the three always have the best of the argument."

Malemort gave vent to a roar of anguish at seeing himself miss such a splendid chance of getting a fresh wound; but he took the advice of Pilletrousse, and yielded to the judgment of the majority, although he by no means concurred in its soundness.

During this time Lactance and Maldent were each busy striking a light, and, as both bands were anxious to have a clear view of the situation, two pine torches, covered with tow and smeared with pitch, burst into flame at the same moment, and illuminated the cave and its tenants with their double glare.

We have explored the cave; we have made the acquaintance of its tenants. We have, therefore, no longer any need to describe the one or depict the other; all that remains for us is to describe and depict the fashion in which they were grouped.

At the back of the grotto were stationed Pilletrousse, Malemort, Lactance, and Fracasso; in front the two Scharfensteins, Maldent, and Procope.

Pilletrousse had kept his position in the van; behind him Malemort was biting his fist with rage; near Malemort was Lactance, with a torch in his hand, and trying to soothe his bellicose companion; Fracasso, on his knees, was, like Agis at the tomb of Leonidas, tying his sandal, in order, like that hero, to be prepared for war while invoking peace.

The two Scharfensteins formed, as we have already stated, the vanguard on the opposite side; about a yard behind them was Maldent; and a yard behind him was Procope.

The two torches lighted all the circular part of the grotto. A single recess near the door, containing quite a heap of fern, intended, no doubt, to become the bed of the future anchorite, who might fancy the cavern for a home, remained in shadow.

A beam of light, gliding through the opening of the grotto, was making vain efforts to struggle with its palish tint against the almost blood-red glare cast by the two torches.

The whole formed a gloomy and warlike spectacle, and would have made an admirable scene in one of our modern dramas.

Our adventurers, for the most part, knew one another already: they had already seen what they could severally do on the field of battle; but there they were struggling against the common enemy, not making preparations for mutual slaughter.

Fearless as were their hearts, every man of them was not the less impressed by the seriousness of the situation.

But the one who took the clearest and most impartial view of the momentous issue was decidedly our legist Procope.

So he advanced toward his adversaries, without, however, passing beyond the line the two Scharfensteins traced.

"Gentlemen," he said, "we have been united in desiring to see one another, and our desire is fulfilled. It is something gained: you see us, and we see you; therefore both sides know their chances. We are four against four, but with us are these two gentlemen—just look at them" (and he pointed to Heinrich and Franz Scharfenstein)—"which authorizes me to say almost that we are eight against four."

At this imprudent gasconade, not only did one simultaneous cry burst forth from the mouths of Pilletrousse, Malemort, Lactance, and Fracasso, but their swords again leaped from their scabbards.

Procope saw that he had forgotten his usual tact, and had made a blunder. He tried to recover ground.

"Gentlemen," he said, "I do not claim that even with eight against four the victory would be certain when these four are named Pilletrousse, Malemort, Lactance, and Fracasso."

This sort of postscript seemed to smooth matters down a little, though Malemort continued to growl under his breath.

"Well, come to the point, then!" cried Pilletrousse.

"Yes," answered Procope, "*ad eventum festina*. Well, then, gentlemen, I was about to say that, putting aside the uncertain chances of a combat, we ought to try to come to some arrangement. Now, we are engaged in a kind of lawsuit, *jacens sub judice lis est;* how shall we bring this lawsuit to a close? In the first place, by a pure and simple statement of the case; this will prove we have right on our side. Who got the idea yesterday of seizing the little farmhouse, or, as you prefer calling it, the little Chateau du Parcq? I and those gentlemen. Who left Doullens to put the plan in execution? I and those gentlemen. Who came to this grotto to arrange the proper course to be pursued during the approaching night? I and those gentlemen again. Finally, who has matured the plan, developed it in your presence, and so inspired you with the desire of becoming partners in our association? I and those gentlemen, of course. Answer, Pilletrousse, and tell us whether the conduct of an enterprise, without let or hindrance, does not belong to those who have had the priority both of the idea and its execution? *Dixi!*"

Pilletrousse burst out laughing; Fracasso shrugged his shoulders; Lactance shook his torch; and Malemort murmured, "A fight!"

"What makes you laugh, Pilletrousse?" asked Procope, gravely, disdaining to address the others, and determined to hold a parley only with the person who seemed for the moment to have become chief of the band.

"What makes me laugh, my dear Procope," replied the adventurer to whom the question was addressed, "is the profound assurance with which you set forth your rights, especially as this very exposition of yours, if we were to admit the principles on which you base it, does not leave you and your companions a leg to stand on. Yes, I admit that the conduct of an enterprise belongs, without let or hindrance, to those who have the priority both of idea and execution—"

"Ah!" interrupted Procope, triumphantly.

"Yes, but excuse me a moment; the idea of seizing the Chateau du Parcq, as you prefer to call it, came to you yesterday evening, did it not? Well, it came to us the day before yesterday. You left Doullens this morning to execute the idea? We left Montreuil-sur-Mer yesterday evening with the same object. You entered the grotto an hour ago? We have been here for the last four hours. You have matured and developed the plan *before* us, but we had already matured and developed the plan long before you. You intend attacking the farmhouse this night? We claim priority of idea and execution, and consequently the right to conduct the enterprise without let or hindrance."

And, parodying the classic manner in which Procope had finished his discourse, "*Dixi!*" added Pilletrousse, with not less coolness and emphasis than the legist.

"But," asked Procope, a little disturbed by the argument of Pilletrousse, "how do I know you are speaking the truth?"

"My word as a gentleman!" said Pilletrousse.

"I would rather prefer another security."

"On the faith of a freebooter, then!"

"Hem!" muttered Procope, imprudently.

The temper of the community was growing warm; the doubt expressed by Procope as to the value of Pilletrousse's word exasperated his followers.

"Well, then, a fight be it!" cried Fracasso and Lactance together.

"Yes, a fight! a fight! a fight!" howled Malemort.

"Fight away, then! since you will have it," said Procope.

"A fight by all means! since there is no other way out of it," said Maldent.

"A fight!" repeated Franz and Heinrich Scharfenstein, drawing their swords.

And then, as everybody appeared agreed, there was a general drawing of swords or daggers, or else a seizure of axe or club; each looked his enemy square in the face, and with curses on the lips, fury in the eyes, and death in the hands, prepared to rush on him.

Suddenly the pile of fern heaped up in the recess near the entrance of the grotto was seen to move; a young man elegantly clad darted out, and with a bound beyond the circle of darkness, appeared in the circle of illumination, extending his arms like Hersilia in the picture of the "Sabines," and crying—

"Down with your arms, comrades! I undertake to arrange this matter to the general satisfaction."

All eyes were turned on the new personage who entered on the scene in so abrupt and unexpected a fashion, and all cried in unison—

"Yvonnet!"

"But where the devil have you come from?" asked Pilletrousse and Procope at the same time.

"You are about to learn," said Yvonnet; "but first return swords and daggers to the scabbards. The sight of all these naked blades sets every one of my nerves quivering horribly."

All the adventurers obeyed except Malemort.

"Come, come, comrade," said Yvonnet, addressing him directly, "what is the meaning of that?"

"Ah!" sighed Malemort, as if his heart were broken, "are we never then to have a little quiet cutting and thrusting!"

And he sheathed his sword with a gesture full of vexation and disappointment.

IV

THE DEED OF PARTNERSHIP

YVONNET cast a look around him, and, recognizing that, if anger was not entirely banished from the hearts of our adventurers, at least swords and daggers were returned to their scabbards, he turned alternately to Pilletrousse and Procope, who, as they remind him, have just had the honor of putting him the same question.

"Where have I come from?" he repeated. "*Pardieu!* a nice question that! I have come from that heap of fern, under which I threw myself when I saw Pilletrousse, Lactance, Malemort, and Fracasso enter, and from which I thought it time to get out when I saw them followed by Procope, Maldent, and the two Scharfensteins."

"But what were you doing in the grotto at such an hour of the night? for when we came here it was yet hardly daylight."

"Ah!" replied Yvonnet, "that's my secret, which I will tell you immediately, if you are very good; but, first, let us come to the main point."

Then, addressing Pilletrousse—

"So, then, my dear Pilletrousse," said he, "it was your intention to pay a little visit to the Chateau du Parcq, as you are pleased to call it?"

"Yes," said Pilletrousse.

"And yours, too?" asked Yvonnet of Procope.

"And ours, too," replied Procope.

"And you were about fighting to settle the priority of your rights?"

"We were about fighting," replied Pilletrousse and Procope together.

"Shame!" exclaimed Yvonnet; "comrades, Frenchmen, or, at least, serving the cause of France!"

"Faith, we couldn't help it, as these gentlemen refused to renounce their claim," said Procope.

"We could not act otherwise, since these gentlemen refused to give way," said Pilletrousse.

"We couldn't help it! we could not act otherwise!" repeated Yvonnet, mimicking the voice of the two disputants. "You could not help massacring each other; you could not act otherwise than cutting each other's throats, eh? And you were there, Lactance, and you saw the preparations for the slaughter, and your Christian soul did not utter a groan?"

"Yes, it did, and a heartfelt groan at that!"

"And that is all wherewith your holy religion inspires you—a groan?"

"After the fight," returned Lactance, a little humiliated by the reproaches of Yvonnet, the justice of which he felt—"after the fight I would have prayed for the dead."

"What a benevolent creature!"

"What would you have had me do, pray, my dear Monsieur Yvonnet?"

"Ah, *pardieu!* I would have had you do what I am doing—I who am not a devotee, nor a saint, nor a swallower of *Pater Nosters* like you. What would I have had you do? Throw yourself between those swords and blades, *inter gladios et enses*, to speak after the manner of our legist Procope, and say to your misguided brethren, with that air of compunction which so well becomes you, the words I am about to say to them now: 'Comrades, when there is enough for four, there is enough for eight; if the first job does not bring in all we expected, we shall soon have another on hand. Men are born to aid one another on the rough pathways of life, not to encumber with stumbling-blocks the roads that are hard enough to make one's way over as it is. Instead of dividing, let us unite. What four cannot attempt without enormous risks, eight can achieve without danger. Let us keep our hatreds, our daggers and swords, for our enemies, and for ourselves let kindly words and courteous deeds be our only weapons. God, who protects France when He has nothing more pressing to occupy His time, will smile on our fraternal unity and give it a fitting reward!' This, my dear Lactance, is what you ought to have said and what you have not said."

"It is true," replied Lactance, smiting his breast; "*mea culpa! mea culpa! mea maxima culpa!*"

And, extinguishing the torch, he fell on his knees and began to pray with fervor.

"Well, then, I have said it in your place," continued Yvonnet, "and I add, The divine reward which Lactance would have promised, I bring, comrades."

"You, Yvonnet?" said Procope, with an air of doubt.

"Yes, I, who had the same desire as you, and even before you."

"What!" said Pilletrousse, "you, too, had the idea of entering the chateau we all have our eyes on?"

"Not only had I the idea," returned Yvonnet; "but, more than that, I have begun to execute it."

"Impossible!" exclaimed all his hearers, lending him, though, a closer attention than ever.

"Yes, I have a friend in the place—a charming little soubrette, named Gertrude," he added, twirling his mustache, "who for my sake is willing to deny father, mother, and mistress; she is mine, body and soul."

Lactance heaved a sigh.

"And you say you have been in the chateau?"

"I left it this night; but you know how much I dread a walk in the night, particularly alone. Rather than spend three leagues in reaching Doullens, or six leagues in reaching Abbeville or Montreuil-sur-Mer, I spent a quarter of a league in making my way to this grotto, with which I was well acquainted, as it was the scene of my first assignation with my divinity. I made acquaintance with the bed of fern, and had fallen asleep there, and had intended to acquaint the first of you I met with my plan, when Pilletrousse arrived with his band, and then Procope with his. Each came here with the same object. And this would have undoubtedly led to a tragedy, did I not judge it time to interfere, as I have interfered. Now I have to say to you: Instead of fighting, become partners. Why not enter the place by craft instead of by violence? Would you not rather have the doors opened for you than broken in? Instead of having to rummage for gold and jewelry, would you not prefer to have them put into your hands? Then, shake! I'm your man! And to show how disinterested I am, I say, let us share. In spite of the service I am rendering you, I only ask an equal share. If any one has anything to say against this, let him say it; I am willing to listen!"

A thrill of admiration ran through the assembly. Lactance forgot to pray for a while, and ran to kiss the hem of his jerkin. Pilletrousse, Maldent and Fracasso grasped his hand. The two Scharfensteins almost choked him with their embraces. Malemort alone growled in his corner:

"There won't be a single thrust or parry. Ah, *dame!*"

"Well, now," said Yvonnet, who had been for a long time looking forward to just such an association, and who, seeing the opportunity within his reach, had no notion to let it slip—"well, now, don't let us lose a moment! Here we are, nine blades who fear neither God nor the devil—"

"Oh, excuse me," interrupted Lactance; "we fear God!"

"Oh, yes, of course! It's a way we have of speaking, Lactance; I meant to say, Here we are, nine blades come hither by chance—"

"By Providence, Yvonnet!" interrupted Lactance, again.

"By Providence, granted. By good luck, we have among us a legist Procope, and, by more good luck, he happens to have a pen and ink at his girdle, and, I am quite sure, also a stamp of our good King Henry II.—"

"Yes, faith, I have one," replied Procope; "and, as Yvonnet says, it's luck."

"Then let us come to the point. Draw up a deed of partnership, while one of us, stationed in the forest, and at the end of the path that leads to the grotto, may see that we are not disturbed."

"I will be the sentinel," said Malemort. "I'll see to it that if Englishmen, Spaniards, or Germans are prowling about the forest, they'll soon be dead men!"

"But, my dear Malemort," said Yvonnet, "that's the very thing we don't want. In our present position—that is to say, within two hundred yards of the camp of the Emperor Charles V., with a man whose ear is so finely and accurately trained as that of Monseigneur Emmanuel Philibert of Savoy—we must not kill all that we should like to kill, especially as we can't be sure always of killing the right person. We perhaps only wound him; and the wounded scream like the eagles. Everybody hurries to the rescue of the wounded; and if this wood is once occupied, God only knows what will become of us! No, my dear Malemort, you must stay here, and one of the two Scharfensteins will mount guard. Both are Germans. If one of our sentinels is discovered, he can say he is a lansquenet of the Duke of Aremberg or a trooper of Count Waldeck."

"Better of Count Waldeck," said Heinrich Scharfenstein.

"This colossus is full of intelligence," said Yvonnet. "Yes, my worthy fellow. Better of Count Waldeck, because Count Waldeck is a freebooter, like the rest of us. That's what you mean, is it not?"

"Ya; I mean just that."

"And is there anything wonderful in a freebooter like him lurking in this wood?"

"Nein; nothing wonderful at all."

"The only thing of importance is, that whichever of the Scharfensteins acts as sentinel does not fall into the hands of the Duke of Savoy; for he has little respect for highwaymen, and gives short shrift to marauders!"

"Yes," said Heinrich; "he hanged two soldiers yesterday!"

"Three!" said Franz.

"Well, which of you is willing to act as sentry?"

"I," replied uncle and nephew together.

"My friends," replied Yvonnet, "such devotion is appreciated by your comrades. But only one sentinel is needed. Draw lots, then; a post of honor remains for him who has to remain here."

The two Scharfensteins consulted together for a moment.

"Franz has good eyes and good ears; he will be sentinel," said Heinrich.

"Good! let Franz go to his post, then."

Franz left the grotto, with his ordinary tranquillity.

"You understand, Franz? If you are caught by others, it doesn't matter; but if you are taken by the Duke of Savoy, you are hanged!"

"No one shall catch me; make your mind easy," said Franz, tranquilly.

And he left the grotto to take the post assigned him.

"And the post of honor," asked Heinrich—"where is it?"

Yvonnet took the torch from the hands of Maldent and presented it to Heinrich.

"There you are!" he said; "stand quiet, and don't stir for your life."

"I won't stir, you may be sure," replied Heinrich.

Procope sat down, took his paper from his pocket, and his pen and ink-bottle from his belt.

We have seen him at work at the very time we entered the grotto of Saint-Pol-sur-Ternoise—a spot usually so lonely, but now, by a fortuitous concurrence of circumstances, so strangely tenanted to-day.

We trust we have made our readers come to the conclusion that it was not a work very easily managed that Procope was devoting himself to between eleven in the morning and three in the afternoon of this 5th of May, 1555.

And so, just as in a bill discussed in our modern parliaments, every one brought forward his amendments and clauses, and so forth.

The said amendments and clauses were passed by a majority of votes, and, it must be said to the honor of our freebooters, with a justice, decorum, and impartiality not often found in more pretentious assemblies.

There are really wrong-headed people who maintain, shameless calumniators that they are, that a code of law drawn up by robbers is likely to be more thorough and equitable than a code drawn up by honest men.

We pity the blindness of such people, just as we pity the blindness of Calvinists and Lutherans for their errors, and we pray to God to pardon both.

Finally, at the very moment when the watch of Yvonnet marked a quarter-past three—watches were rare at the period, but our dandy adventurer had one—finally, we repeat, at a quarter-past three, Procopo raised his head, took his pen in his hand, and produced his paper. Thereat, feeling an emotion of joy, he could not help exclaiming—

"Ah! it's done, and well done—*Exegi monumentum!*"

At this announcement, Heinrich Scharfenstein, who had been holding the torch for three hours and twenty minutes, stretched his arm, as he felt rather tired; Yvonnet interrupted his oration; Malemort completed the bandaging of his wound; Lactance hurried through his last *Ave*; Maldent drew himself up to his full height, his hands still resting on the table; Pilletrousse sheathed his dagger, now sharpened to his satisfaction; and Fracasso awoke from his poetic revery, satisfied with having captured the rhymes he had been in search of for a sonnet during the past month.

All approached the table, with the exception of Franz, who, leaving to his uncle the discussion of their common interests, had placed himself, or rather lain down, within twenty yards of the entrance to the grotto, with the determined resolution, not only of watching over his companions, but of keeping out of the way of that rough justiciary, Emmanuel Philibert of Savoy.

"Gentlemen," said Procope, glancing at the members of the circle that had formed around him with as much regularity as the officer is accustomed to behold when he calls his soldiers to order—"gentlemen, are we all here?"

"Yes," replied the adventurers in chorus.

"Then every one is ready to hear the document which we have drawn up in eighteen articles, severally and conjointly, and which is hereby constituted a deed of partnership thereunto founded and established."

The reply was affirmative and unanimous, Heinrich Scharfenstein, as a matter of course, answering for himself and his nephew.

"Then listen," said Procope.

And, after coughing and spitting, he began:

"We, the undersigned—"

"Excuse me," interrupted Lactance; "I do not know how to sign."

"*Parbleu!*" said Procope; "as if it mattered! you will make a cross."

"Ah!" murmured Lactance, "that will make the pledge only the more sacred. Continue, my brother."

Procope resumed—

"We, the undersigned: Jean Chrysostome Procope—"

"You haven't a low opinion of yourself," said Yvonnet; "you don't object to lead off."

"Somebody had to be first," returned Procope, innocently.

"Good!" said Maldent; "continue."

Procope continued—

"Jean Chrysostome Procope, attorney-at-law, admitted to practice at the bar of Caen, as also before the court of Rouen, Cherbourg, Valognes—"

"*Corbleu!* I am no longer surprised at the business taking up three hours and a half, if you have given every one all his titles and degrees. What does surprise me is that you should have got to the end of it at last."

"No," said Procope; "I have comprised you all under the same title. But, as the person responsible for the instrument, I judged it not only proper, but absolutely necessary to give a full exposition of all my titles, degrees, and qualities."

"Oh, I see!" said Pilletrousse.

"Ah! get on, will you!" growled Malemort. "We shall never get to the end if every fellow interrupts at each word. I want to come to the fighting—that's what I want!"

"Faith," said Procope, "I'm not the one that interrupts, as far as I can see."

And he continued—

"Jean Chrysostome Procope, etc., Honoré Joseph Maldent, Victor Felix Yvonnet, Cyrille Nepomucene Lactance, César Hanibal Malemort, Martin Pilletrousse, Vittorio Albani Fracasso, and Heinrich and Franz Scharfenstein—all captains in the service of King Henry II.—"

A flattering murmur interrupted Procope, and no one any longer dreamed of interfering with the titles and qualities he had given himself, for each was busy in arranging on his person a scarf, a napkin, a handkerchief, any rag that could be made to look like a symbol of the rank in the French service he had just received.

Procope gave time for the murmurs of applause to cease, and continued—

"Have hereunto set forth, resolved, and—"

"Excuse me," said Maldent; "but the deed is null."

"Null! How?" said Procope.

"You forgot only one thing in your deed."

"What?"

"The date."

"The date is at the end."

"Oh," said Maldent, "that is another thing; still, it would have been better if you had put it at the beginning."

"The beginning or the end's all one," said Procope. "The Institutes of Justinian say, positively: *Omne actum quo tempore scriptum sit, indicato; seu initio seu fine ut paciscentibus libuerit:* which means: 'Every deed must bear its proper date; but the contracting parties are at liberty to place the date at the beginning or at the end of the said deed.'"

"What hideous gibberish your law Latin is!" said Fracasso, "and how far removed from the language of Virgil and Horace!"

And he began to scan lovingly those verses from the third Eclogue of Virgil—

"Malo me Galatea petit, lasciva puella,
Et fugit ad salices, et se cupit ante videri."

"Silence, Fracasso!" said Procope.

"Oh, silence as much as you like," replied Fracasso. "But it is not the less true that, great a man as was Justinian the First, I prefer Homer the Second to him, and I would rather have made the Bucolics, the Eclogues, or even the Æneid, than the Digest, Pandects, Institutes, and the whole *Corpus juris civilis.*"

There was undoubtedly going to be a dispute between Fracasso and Procope on this important point—and only God knows where it would have led the disputants!—when a kind of stifled cry was heard outside the grotto, and the attention of the adventurers was drawn to the direction whence it came.

Soon it was seen that the light of day was intercepted by some opaque body which interposed between the artificial and ephemeral glow of the torches and the divine and inextinguishable illumination of the sun. At last, a being whose species it was impossible to discern, so indefinite were its lines in the demi-obscurity in which it moved, appeared, and advanced into the centre of the circle, all making way before it.

Then only, by the glare of the torch which lighted the

distorted group, was Franz Scharfenstein recognized, holding a woman in his arms, with his huge hand pressed against her mouth, and doing duty as a sort of gag.

Each waited for the explanation of this new incident.

"Comrades," said the giant, "here is a little woman I found prowling about the grotto; I caught her, and have brought her to you. What is to be done with her?"

"*Pardieu!*" said Pilletrousse, "release her. She won't eat the whole nine of us, perhaps!"

"Oh! I'm not afraid of her eating the whole nine of us either," said Franz, with his enormous laugh. "Wouldn't I like to have the eating of her alone by myself, though! Ja wohl!"

And, as Pilletrousse had invited him to do, he set her in the middle of the circle, on her two feet, and withdrew to the rear quickly.

The woman, who was young and pretty, and seemed, by her costume, to be a respectable cook in some well-to-do family, gave a frightened glance around her, and then at each individual, as if to take stock of the company in the centre of which she stood, and which her eyes told her, at the first look, seemed rather mixed.

But her glance did not take in the whole circle, either; it stopped at the youngest and most elegant of the adventurers.

"Oh, Monsieur Yvonnet," she cried, "in the name of Heaven, protect, defend me!" And, trembling, she ran and threw her arms round the neck of the young man.

"Why!" said Yvonnet, "it is Mademoiselle Gertrude!"

And, pressing the young girl against his breast, to reassure her, he said, "*Pardieu!* gentlemen, we shall now have fresh news from the Chateau du Parcq; for this fair lady has just come from it."

Now, as any news promised by Yvonnet which should come through the mouth of Mademoiselle Gertrude interested every one of them to the extremest degree, our adventurers at once abandoned, for the time, their deed of partnership, and thronged round the two young persons, waiting impatiently until the emotion to which Mademoiselle Gertrude was a prey permitted her to speak.

V

COUNT WALDECK

THERE was silence still for a few moments, after which Mademoiselle Gertrude, evidently reassured by the consoling words which Yvonnet whispered into her ear, at last began her story.

But as this story, at one time interrupted by her own excitement, at another by the interrogatories put to her by the adventurers, might not have, for our readers, the limpid clearness desirable, we shall, with their kind permission, substitute our prose for that of the fair narrator, and, grasping the entire situation, relate, as plainly as we can, the tragic event that forced the young girl to quit the Chateau du Parcq, and led her into the midst of the adventurers.

Two hours after the departure of Yvonnet, at the moment when Mademoiselle Gertrude, doubtless a little fatigued after her nocturnal conversation with the handsome Parisian, decided at last to leave her bed and go down to her mistress, who was for the third time calling her, a young boy named Philippin, the son of the farmer, about sixteen years old, entered the chamber of his mistress, quite scared, and announced that a troop of forty or fifty men, belonging, he thought from their black and yellow scarfs, to the army of the Emperor Charles V., was riding toward the chateau, after making his father, who happened to be working in the fields, prisoner.

Philippin, who was working himself some hundred yards from the farmer, had seen the capture, and guessed by the gestures of the soldiers and the prisoner that they were speaking of the chateau. Then he had crept along until he came to a path, which he saw would hide him from the view of the troopers, and ran like the wind to give his mistress notice of what was passing, and time to adopt the proper resolution.

The chatelaine rose, went to the window, and, in fact, saw that the troop was hardly a hundred yards from the chateau. It consisted of about fifty men, as Philippin had said, and appeared to be commanded by three leaders. The farmer was walking beside one of them, with his hands tied behind his back. The officer near whom he walked held the end of the cord, undoubtedly with the object of preventing the farmer from attempting to escape, or, if he should attempt, bringing him to a halt on the moment.

This sight was anything but reassuring. However, as the horsemen, who were hastening to visit the chateau, wore, as we have said, the scarf of the Empire; as the three leaders who rode at their head had crowns on the crests of their helmets and escutcheons on the breastplates of their cuirasses; as the orders of Duke Emmanuel Philibert with regard to pillaging and marauding were positive; as, in fine, there was no way of escape, especially for a woman—the chatelaine resolved to receive the arrivals in the best manner possible. Consequently, she left her chamber, and, descending the staircase, went, as a mark of honor to her visitors, to receive them on the first step of the perron.

As to Mademoiselle Gertrude, her terror at the sight of these men was so great that, instead of following her mistress, as was perhaps her duty, she threw herself on Philippin, begging him to point out some retreat where she could hide during the stay of the soldiers in the chateau, and where he, Philippin, could come from time to time, and give her intelligence as to how the affairs of her mistress were going on; for they certainly appeared to be in a bad way at present.

Although Mademoiselle Gertrude had been a little rough with Philippin for some time, and the latter, who had vainly sought for the cause of the change, had promised to himself that, should she ever need his services, he would be in no hurry to offer them, yet was Mademoiselle Gertrude so beautiful in her terror, so seductive in her attitude of entreaty, that Philippin allowed himself to relent, and led Mademoiselle Gertrude by the private staircase into the yard, and from the yard into the garden, and there hid her in a corner of the cistern, where his father stored his gardening tools usually.

It was not likely that soldiers whose evident intention it was to devote their attention to the pantries and cellars of the chateau would search for her in a place where, as Philippin wittily said, there was nothing to drink but water.

Mademoiselle Gertrude would have liked to keep Philippin, and Philippin, perhaps, on his side, would have asked nothing better than to remain with Mademoiselle Gertrude; but the beautiful child was even more curious than timid, so that her desire for news got the better of her dread of remaining alone.

For more security, moreover, Philippin put the key of the cistern in his pocket, which at first disturbed Mademoiselle Gertrude somewhat, but, after due reflection, seemed, on the contrary, rather reassuring.

Mademoiselle Gertrude held her breath and listened with both her ears; she heard at first a great noise of arms and horses, shouting and neighing; but, as Philippin had foreseen, the shouting and neighing seemed to be concentrated in the chateau and its courts.

The prisoner was trembling with impatience and burning with curiosity. She had been at the door more than once, and tried to open it. If she had succeeded, she would very certainly, although at the risk of encountering some unpleasant mishap in the enterprise, have tried to hear what was saying or see what was doing by listening at the doors and looking above the walls.

At last a step, as light as that of nocturnal animals prowling around poultry-yards and sheep-folds, drew near the cistern; a key was introduced cautiously, turned gently in the lock, and the door, slowly opened, was quickly shut after giving entrance to Master Philippin.

"Well?" asked Gertrude, before even the door was closed.

"Well, Mademoiselle Gertrude," said Philippin, "it seems they are, in fact, gentlemen, just as Madame la Baronne had surmised. But what gentlemen, good God! If you heard them curse and swear you would take them for genuine pagans!"

"Great heavens! what is that you're telling me, Monsieur Philippin?" exclaimed the young girl, now quite scared.

"The truth, mademoiselle; nothing but God's pure truth! When the chaplain reprimanded them, they answered that if he did not keep a quiet tongue in his mouth they would make him sing Mass with his feet up and his head down, and the rope of the belfry about his neck; while their chaplain, a regular heathen with beard and mustaches, would read a service in which there were neither responses nor questions."

"But, then," said Mademoiselle Gertrude, "they are not real gentlemen, are they?"

"*Pardieu!* they are; and among the best in Germany, even! They were not ashamed to tell their names; and that, you must acknowledge, was no small bravado, after the way they conducted themselves. The oldest, a man of fifty, or thereabout, is named Count Waldeck, and commands four thousand reiters in the army of his Majesty Charles V. The two others, who may be from twenty-four to twenty-five, and from nineteen to twenty, are his legitimate son and his bastard. Only, from what I have seen—and the thing is not unusual—he appears to be fonder of the bastard than of the lawful heir. The legitimate son is a handsome young man, with pale complexion, large brown eyes, black hair and mustaches, and I have a fancy he might be brought to listen to reason. The same can't be said of the bastard, who is red-headed, and has the eyes of an owl.

Oh, mademoiselle, he's a regular devil, that fellow! God preserve you from meeting him! The way he looked at Madame la Baronne!—It makes one shiver to think of it!"

"You don't say so?" said Mademoiselle Gertrude, who was evidently curious to know what kind of a look is that which makes one shiver.

"Oh, good God, yes," said Philippin, by way of peroration; "and it was thus I left them— Now I am going back for further news, and as soon as I have any, I'll let you know."

"Yes, yes," said Gertrude, "go! and return soon; but take care that nothing happens to you."

"Oh, don't be afraid, mademoiselle," replied Philippin; "I never show myself except with a bottle in each hand; and, as I know where to find the best wine, the rascals have the greatest respect for me."

Philippin left, and shut up Mademoiselle Gertrude, who at once began to think within herself what kind of looks those are that make one shiver. She had not yet solved the difficulty, although she spent nearly an hour in trying, when the key turned anew in the lock, and the messenger reappeared.

It was not that of the ark, and he was far from holding an olive branch in his hand. Count Waldeck had, by threats and even ill-treatment, forced the baroness to surrender her jewels, plate, and all the gold she had in the chateau. But this had not satisfied them; and, after the first ransom had been paid, the poor woman, at the very moment she believed herself about to be rid of the noble bandits who had asked her hospitality, had been, on the contrary, seized, garroted, and locked up in her chamber, with the assurance that if in two hours she did not find two hundred rose nobles in her own purse or in that of her friends, the chateau would be set on fire.

Mademoiselle Gertrude bewailed, according to all the rules of propriety, the fate of her mistress; but, as she had not two hundred crowns to lend her, and thus extricate her from her embarrassment, she tried to think of something else, and asked Philippin what that infamous bastard of Waldeck, of the red hair and terrible eyes, was doing?

Philippin replied that the bastard of Waldeck was doing his best to get drunk—an occupation in which he was powerfully seconded by his father. The Vicomte Waldeck alone was preserving, as far as possible, his coolness in the midst of the pillage and the orgies.

Mademoiselle Gertrude had a furious craving to form some idea of what these orgies might be, and to see them with her own eyes. As to pillage, she knew that already, having been present at the sack of Thérouanne, but of what are called orgies she had no notion.

Philippin explained that it was a meeting of men who drank, and ate, and indulged in loose conversation, and committed every sort of outrage on any woman that fell into their hands.

The curiosity of Mademoiselle Gertrude was immensely increased by this picture, which would have made a heart less courageous than hers shudder. She therefore begged Philippin to let her out, if it were only for ten minutes; but he repeated to her so often and so seriously that by leaving she ran a risk of her life, that she decided to remain in her hiding-place, and await the third return of Philippin, before settling, finally, on what she was to do.

This she had done before the return of Philippin. It was, no matter what might happen, to force a passage out, gain the chateau, slip along the secret corridors and private staircases, and see with her own eyes what was passing—any narrative, however eloquent, being always inferior to the scene it attempts to paint.

As soon as she heard, for the third time, the key turn in the lock, she prepared to dart from the cistern, whether Philippin liked it or not; but when she saw his face, she recoiled in terror.

Philippin was as pale as a corpse; his lips stammered forth disconnected words, and his eyes had the haggard expression of a man who has just witnessed some awful and sombre event.

Gertrude wished to question him, but at the contact of this unknown terror she felt frozen; the paleness of his cheeks passed into her own, and, face to face with this grewsome dumbness, she became dumb herself.

The young man, without saying anything, but with that strength given by fright which is irresistible, seized her by the wrist and dragged her toward the little gate of the garden opening on the plain, stammering only these words—

"Dead—assassinated—stabbed!"

Gertrude made no resistance; Philippin let her go a moment to shut the gate behind them—a useless precaution, for no one dreamed of pursuing them.

But the shock received by Philippin had been so rough that the momentum impressed on him could not cease until his strength failed him. At the end of five hundred yards he fell, breathless, murmuring, in a hoarse voice, like that of a man in the last agony, those frightful words, the only ones he could utter—

"Dead—assassinated—stabbed!"

Then Gertrude cast her eyes around her: she was not more than two hundred yards from the border of the forest; she knew the forest, she knew the grotto; it was doubly a refuge; besides, in the grotto she might perhaps find Yvonnet.

She was quite remorseful at the notion of leaving poor Philippin unconscious on the edge of a ditch; but she perceived four or five horsemen coming in her direction. Perhaps these men might be some of Count Waldeck's reiters; she had not a second to lose if she wanted to escape. She darted toward the forest, and, without looking behind her, ran, frantic and dishevelled, until she crossed the border of the wood. Then only did she stop, and, leaning against a tree so as not to fall, she cast her eyes over the plain.

The horsemen reached the place where she had left Philippin unconscious. They raised him up; but, seeing that he could not move a step, one of them laid him across the pommel of his saddle, and, followed by his comrades, transported him to the camp.

The intentions of these men, however, seemed to be good; and Gertrude began to think that the best thing for Philippin was to fall into such humane hands.

Then, no longer anxious for the fate of her companion, and having regained her breath in this halt, Gertrude began again to run in the direction, or rather toward the point she believed in the direction, of the grotto. She naturally went astray; and it was only at the end of an hour that she found herself, by accident, chance, or instinct, in the neighborhood of the grotto, and within reach of Franz Scharfenstein.

It is easy to guess the rest: Franz stretched out one hand and encircled the waist of Gertrude, placed the other on her mouth, and carried her as if she was a feather, then set her in the midst of the adventurers in an altogether scared condition, until, reassured by the sympathetic words of Yvonnet, she was able to begin the tale we have just told, and which was received with a general cry of indignation by the adventurers.

But, let not the reader be deceived, this indignation sprang from an entirely selfish cause. The adventurers were not indignant at the little morality displayed by the marauders in connection with the Chateau du Parcq and its inhabitants. No; they were indignant at Count Waldeck and his sons having pillaged in the morning a chateau which they had reckoned on pillaging in the evening.

This indignation was succeeded by a general hubbub, which, in turn, was followed by a resolution, adopted unanimously, to go into the open and see at once what was passing in the direction of the camp, whither Philippin had been transported, and in the direction of the chateau, where had been accomplished the drama just related by Gertrude with all the eloquence and all the energy of terror.

But the indignation of the adventurers did not exclude prudence. It was then decided that a man of goodwill should begin by exploring the wood, and render an account of the present condition of things to the adventurers. Their action would depend on the motives for fear or security supplied by this exploration.

Yvonnet offered to beat the wood. He was, besides, the very man for the work: he knew all the turnings and twistings of the forest; he was as agile as a stag and cunning as a fox.

Gertrude broke into loud cries, and tried to prevent her lover going on a dangerous mission. But she was made to understand, without much ceremony, that the moment was badly chosen for the display of her amorous susceptibilities, which were likely to be anything but favorably appreciated by the rather practical people among whom she found herself. She was a sensible girl at bottom; she grew calm when she saw that her cries and tears would not only have no result, but might even turn out badly for her. Besides, Yvonnet explained to her, in a low voice, that an adventurer's mistress ought not to affect the nervous sensibility of a princess of romance, and, having placed her in the hands of his friend Fracasso and under the special guard of the two Scharfensteins, he quitted the grotto to accomplish the important mission which he had just undertaken.

Ten minutes after, he was back. The forest was perfectly deserted, and did not appear to offer any danger.

As the curiosity of the adventurers was almost as keenly aroused in their grotto by the story of Mademoiselle Gertrude as the curiosity of Mademoiselle Gertrude had been excited in her cistern by the story of Philippin, and as old freebooters of their stamp could not have the same motives of prudence as those that direct the actions of a beautiful and timid young girl, they left the cavern, abandoning Procope's deed of partnership to the guardianship of the genii of the place, invited Yvonnet to place himself at their head, and, guided by him, they directed their course toward the border of the wood, not without each making sure that his dagger or sword had not rusted in the scabbard.

VI

THE JUSTICIARY

ACCORDING as our adventurers advanced toward that point of the forest which we have said stretched out in the form of a lance-head in the direction of Hesdin, stopping within a quarter of a league of it, and separating the two basins of the plain already known to our readers, a thick copse succeeded the larger trees, and by the closeness of the trunks and the interlacing of the branches afforded still greater security to such as took advantage of its shade. It was, then, without being seen by any living soul that the little band made its way to the outskirts of the forest.

Nearly fifteen yards from the ditch that separated the forest from the plain—a ditch which ran along the road brought to the notice of our readers in the first chapter of this work and forming a means of communication between the Chateau du Parcq, the camp of the emperor, and the neighboring villages—our adventurers halted.

The spot was well selected for such a purpose; a huge oak, remaining with a few other trees of the same height and the same size, to indicate the sort of giants that had formerly fallen under the axe, spread its dome of foliage above their heads, while, by advancing a few steps forward, they could take in at a glance the whole plain, unseen themselves.

All raised their eyes at the same time to the leafy crown of the venerable tree. Yvonnet understood what was expected of him; he nodded consent and borrowed Fracasso's tablets, containing one last, immaculate leaf, which the poet showed him, at the same time recommending him to respect the others, the depositaries of his romantic reveries. He planted one of the two Scharfensteins against the gnarled trunk, not to be embraced, even by that giant's arms, placed a foot on each of the German's hands, climbed to his shoulders, from his shoulders to the branches, and was soon seated astride, on a stout bough, with as much ease and security as is a sailor on the yard of the maintop or jib-boom.

During the ascent, Gertrude followed him with an anxious eye; but she had already learned to restrain her fears and repress her cries. Besides, on seeing the carelessness with which her lover took his station on the branch, the readiness with which he turned his head left and right, she knew that he was at least in no danger from one of those fits of dizziness to which he was liable when nobody was looking on.

But Yvonnet, in the meanwhile, with one hand shading his eyes, was looking now north, now south, and appearing to divide his attention between two spectacles equally interesting.

These multiplied motions of the head strongly excited the curiosity of the adventurers, who, lost in the depths of the coppice, could see nothing of what Yvonnet was seeing from the elevated region in which he was domiciled.

Yvonnet could understand their impatience, of which they gave many signs by throwing back their heads, questioning him by a look, and even venturing to cry, in suppressed tones, "What is happening?"

And among those who questioned by voice and gesture we may be sure Mademoiselle Gertrude was not the least animated.

Yvonnet made a sign with his hand, which meant that if they waited a few seconds they should know as much as he. He opened the tablets of Fracasso, tore out the last blank page, wrote on this page a few lines in pencil, rolled the paper between his fingers, in order that the wind might not bear it away, and dropped it. All hands were stretched out to catch it, even the white little hands of Mademoiselle Gertrude; but it was between the huge paws of Franz Scharfenstein that the paper fell.

The giant laughed at his good luck, and, passing the paper to his neighbor, said, "Take it, Monsieur Procope; I don't know how to read French."

Procope, not less curious than the others to know what was passing, unfolded the paper, and amid general silence read the following lines:

"The Chateau du Parcq is on fire.

"Count Waldeck, his two sons, and forty reiters have appeared in the plain and are taking the direction of the camp.

"They are about two hundred yards from the point of the wood in which we are hidden.

"So much for my right.

"Now another little troop is following the road from the camp to the chateau.

"It consists of seven men, a leader, squire, page, and four soldiers.

"As well as I can judge from here, the leader is Duke Emmanuel Philibert.

"His troop is nearly at the same distance on our left that Waldeck's is on our right.

"If the two troops march at the same speed, they ought to meet at the point of the wood and find themselves face to face at the moment they least expect it.

"If Duke Emmanuel has been informed by M. Philippin, as seems probable, of what occurred at the chateau, we are about to see something curious.

"Attention, comrades; it is the duke, beyond doubt."

Here the note of Yvonnet ended. It was impossible to say more things in fewer words, and to promise with more simplicity a spectacle which, in truth, was likely to be very curious, if the adventurer was not mistaken on the identity and intentions of the parties.

Naturally, therefore, the several companions drew near the outskirts of the wood with all sorts of precautions, in order to witness with the greatest possible comfort and the least possible danger the spectacle promised by Yvonnet, and for observing which chance had given him the best place.

If the reader will follow the example of our adventurers, we shall not trouble ourselves about Count Waldeck and his sons, whose acquaintance we have made already through the medium of Mademoiselle Gertrude, and, stealing across the left border of the wood, we, too, shall put ourselves in communication with the new personage announced by Yvonnet, who, indeed, is no less a personage than the hero of our story.

Yvonnet was not mistaken. The leader, advancing between his squire and page, and preceding a little troop of four men-at-arms, as if there was only question of an ordinary patrol, was really Duke Emmanuel Philibert, generalissimo of the forces of the Emperor Charles V. in the Low Countries.

He was the more easily recognized because, instead of wearing his helmet on his head, it hung on the left side of his saddle, its constant position, in rain and sun, and even sometimes in battle; from whence it was said his soldiers, seeing his insensibility to cold and heat and blows, gave him the name of *Tête de Fer*.

He was at the present time a handsome young man of twenty-seven, of middle height, but vigorously built, with hair cut very short, very clearly marked brown eyebrows, keen blue eyes, and straight nose. He had a heavy mustache, and a beard trimmed to a point; in fine, his neck seemed pressed down on his shoulders, as happens almost always in the case of the descendants of those warlike races whose ancestors have worn the helmet for many generations.

When he spoke, his voice had at once infinite sweetness and remarkable firmness. A strange characteristic of it was that it could ascend to the expression of the most violent menace without rising more than one or two tones; the ascendant gamut of anger was concealed in the almost imperceptible gradations of the accent.

As a result, only his most intimate friends knew what perils awaited those imprudent enough to arouse and brave his anger—an anger so carefully restrained that its strength could only be understood, and its extent measured, at the moment when, preceded by the lightning of his eyes, it burst forth, thundered, and pulverized like a bolt from heaven. Then, the thunderbolt once fallen, the storm at once ceases, and the weather is again serene; the explosion over, the physiognomy of the duke recovered its habitual serenity and calm; his eyes their look of placidity and strength; his mouth its benevolent and royal smile.

As to the squire, riding at his right, with his visor up, he was a fair young man of nearly the same age and of exactly the same build as the duke. His clear blue eyes, full of boldness and energy, his beard and mustaches, fair, but with a warmer tint than that of his hair, his nose, with the nostrils dilated like those of a lion, his lips, whose plumpness and ruddiness the mustaches could not hide, his complexion, rich with the double coloring of health and exercise—all indicated the possession of the very highest degree of physical strength. At his back—not girt to his side—hung one of those terrible two-handed swords of which François I. broke three at the battle of Marignano, and which, from their length, could only be drawn from over the shoulder, while at the saddle-bow was one of those battle-axes that had a blade on one side, was a club on the other, and had a lance-head at the end, so that it could, when occasion required, be used as a hammer to knock a man down, an axe to cleave him in two, and a poniard to stab him.

On the left of the duke was the page, a handsome lad of from sixteen to perhaps, though scarcely, eighteen, with blue-black hair, cut after the German fashion, as it is worn in Holbein's knights and Raphael's angels. His eyes, shaded by long velvety lashes, were endowed with that elusive shade which floats between chestnut and violet, and is only met in Arab or Sicilian eyes. His olive complexion, of that fine olive peculiar to the northern countries of the Italian peninsula, resembled Carrara marble, whose paleness had been longingly and amorously absorbed by a Roman sun. His hands, small, white, and tapering, managed, with wonderful skill, a little Tunis horse whose sole saddle was a leopard's skin, with eyes of enamel, teeth and claws of gold, a slender silken cord serving for bridle. As to his dress, at once simple and full of elegance, it was composed of a doublet of black velvet, opening on a cherry-colored vest with white satin facings, and drawn in at the bottom by a gold cord supporting a dagger, the handle of which was a single agate. His feet, beautifully modelled, were shod with morocco boots, and came up above the knee, the hose of the same material and color as the doublet.

In fine, his forehead was covered by a cap of the same stuff and color as the entire exterior part of his clothing. A diamond agrafe held in front a cherry-colored plume which rolled around it, floating at the least breath of air, and falling gracefully between his shoulders.

And now that we have introduced our new characters, we shall return to the action, which, interrupted for a moment, is about to unfold itself with still more vigor and firmness than before.

In fact, during this description, Duke Emmanuel Philibert, his two companions, and the four men of his suite were proceeding on their way, without hurrying or slackening their horses' steps. Only, when they approached the point of the wood, the face of the duke grew more sombre, as if he had a presentiment that some spectacle of desolation would meet his eyes, once that point was passed. But suddenly, on arriving simultaneously at the extremity of the angle, as had foreseen Yvonnet, the two troops found themselves face to face, and, strange to say! it was the stronger of the two that stopped, nailed to the spot by a feeling of surprise, with which a little fear was obviously mingled.

Emmanuel Philibert, on the contrary, without indicating

by a start, by a gesture, by a motion of his countenance, the feeling, whatever it might be, which agitated him, continued his course, riding straight up to Count Waldeck, who awaited him, placed between his two sons.

At ten paces from the count, Emmanuel made a sign to his squire, his page, and four soldiers, who halted with a regularity and obedience quite military, and allowed him to go on alone.

When he was just within reach of Vicomte Waldeck, who happened to be stationed as a rampart between him and his father, the duke halted in turn.

The three gentlemen saluted by raising their hands to their helmets; but in raising his, the bastard of Waldeck lowered his visor, as if to be ready for any eventuality.

The duke replied to the triple salutation by an inclination of his bare head.

Then, addressing Vicomte Waldeck in that dulcet voice that made a harmony of his words—

"Vicomte," he said, "you are a brave and worthy gentleman, one of those gentlemen whom I love, and whom my august master, the Emperor Charles V., loves. I have been a long time thinking of doing something for you; but a quarter of an hour ago the opportunity has presented itself, and I have seized it. I have just been informed that a company of a hundred and twenty lances which I have ordered to be levied, by command of his Majesty the Emperor, on the left bank of the Rhine, is assembled at Spires; I have named you captain of this company."

"Monseigneur—" stammered the young man, astonished, and blushing with pleasure.

"Here is your commission, signed by me, and sealed with the seal of the Empire," continued the duke, drawing from his breast a parchment which he presented to the viscount; "take it, set out on the very instant, and without a minute's delay. Go, M. le Vicomte de Waldeck; show yourself worthy of the favor granted you, and God keep you!"

The favor was, in fact, great. And so the young man, obedient to the order given him to set out at once, immediately took leave of his father and brother, and, turning to Emmanuel—

"Monseigneur," said he, "you are truly a *justiciary*, as you are called, for evil as well as for good, for the wicked man as well as for the good man. You have had confidence in me; that confidence shall be justified. Adieu, monseigneur." And, spurring his horse to a gallop, the young man disappeared at a corner of the wood.

Emmanuel Philibert followed him with his eyes until he was entirely out of sight. Then, turning round, and fixing a severe look on Count Waldeck—

"And now it is your turn, M. le Comte!" he said.

"Monseigneur," interrupted the count, "let me first thank your Highness for the favor you have just granted my son."

"The favor I have granted Vicomte Waldeck does not deserve thanks," coldly replied Emmanuel, "since he has merited it. But you heard what he said: I am a justiciary for evil as well as for good, for the wicked man as well as for the good man. Surrender your sword, M. le Comte!"

The count started, and, in an accent that clearly indicated he would not easily obey the order just given him—

"Surrender my sword! And why?"

"You know my orders forbidding pillage and marauding, under penalty of the lash for the common soldiers, and court-martial or imprisonment for the officers. You have violated my orders by forcibly entering the Chateau du Parcq, in spite of the protest of your eldest son, and stealing the gold, jewelry and plate of the chatelaine inhabiting it. You are a marauder and a pillager; surrender your sword, M. le Comte de Waldeck!"

The duke pronounced these words without the tone of his voice visibly changing, except for his squire and page, who, beginning to comprehend the situation, looked at each other with a certain anxiety.

Count Waldeck turned pale; but, as we have said, it was difficult for a stranger to guess by the sound of Emmanuel Philibert's voice the menacing nature of his anger or his justice.

"My sword, monseigneur?" said Waldeck. "Oh! I must have committed some other misdeed? A gentleman does not surrender his sword for such a trifle!" And he tried to laugh disdainfully.

"Yes, monsieur, yes," returned Emmanuel, "you have committed something else; but for the honor of the German nobility I was silent about it. Do you wish me to speak? Be it so; then listen. It did not suffice you to rob the mistress of the house of her gold and jewelry and plate; you had her tied to the foot of her bed, and you said to her, 'If, in two hours, you do not put two hundred rose nobles in our hands, I shall set fire to your chateau!' You said this; and as, at the end of the two hours, the poor woman, who had given you her last pistole, found it impossible to hand over the sum demanded, in spite of the prayers of your eldest son, you set fire to the farm-buildings, in order that the unhappy victim might have time to make her own reflections before the fire gained the chateau. Hold! you will not attempt to say this is untrue: the smoke and flame can be seen from here. You are an incendiary; surrender your sword, M. le Comte!"

The count ground his teeth, for he was beginning to comprehend the extent of the resolution in the calm but firm words of the duke.

"Since you are so well informed as to the beginning, monseigneur," he said, "you are no doubt equally so as to the end?"

"You are right, monsieur, I know everything; but I wanted to spare you the cord, which you deserve."

"Monseigneur!" cried Waldeck, in a menacing tone.

"Silence, monsieur!" said Emmanuel Philibert; "respect your accuser, and tremble before your judge! The end? I am about to tell it to you. By the glare of the flame already mounting into the air, your bastard, who had the key of the room in which the prisoner was garroted, entered that room. The unfortunate woman had not cried on seeing the fire approaching her; that was only death. She cried on seeing your bastard advance and seize her in his arms, for that was dishonor! Vicomte Waldeck heard these cries, and ran up. He summoned his brother to restore the woman he was outraging to liberty; but instead of answering the appeal, he flung his prisoner, still garroted, on the bed, and drew his sword. Vicomte Waldeck also drew his, resolved to save this woman, even at the peril of his life. The two brothers attacked each other furiously, for there had been bitter hate between them for a long time. You then entered, and, believing your sons to be fighting for the possession of this woman, 'The fairest woman in the world,' you said, 'is not worth a single drop of blood from the veins of a soldier. Sheathe your swords, boys; I will make you friends again.' Then both the brothers lowered their weapons at your command; you stepped between them; both followed you with their eyes, for they did not know what you were about to do. You approached the woman, and before either of your sons had time to prevent the infamous deed, you drew your dagger and plunged it in her breast. Do not say that this is not so; do not say that this is not true; your dagger is still wet and your hands are still bloody. You are an assassin; surrender your sword, Count Waldeck!"

"That is easily said, monseigneur," replied the count; "but a Waldeck would not surrender you his sword, prince though you be, even if he stood alone against you seven; for a stronger reason, he will not, when he has his son on his right and forty soldiers at his back."

"Then," said Emmanuel, with a slight change in his voice, "if you will not surrender it voluntarily, I must take it by force." And, with a single bound, his horse was side by side with Count Waldeck's.

The latter was pressed too close to be able to draw his

sword; he reached his hand to his holsters; but, before he could open them, Emmanuel Philibert had plunged his hand in his, which were open beforehand, and drew a pistol, ready loaded, from them.

The movement was so rapid that neither the bastard of Waldeck, nor the squire, nor the page of the duke, nor Count Waldeck himself foresaw it. Emmanuel Philibert, with a hand steady and sure as that of justice, discharged it at such close quarters that he burned the count's face, as well as blew out his brains.

The count had hardly time to utter a cry; he opened his arms, fell back slowly on the croup of his horse, like an athlete whom some invisible wrestler was bending backward, lost the spur from his left foot, then from his right, and rolled heavily on the ground.

The justiciary had done justice: the count was killed on the spot.

During all the time the scene lasted, the bastard of Waldeck, entirely sheathed in his iron mail, had remained as motionless as an equestrian statue; but when he heard the pistol-shot and saw his father fall, he uttered a hoarse cry of rage, which was further roughened through the visor of his helmet. Then, addressing the stupefied and frightened reiters—

"Help, comrades!" he shouted in German; "this man is not one of us. Death! death to Duke Emmanuel Philibert!"

But the only reply of the reiters was a shake of the head in sign of refusal.

"Ah!" cried the young man, allowing himself to grow more and more enraged—"ah! you do not listen to me! You refuse to avenge one who loved you as his children, who loaded you with gold, who gorged you with booty! Well, then, I will avenge him, since you are ingrates and cowards!"

And he drew his sword, about to rush upon the duke. But two reiters jumped to the head of his horse, seizing the rein on each side of the bit, while a third clasped him in his arms.

The young man struggled furiously, overwhelming those who held him with insults.

The duke gazed on the spectacle with a certain pity; he understood the despair of this son who had just seen his father fall at his feet.

"Your Highness," said the reiters, "what orders have you to give regarding this man, and what are we to do with him?"

"Let him go free," said the duke. "He threatened me. If I arrested him, he might believe I was afraid."

The reiters tore the sword from the hands of the bastard and left him free.

The young man spurred his horse, which, at a single bound, cleared the distance between him and Emmanuel Philibert.

The latter awaited him with his hand on the trigger of his second pistol.

"Emmanuel Philibert, Duke of Savoy, Prince of Piedmont," cried the bastard of Waldeck, extending his hand toward him threateningly, "you understand, do you not, that from this day there is between me and you mortal hatred? Emmanuel Philibert, you have slain my father." He lowered his visor. "Look well at my face, and every time you see it again, by night or by day, at festival or in battle, woe to you, Emmanuel Philibert!"

And he set out at full gallop, shaking his hand, as if to hurl one more malediction at the duke, and crying again, for the last time, "Woe!"

"Wretch!" shouted the squire of Emmanuel, spurring his horse, in order to pursue him.

But the duke, making an imperative sign with his hand—

"Not a step further, Scianca-Ferro!" he said; "I forbid you!"

Then, turning to his page, who, pale as death, seemed ready to drop from the saddle—

"What is the matter, Leone?" he said, approaching, and offering his hand. "In truth, seeing you thus, wan and trembling, one would take you for a woman!"

"Oh, my beloved duke," murmured the page, "say again that you are not wounded, or I die—"

"Child!" said the duke, "am I not under the hand of God?"

Then, addressing the reiters—

"My friends," he said, pointing to the dead body of Count Waldeck, "give this man Christian burial, and let the justice I have executed on him be to you a proof that in my eyes, as in those of the Lord, there are neither great nor little."

And making a sign of the head to Scianca-Ferro and Leone, he took the road to the camp with them, without any trace remaining on his countenance of the terrible event that had just taken place, except that the usual thoughtful furrow on his forehead seemed a little more deepened than customarily.

VII

HISTORY AND ROMANCE

WHILE the adventurers, visible witnesses of the catastrophe we have related, after casting a melancholy glance on the smoking ruins of the Chateau du Parcq, are regaining their grotto, where they will put their signatures to the deed of partnership, become useless for the present, but likely to bear the most marvellous results in the future for their nascent association; while the reiters, obedient to the order given, or rather to the recommendation made, to procure Christian sepulture for their dead leader, are about to dig the grave of him who, having received the punishment of his crime on earth, rests now in the hope of divine mercy; while, in fine, Emmanuel Philibert reaches his tent with his squire and page on each side of him—let us, abandoning the prologue, *mise en scène*, and secondary characters of our drama for the real action and principal characters about to come on the stage, let us venture, in order to give the reader a more ample knowledge of their disposition and moral and political situation, on an excursion at once historical for some, and romantic for others, into the domain of the past, that splendid realm of the poet and historian, which no revolution can wrest from them.

Emmanuel Philibert, third son of Charles III. the Good and Beatrix of Portugal, was born in the castle of Chambéry on the 8th of July, 1528.

He received his double name Emmanuel Philibert for the following reasons: Emmanuel, in honor of his maternal grandfather Emmanuel, King of Portugal, and Philibert, in virtue of a vow made by his father to Saint Philibert of Tournus.

He was born at four in the afternoon, and appeared so weak at his entrance into life that the respiration of the infant was supported solely by the breath introduced into his lungs by one of the women of his mother; and until he was three years old he remained with his head inclined on his breast, and was unable to stand on his legs. So, when his horoscope was drawn, as was then customary at the birth of every prince, and it was predicted that the new-born child was to be a great warrior, and glorify the House of Savoy with a splendor brighter than it had received from Peter, surnamed the Little Charlemagne, or Amadeus V., called the Great, or Amadeus VI., vulgarly styled the *Green Count*, his mother could not help shedding tears, and his father, a resigned and pious prince, saying, with a shake of the head and an expression of doubt, to the mathematician who made the prediction:

"May God hear you, my friend!"

Emmanuel Philibert was the nephew of Charles V. by his mother Beatrix of Portugal, the fairest and most accomplished princess of her time, and cousin of François I., by his aunt, Louise of Savoy, under whose pillow the Connétable de Bourbon claimed to have left the cordon of the Order of the Holy Ghost, which François I. ordered him to return.

Another of his aunts was that vivacious Margaret of Austria, who left a collection of songs in manuscript still to be seen in the national library of France, and who, when attacked by a storm at the time she was going to Spain to marry the son of Ferdinand and Isabella, after having been betrothed to the Dauphin of France and to the King of England, made, under the impression she was going to die, this curious epitaph on herself—

> Weep, Loves, the fate of Margaret here laid,
> Who thrice betrothèd was, yet died a maid.

As to Emmanuel Philibert, he was, as we have said, so weak that, in spite of the prediction of the astrologer that he would be a powerful warrior, his father destined him for the Church. So, at the age of three, he was sent to Bologna to kiss the feet of Pope Clement VII., who, coming thither to give the crown to his uncle, the Emperor Charles V., and on the recommendation of the latter, the young prince obtained the promise of a cardinal's hat. Hence his surname of the Cardinalin, given him in childhood, and which used to enrage him.

Why should this name enrage the child? We are about to see.

The reader remembers that woman, or rather that friend, of the Duchess of Savoy, who had breathed life into the little Emmanuel Philibert an hour after his birth, and just as he was about to expire. Six months before, she had had a son who came into the world as strong and vigorous as that of the duchess had come weak and languishing. Now, the duchess, seeing her son thus saved, said to her:

"My dear Lucrezia, this child is now as much yours as mine; I give him to you. Take him, nourish him with your milk as you have nourished him with your breath, and I shall owe you more than even he does; for he will only owe you life, but I shall owe you my child!"

Lucrezia received the child, of whom she was now made the mother, as a sacred trust. And yet it looked as if this must work some injury to the little Rinaldo—it was the name of her own son—if the heir of the Duke of Savoy was to recover life and strength by depriving his foster-brother of a portion of that nutriment which was his due.

But Rinaldo at six months was stronger than another child would have been at the end of a year. Besides, Nature has her miracles, and the two infants drew life from the same paps without the source of the maternal milk being for a moment exhausted.

The duchess smiled as she saw, hanging from the same living trellis, this stranger child so strong, and her own child so feeble.

For that matter, it might be said that little Rinaldo understood this feebleness, and had compassion on it. Often the capricious ducal baby wanted the pap at which the other was drinking; and the latter, a smile on his lips white with milk, gave place to his imperious foster-brother.

Thus the two children grew on the knees of Lucrezia. At three Rinaldo seemed to be five; at three, as we have said, Emmanuel Philibert hardly walked, and only with an effort raised his head from his breast. This was the time of the journey to Bologna, when Pope Clement VII. promised him the cardinal's hat.

It looked as if this promise brought him good fortune, and this name of Cardinalin won him the protection of God; for when he passed his third year, his health improved and his body grew vigorous.

But the one who in this respect made the most marvellous progress was Rinaldo. His most solid playthings flew into pieces under his fingers; he could not touch any one of them without breaking it.

Then his toys were made of steel, but he broke them as

if they were china. And so it was that the good Duke Charles III., who amused himself with seeing the children at their games, called the companion of Emmanuel Philibert *Scianca-Ferro*, which in the Piedmontese *patois* signifies, *Brise-Fer*.

The name remained to him. And the remarkable thing was that Scianca-Ferro never used this miraculous strength except to protect Emmanuel, whom he adored instead of being jealous of him, as might perhaps have happened in the case of another child.

As to young Emmanuel, he envied very much his foster-brother's strength, and would have willingly exchanged his nickname of Cardinalin for that of Scianca-Ferro.

However, he seemed to gain a certain vigor from this companionship with a vigor greater than his own. Scianca-Ferro, bringing his strength down to the level of the young prince's, wrestled with him, ran with him, and, not to discourage him, allowed himself sometimes to be outstripped in the race and vanquished in the wrestling-bout.

All exercises—riding, swimming, fencing—were common to them. In all, Scianca-Ferro was the superior. But it was, after all, only an affair of chronology; and Victor Emmanuel, though holding back, had not yet said his last word.

The two children were inseparable, and loved each other like brothers. Each was jealous of the other, as a mistress might have been of her lover; and yet the time was approaching when a third companion, whom they would adopt with equal affection, was to mingle in their games.

One day when the court of Charles III. was at Verceil, on account of certain disturbances that had broken out at Milan, the two lads, in company with their riding-master, made a lengthy journey on horseback along the left bank of the Sesia, passed by Novara, and ventured almost up to the Ticino. The horse of the young duke was in front, when suddenly a bull, shut up in a pasture-field, breaking through the barriers by which he was imprisoned, frightened the horse of the prince. The animal ran away with him, crossing meadows, and leaping over streams, bushes, and hedges. Emmanuel was an admirable rider, so there was nothing to be feared; however, Scianca-Ferro rushed after him, taking the same course he did, and, like him, leaping over all the obstacles he encountered. The riding-master, more prudent, went round by a circular line, which was likely to lead him to the point the two young people were making for.

After a quarter of an hour's reckless racing, Scianca-Ferro, no longer seeing Emmanuel, and fearing he had met with some accident, called with all his might. Two of these appeals remained unanswered; at last he thought he heard the prince's voice in the direction of Oleggio. He turned his horse on that side, and soon, in fact, guided by the voice of Emmanuel, he found his comrade on the banks of an affluent of the Ticino.

At his feet was a dead woman, and in her arms a little boy, almost dying, of from four to five years.

The horse, which had grown calm, was quietly browsing the young shoots of the trees, while his master was trying to restore consciousness to the child. As to the woman, nothing could be done for her; she was quite dead.

She appeared to have succumbed to fatigue, misery, and hunger. The child, who had undoubtedly shared the misery and fatigue of his mother, seemed nearly dead from exhaustion.

The village of Oleggio seemed only a mile from there. Scianca-Ferro set his horse to a gallop, and disappeared in the direction of the village.

Emmanuel would have gone there himself, instead of sending his brother; but the child clung to him, and, feeling that there was still a bare chance for its life, he did not wish to leave it.

The poor little thing had drawn him quite near the woman, and was saying, with that heartrending accent of childhood, unconscious of its misfortune—

"Wake up, mamma! please waken, mamma!"

Emmanuel wept. What could he do, poor child, now

seeing, for the first time, the spectacle of death? He had only his tears, and he gave them.

Scianca-Ferro reappeared; he brought bread and a flask of Asti wine. They tried to introduce a few drops between the lips of the mother—a vain effort: she was but a corpse. There was nothing to be done, therefore, except for the child.

The child, while weeping because his mother would not waken, drank and ate, and recovered a little strength.

At this moment the peasants, whom Scianca-Ferro had summoned, arrived. They had met the riding-master, who was quite scared at the disappearance of his two pupils, and led him to the place appointed by Scianca-Ferro.

They then knew that they were acting for the young Prince of Savoy; and as Duke Charles was adored by his subjects, they at once offered to execute whatever orders Emmanuel might give with regard to the mother and child.

Emmanuel selected from among the peasants a woman who looked kind-hearted and good; he gave her all the money he and Scianca-Ferro had on them, took her name down in writing, and begged her to see after the mother's funeral and the most pressing needs of the child.

Then, as it was growing late, the riding-master insisted on his two pupils turning their horses' heads toward Verceil. The little orphan wept bitterly; he did not want to quit his good friend Emmanuel, for he knew his name, though not his rank. Emmanuel promised to return to see him; this promise quieted him somewhat; but as long as he could see him he continued to stretch out his arms toward the savior chance had brought him.

And, in truth, if the succor sent by chance, or rather, by Providence, to the poor child, had been delayed even two hours, he would have been found dead beside his mother.

Notwithstanding all the diligence of the riding-master, the evening was far advanced when they reached the castle of Verceil. There had been considerable anxiety about them, and messengers sent in all directions. The duchess was preparing to give them a good scolding when Emmanuel began his story, relating it in his sweet voice, whose tones were instinct with the sadness the gloomy event had impressed on his soul. The story finished, no one thought of scolding, but rather of praising the children; and the duchess, sharing the interest felt in the orphan by her son, declared that on the day after the funeral of the mother, she would pay him a visit.

And on the day appointed, the duchess set out in a litter, accompanied by the two young comrades on horseback.

On arriving near the village, Emmanuel could not restrain himself; he set spurs to his horse and rode at full speed to see the little orphan again.

His arrival was a great joy for the unfortunate child. It had been necessary to tear him away from the body of his mother; he would not believe she was dead, and never ceased crying—

"Do not put her in the ground; do not put her in the ground! I promise you she will awaken!"

Ever since his mother had been borne from the house, they had had to lock him up; he wanted to go and stay with her.

The sight of his savior consoled him a little.

Emmanuel told him his mother desired to see him, and was about to arrive.

"And you have a mamma also?" said the orphan. "Oh, I shall pray to God not to let her go to sleep so as not to waken any more!"

It was great news that Emmanuel gave the peasants— this coming of the duchess into their house; and as they told it everywhere, people flocked from all quarters of the village in the direction she was coming.

So there was soon quite a procession, which arrived, preceded by Scianca-Ferro, who had gallantly remained to act as squire to the duchess.

Emmanuel presented his *protégé* to his mother. The

duchess asked the child what Emmanuel had forgotten to ask him; that is to say, what was his name, and who was his mother.

The child replied that he was called Leone and his mother Leona; but he would not give any other details, answering to all the questions put to him, "I do not know."

And yet, strange to say, it was easy to guess that this ignorance was feigned and that it concealed a secret.

Undoubtedly, his mother, when dying, had advised him to only answer as he answered; and, indeed, nothing but the last recommendation of a dying mother could make such an impression on a child of four years.

Then the duchess studied the child with a curiosity altogether feminine. Although his dress was coarse, the hands were delicate and white; it was easily seen that a mother, and an elegant and refined mother, had taken care of those hands. At the same time, his language was that of the aristocracy, and he spoke French and Italian equally well.

The duchess ordered the dress of his mother to be brought to her; it was that of a peasant.

But the peasants who had undressed her said they never had seen a whiter skin, more delicate hands, or feet more small and elegant.

Moreover, one circumstance betrayed the class of society to which the poor woman must have belonged; though her garb was that of a peasant, rough shoes and drugget gown, she wore silk stockings.

Clearly she had fled in disguise; and of all her garments had only kept the silk stockings which betrayed her after her death.

The duchess returned to Leone and questioned him on all these points; but his constant answer was, "I do not know." She could not get any other reply from him. She recommended anew the poor orphan to the care of the worthy peasants, giving them double the sum they had already received, and charged them to make inquiries about the mother and child in the neighborhood, promising them a liberal reward if they were able to give her any information.

Little Leone made the greatest efforts to follow Emmanuel; and Emmanuel was very near begging his mother to let him take him with him, so genuine was the pity he felt for the orphan. He promised Leone then that he would return to see him as soon as possible, and the duchess herself declared she would pay him a second visit.

Unfortunately, about this same period occurred events that compelled the duchess to break her promise. For the third time François I. declared war on Charles V., on account of the duchy of Milan, which he claimed to inherit through Valentine Visconti, wife of Louis d'Orléans, brother of Charles VI.

The first time François had won the battle of Marignano. The second time he had lost the battle of Pavia.

After the treaty of Madrid, after the prison of Toledo, after, above all, he had pledged his faith, it would have been allowable to imagine that François I. had renounced all claim to this unfortunate duchy, which, if won by him, would have made the King of France a vassal of the Empire. But it was quite the contrary; he was only waiting for an opportunity to lay claim to it again, and he seized the first that presented itself.

It was good, luckily; but if it had been bad, he would have seized it all the same.

François I., we know, was not scrupulous as to a violation of those silly delicacies that often hamper those donkeys known by the name of honest men.

The following, then, was the opportunity placed within his reach.

Maria Francesco Sforza, son of Ludovico the Moor,[1] was reigning over Milan; but he was reigning under the complete guardianship of the Emperor, from whom he had purchased, on the 23d of December, 1529, his duchy for

---

[1] Many historians believe that he derived his surname, *il Moro*, not from his swarthy complexion, but from the mulberry-tree in his coat of arms.

two hundred thousand ducats, payable during the first year of his reign, and five hundred thousand payable in the two following years.

As security for these payments, the castle of Milan, Como, and Pavia remained in the hands of the Imperialists.

Now it happened that, toward 1535, a Milanese gentleman, whose fortune François I. had made, was accredited as ambassador of France at the court of Duke Sforza.

This gentleman was named Francesco Maraviglia. Having grown very rich at the court of France, Francesco Maraviglia was at once proud and happy to return to his natal city with all the pomp of an ambassador.

He brought with him his wife and daughter, then three years old, leaving in Paris, among the pages of King François, his son Odoart, aged twelve years.

How did this ambassador come to offend Charles V.? Why did he invite Sforza to get rid of him on the first opportunity? This is unknown, and can only be known when the secret correspondence of the Emperor with the Duke of Milan is discovered, as was his secret correspondence with Cosmo de Médicis. But, however, it happened that when there was an accidental quarrel between some subjects of Sforza and the servants of the ambassador, in which two of the former were slain, Maraviglia was arrested and conducted to the castle of Milan, held, as we have said, by the Imperialists.

What became of Maraviglia? No one ever knew for certain. Some said he had been poisoned; others, that, having missed his footing, he had fallen into an *oubliette*, the neighborhood of which they neglected to warn him of. In fine, the most probable version and the one most believed was that he had been executed, or rather assassinated, in prison. The certain fact, however, is that he had disappeared, and with him, almost at the same time, his wife and daughter, without leaving a trace behind them.

These events had occurred quite recently, scarcely more than a few days before the meeting between Emmanuel and

CAPTAIN PLANCHET *Dumas, Vol. Twenty*

the dead woman and her abandoned child on the banks of a little stream. They were to have a terrible effect on the destiny of Duke Charles.

François I. seized the opportunity by the hair.

It was not the lamentations of the child beside him demanding vengeance for the murder of his father; it was not the royal majesty outraged in the person of an ambassador; it was not, in fine, the law of nations violated by an assassination, which inclined the balance to the side of war. No; it was the old leaven of vengeance fermenting in the heart of him who had been vanquished at Pavia and a prisoner in Toledo.

A third expedition to Italy was resolved on.

The moment was well chosen. Charles V. was in Africa fighting against the famous Khaïr-Eddin, surnamed Barbarossa.

But to accomplish this fresh invasion, it was necessary to pass through Savoy. Now Savoy was held by Charles the Good, father of Emmanuel Philibert, uncle of François I., and brother-in-law of Charles V.

For whom would Charles the Good declare himself? Would it be for his nephew? It was an important thing to know.

But it was suspected what his action would be; all the probabilities pointed to the Duke of Savoy being the ally of the Empire and the enemy of France.

In fact, as a pledge of his faith, the Duke of Savoy had intrusted to Charles V. his eldest son Louis, Prince of Piedmont. He had refused to receive the order of Saint Michael from François I. and a company of artillery with a pension of twelve thousand crowns; he had occupied the lands of the marquisate of Saluce, a transferable fief in Dauphiné. He refused homage to the crown of France for that of Faucigny. He had expressed his satisfaction at the defeat of Pavia in letters to the Emperor. In fine, he had loaned money to the Connétable de Bourbon, when the latter traversed his states in order to go and get killed by Benvenuto Cellini at the siege of Rome.

Still, it was necessary to be sure if the doubts were well founded.

With this object, François I. sent to Turin Guillaume Poyet, President of the Parliament of Paris. The latter was instructed to ask Charles two things—

The first was a passage for the French army through Savoy and Piedmont.

The second, the delivery, as places of security, of Montmélian, Veillane, Chivas, and Verceil.

In exchange, he offered to Duke Charles to give him lands in France, and to give his daughter Marguerite in marriage to Prince Louis, eldest brother of Emmanuel Philibert.

Charles III. deputed Purpurat, the Piedmontese president, to discuss matters with Guillaume Poyet, the President of the Parliament of Paris. The former was authorized to permit the passage of the French troops through the two provinces of Savoy and Piedmont; but he was first to parry diplomatically the demand for the surrender of the fortresses, and then, if Poyet insisted, to give an absolute refusal.

The discussion grew warm between the two plenipotentiaries, until at last Poyet, routed by the reasoning of Purpurat, exclaimed:

"It shall be so, because the king wills it!"

"Excuse me," replied Purpurat; "but I do not find that law among the laws of Piedmont."

And, rising, he abandoned the future to the omnipotent will of the King of France and to the wisdom of the Most High.

The conferences were broken up, and in the course of the month of February, 1535, Duke Charles being in his castle of Verceil, a herald was introduced into his presence, who declared war against him in the name of King François I.

The duke heard him tranquilly, then when he had finished his warlike message—

"My friend," he said in a calm voice, "I have rendered only services to the King of France, and I have thought that the titles of ally, friend, servant, and uncle might have met with a better return. I have done what I could to live on a good understanding with him; I have neglected nothing that could prove to him how wrong he is to be irritated against me. But since he will in no manner listen to reason, and appears determined to take possession of my states, tell him that he shall find me on the frontier, and that, seconded by my friends and allies, I hope to defend and preserve my country. The king my nephew knows, besides, my motto: 'Nothing fails him to whom God is left!'"

And he dismissed the herald, after ordering a very rich dress and a pair of gloves filled with crowns to be given him.

After such a reply there was nothing for it but to prepare for war.

The first resolution adopted by Charles III. was to secure the safety of his wife and son by placing them in the fortress of Nice.

The departure for Nice was therefore announced as very near.

Then Emmanuel Philibert decided that the time had come to obtain from his mother a favor he had delayed asking until now; namely, permission to take Leone away from his peasant home, where, for that matter, he had been left only provisionally, as it had been agreed to make him, as well as Scianca, a companion of the young prince.

The Duchess Beatrix, as we have already said, was a woman of judicious mind. Everything she had remarked in the orphan—the delicacy of his features, the fineness of his hands, the distinction of his language—led her to believe that some great mystery was hidden under the rude garb of mother and child. The duchess, besides, was a woman of religious heart; she saw the hand of God in this meeting between Leone and Emmanuel, brought about by an accident—an accident almost providential, since it had no other result than to conduct the young prince to the dead woman and the expiring child. She thought that at the moment when her family was losing everything, when misfortune was approaching her house, and when the angel of darkness was pointing out to her and her husband and child the mysterious road of exile, it was not the hour to repulse the orphan, who, grown to manhood, would perhaps one day become a friend. She recalled the messenger of God presenting himself as a simple traveller on the threshold of the blind Tobias, to whom, by the hands of his son, he restored later joy and light; and, far from resisting the prayer of Emmanuel, at the first word he said, she anticipated it, and with the permission of the duke, authorized her son to transport his *protégé* to Verceil.

From Verceil to Nice, Leone was to make the journey with the two other children.

Emmanuel did not wait longer than the next day to announce the good news to Leone. At daybreak he descended to the stables, saddled himself his little Barbary horse, and, leaving to Scianca the care of the rest, started for Oleggio with all the speed possible.

He found Leone very sad. The poor orphan had also heard that his rich and powerful protectors were, in their turn, visited by misfortune. They had spoken of the departure of the court for Nice—that is to say, for a country whose very name was unknown to Leone; and when Emmanuel arrived, breathless from his race and sparkling with joy, Leone was weeping as if he had a second time lost his mother.

It is through tears especially that children see the angels. We do not exaggerate in saying that Emmanuel appeared like an angel through the tears of Leone.

In a few words everything was said, explained, and settled, and smiles succeeded tears. There is with man—and it is his happy time—a period when tears and smiles touch each other as the night touches the dawn.

Two hours after Emmanuel, Scianca-Ferro arrived with

the first equerry of the prince and two grooms, holding by the bridle the favorite pony of the duchess. A considerable sum of money was bestowed on the peasants, who had for six weeks taken care of Leone. The latter embraced them, weeping again. But this time tears of joy were mingled with tears of regret. Emmanuel assisted him to mount, and for fear any accident might happen to his dear *protégé*, he himself wished to lead the pony by the bridle.

Instead of being jealous of this new friendship, Scianca-Ferro galloped along quite joyous, going and returning, examining the route as if he had been a real captain, and smiling with that fine boyish smile that discloses the teeth and the heart at the same time, on the friend of his friend.

It was in this manner they arrived at Verceil. The duchess and the duke embraced Leone, and Leone was one of the family.

The next day they set out for Nice, which they reached without any accident.

VIII

SQUIRE AND PAGE

IT IS not our intention—God forbid! others having done it much better than we could—it is not our intention, we repeat, to relate the wars of Italy, and write the history of the great rivalry that desolated the beginning of the sixteenth century. No, God has happily, in this case at least, assigned us a more humble task; but still, we must be permitted to say, a task more picturesque for ourselves and more amusing for our readers. We shall, therefore, see, in the narrative about to follow, only the summits of great events, which, like unto the topmost ridges of the Alps, lift above the clouds their peaks covered with eternal snows.

François I. broke through Savoy, crossed Piedmont, and spread over Italy.

For three years the cannon of France and of the Empire thundered, now in Provence, now in the duchy of Milan.

Fair plains of Lombardy, only the Angel of Death can tell how many corpses were needed to give you your inexhaustible fertility.

During this time, under the lovely sky of Nice, all azure in daytime, all flame at night, when the very insects of darkness are winged sparks, the children grew up under the look of the Princess Beatrix, and under the eye of God.

Leone had become an indispensable member of the joyous trinity; he shared in all the sports, but not in all the exercises. The too violent studies of the art of war did not suit his little hands, and his arms seemed to the masters of this art too weak ever to bear in martial fashion the lance or the buckler. It is true Leone was three years younger than his companions. But it appeared as if in reality there were ten years' difference between them, particularly since —undoubtedly by the grace of the Lord, who was reserving him for great things—Emmanuel had begun to grow in health and strength, as if he had set himself the task of gaining in this respect the distance in the race in which he had been outstripped by his foster-brother, Scianca-Ferro.

And so their respective offices fell quite naturally to the companions of the little duke. Scianca-Ferro became his squire, and Leone his page.

Meanwhile news came that Prince Louis, the eldest son of the duke, had died at Madrid.

It was a great sorrow for Duke Charles and Duchess Beatrix. But with the sorrow God gave them the consolation, if in truth there be any consolation for a father and, above all, for a mother, in the death of their offspring. Prince Louis had been for a long time a stranger to his parents; while, under the eyes of the duke and duchess, Emmanuel Philibert, who appeared every day to do more and more credit to the prediction of the astrologer, was flourishing like a lily, growing vigorous as an oak.

But God, who had doubtless wished only to try the exiles, before long struck them with a still more cruel blow. The Duchess Beatrix fell sick of some disease that exhausted all her vitality; and in spite of the art of physicians, and the care of her husband, child, and attendants, she expired on the 8th of January, 1538.

The duke's grief was deep, but religious; that of Emmanuel bordered on despair. Happily the ducal child had near him that other child who knew what were tears. What would have become of him without this gentle companion, who did not try to console him, and who was contented to mingle his own tears with his?—this was all his philosophy.

Undoubtedly Scianca-Ferro also suffered from this loss; if he could have restored life to the duchess by going in search of some terrible giant and challenging him in his castle, or defying some fabulous dragon in his cavern, this paladin of eleven years would have set out on the very instant, and without hesitation, to accomplish this exploit; for though he lost his life in the enterprise, would it not give back joy and happiness to his friend? But this was the limit of all the consolation he could offer; his robust nature did not lend itself kindly to enervating weeping. A wound might make his blood flow; no sorrow would make his tears flow. What was necessary to Scianca-Ferro was dangers to vanquish, not misfortunes to endure.

And so what was he doing while Emmanuel Philibert was weeping, with his head resting on the shoulder of Leone? He was saddling his horse, girding on his sword, hanging his club from his saddle-bows, and wandering through that beautiful stretch of hills which borders the Mediterranean. Like a mastiff whose rage is excited against sticks and stones, which he grinds between his teeth, he was figuring to his imagination that he was dealing blows at the heretics of Germany or the Saracens of Africa, was making fantastic enemies out of insensible and inanimate objects, and, in default of cuirasses to batter and helmets to cleave, was breaking rocks with his mace and splitting pines and oaks with his sword, seeking and finding a relief for his sorrow in the violent exercises suited to his rude organization.

Hours, days, and months slipped by; tears were dried. The grief, living at the bottom of the heart as a gentle regret and tender memory, disappeared gradually from the countenance; eyes that searched in vain for the spouse, mother, and friend here below were raised to heaven, seeking for the angel there.

The heart that turns to God is very close to consolation.

Moreover, events continued their march, imposing on sorrow itself a powerful distraction.

A congress had been decided on, to be participated in by Pope Paul III. (Alexander Farnese), François I., and Charles V. The subjects of discussion were: the expulsion of the Turks from Europe, the creation of a duchy for Louis Farnese, and the restitution to the Duke of Savoy of his states. The congress was to be held at Nice.

Nice had been selected by the Pope and by Charles V., in hopes that François I., in recognition of the hospitality received from his uncle, would be more ready for concessions.

Then there was also a kind of understanding to be brought about between Pope Paul III. and Charles V.

Alexander Farnese had given his eldest son Louis the duchies of Parma and Placentia, in exchange for the principalities of Camerino and Nepi, which he had just taken from him to give to his second son Octavio. This investiture was displeasing to Charles V., who had lately refused to grant the Pope, on the death of Maria Francesco Sforza in 1535, that famous duchy of Milan that was, if not the cause, at least the pretext of this interminable war between France and the Empire; and this he did, disregarding any amount of money offered, however large.

For that matter, Charles V. was quite right; the new

Duke of Parma and Placentia was that infamous Louis Farnese who used to say he did not care to be loved, provided he was feared; who disarmed the nobles, flogged women, and outraged bishops.

The popes of the sixteenth century were not happy in their children.

The congress of Nice had then for object not only to reconcile the Duke of Savoy and the King of France, but also the Pope and the Emperor.

However, Charles III., whom misfortune had rendered cautious, could not see without anxiety his nephew, his brother-in-law, and their holy arbitrator installed in his last fortified place.

Who could assure him that, instead of restoring the states that were taken from him, they would not deprive him of what was left to him?

At all hazards then, and for greater security, he shut up Emmanuel Philibert, his last heir, just as Nice was his last city, in the fortress that commanded the place, charging the governor not to open the castle to any force whatever, though this force came on the part of pope, emperor, or king.

Then he went in person to meet Paul III., who, according to the programme arranged, was to precede the Emperor and King of France by some days.

The Pope was no more than a league from Nice, when a letter reached the governor from the duke, ordering him to prepare the *Pope's lodgings* in the castle.

This letter was brought by his Holiness's captain of guards, who, at the head of two hundred foot-soldiers, demanded to be admitted into the castle, in order to wait on his sovereign.

Duke Charles spoke of the Pope, but he had said nothing of the captain nor of his two hundred men.

The thing was embarrassing; the Pope was expressly asking what the governor was expressly forbidden to grant.

The governor assembled a council.

Emmanuel Philibert was present, although hardly eleven years old.

Without doubt he had been summoned there to give courage to his defenders.

While they were deliberating, the child perceived hanging from the wall the wooden model of the castle now likely to form a bone of contention between the Pope and Charles III.

"By my faith, gentlemen!" he said to the councillors, who had been disputing an hour without being the further advanced for that, "you are very much embarrassed for a trifle. Since we have a castle of wood and a castle of stone, let us give the wooden one to the Pope and keep the stone one for ourselves."

"Gentlemen," said the governor, "we have been taught our duty by the words of a child. His Holiness shall have, if he like, the castle of wood; but I swear by God, he shall not have, while I am alive, the castle of stone!"

The reply of the child and the reply of the governor were carried to the Pope, who did not insist further, and took lodgings in the convent of the Cordeliers.

The Emperor arrived, then the King of France.

Each lodged under his tent on either side of the city, with the Pope between them.

The congress was opened.

Unfortunately the results were far different from what was hoped.

The Emperor claimed, on behalf of his brother-in-law, the states of Savoy and Piedmont.

François I. claimed for his second son, the Duke of Orléans, the duchy of Milan.

In fine, the Pope, who also wanted to settle his son there, demanded that a prince belonging neither to the family of François nor of Charles V. should be elected Duke of Milan, on condition of receiving investitutre from the Emperor and paying a tribute to the King of France.

Each wanted the impossible, since he wanted the exact

contrary of what the others wanted. Everybody, indeed, desired a truce—François I., in order to give a little rest to his soldiers, who were half-exhausted, and to his finances, which were entirely so; Charles V., in order to repress the incursions of the Turks in his two kingdoms of Naples and Sicily; Paul III., in order to make sure of the principalities of Parma and Placentia for his son, since he could not establish him in the duchy of Milan.

A ten years' truce was concluded. François I. himself fixed on the figure.

"Ten years or nothing!" he said peremptorily. And ten years were given him.

It is true that he was the first to break this truce at the end of four.

Charles III., who feared that all these conferences would end in the sequestration of the little territory remaining to him, saw his illustrious guests depart with more joy than he had seen them arrive.

They left him as they had found him, only somewhat poorer by the debts they had incurred in his states and forgotten to pay.

The Pope was the only one who pulled anything out of the fire; he had pulled two marriages—the marriage of his second son Octavio Farnese with Margaret of Austria, widow of Julian de Médicis, who had been assassinated at Florence in the church of Saint Mary of the Flowers; and the marriage of his niece Vittoria with Antoine, eldest son of Charles of Vendôme.

Delivered from his anxiety with respect to François I., Charles V. made at Genoa his preparations against the Turks. These preparations were immense; they lasted two years.

At the end of these two years, when the fleet was on the point of sailing, Duke Charles resolved to pay a visit to his brother-in-law, and present his son Emmanuel Philibert, now entering on his thirteenth year.

No need of our saying that Scianca-Ferro and Leone were

among the travellers. Emmanuel Philibert never took a journey without them.

For some time the young prince had been very much preoccupied. He was busied about the composition of a discourse of which he never thought of speaking to Monseigneur Louis Alardet, bishop of Lausanne, his preceptor, nor to his governors, Louis de Châtillon, lord of Musinens, grand equerry of Savoy, Jean Baptist Provana, lord of Leyni, and Edouard de Genève, baron of Lullens.

He was content with unbosoming himself on the subject to his squire and his page.

It was nothing less than a discourse embodying a petition to the Emperor Charles V. to allow him to accompany him on the expedition against the Barbary pirates.

Scianca-Ferro refused his aid, saying that, if it had been a challenge to carry, he would have been equal to the task; but as to helping in making up a speech, he knew his incompetency.

Leone refused, saying that the mere thought of the dangers Emmanuel Philibert would naturally run in such an expedition disturbed his mind to that degree that he could not begin to put together the very first words of such a petition.

The young prince found then that he must rely on himself alone. Therefore, with the assistance of Titus Livy, Quintus Curtius, Plutarch, and all the makers of discourse of antiquity, he composed the one he reckoned on addressing to the Emperor.

The Emperor was lodging with his friend Andrea Doria, in the fine palace which looks like the king of the port of Genoa, and was following the provisioning of his fleet, while promenading the magnificent terraces from which the splendid admiral, after dining the ambassadors of Venice, had flung his silver plate into the sea.

Duke Charles, Emmanuel Philibert, and their suite were introduced to the Emperor as soon as they were announced.

The Emperor embraced his brother-in-law, and was about

to embrace his nephew also; but Emmanuel Philibert extricated himself respectfully from the august embrace, put one knee on the ground, and with the gravest air in the world, his squire and page at his side, without his father having even the least idea of what he was going to say, pronounced the following words:

"Devoted to the maintenance of your dignity and your cause, which are those of God and of our holy religion, I come freely and joyfully to supplicate you, Cæsar, to receive me as a volunteer among that infinite number of warriors who are present from all quarters to range themselves under your banners; fortunate should I be, O Cæsar, to learn under the greatest of kings and under an invincible emperor the discipline of camps and the science of war."

The Emperor looked at him and smiled; and while Scianca-Ferro was expressing quite loudly his admiration at the discourse of his prince, and Leone, pale with terror, was begging God to inspire the Emperor with the good thought of refusing the offer of Emmanuel's services, the monarch replied gravely:

"Prince, I thank you for this mark of your attachment. Persist in these good sentiments; they will be useful to us both. But you are still too young to follow me to the wars. If, however, you are always moved by the same ardor and determination, you may rest assured that in a few years you shall not want for opportunities."

And, raising the young prince, he embraced him. Then, to console him, he detached his own order of the Golden Fleece and passed it round his neck.

"Ah, *mordieu!*" cried Scianca-Ferro, "that is something better than a cardinal's hat!"

"You have a bold comrade there, fair nephew," said Charles V.; "and we shall give him a chain in lieu of the cross we may bestow on him some time or other."

And, taking a gold chain from the neck of one of his lords, he threw it to Scianca-Ferro, saying:

"For you, fair squire."

But quick as was the movement of Charles V., Scianca-Ferro had time to place a knee on the ground, so that it was in this respectful attitude he received the Emperor's present.

"And now," said the victor of Pavia, "it is right that every one have his share, even the page."

And, drawing a diamond from his little finger, "Fair page," he said, "it is your turn."

But to the great astonishment of Emmanuel Philibert, Scianca-Ferro, and all the spectators, Leone did not respond, and remained motionless in his place.

"Oh, oh!" said Charles V., "we have a deaf page, it would seem." And shrugging his shoulders, "Come forward, fair page," he said.

But instead of obeying, the page took a step backward.

"Leone!" exclaimed Emmanuel, seizing the page's hand and attempting to lead him forward.

But, wonderful to tell, Leone snatched away his hand, uttered a cry, and rushed from the place.

"There is a page for you who is not covetous," said Charles V. "You must tell me where you are able to get such, fair nephew. The diamond I wished to give him is worth a thousand pistoles."

Then, turning to his courtiers, "A good example to follow, gentlemen!" said Charles V.

IX

LEONE-LEONA

ALL the efforts made by Emmanuel Philibert during their return to the Corsi palace, where he lodged with his father, could not induce Leone to tell, not only the cause of his refusal of the diamond, but the reason why, like a wild young falcon, he fled with a scream of terror. The child remained dumb, and no entreaty could draw a word from his lips on the subject.

It was the same obstinacy the Duchess Beatrix made vain efforts to triumph over when she tried to obtain from the child some information about his mother, which he constantly refused to give.

Only how could the Emperor Charles V. be concerned in the catastrophe that had struck the orphan page? This was what it was impossible for Emmanuel Philibert to divine. However it might be, he preferred to find the whole world wrong, even his uncle, rather than for a moment suspect Leone of inconsistency and levity.

Two years had passed since the truce of Nice. It was a very long time for François I. to keep his word. Consequently every one was astonished, and especially Charles V., who during his interview with his brother-in-law could not help feeling anxious as to what the King of France would do when he, Charles V., was no longer there to protect the poor duke.

And, in fact, scarcely had the Emperor set sail, when the Duke of Savoy, on his return to Nice, received a messenger from François I.

François I. proposed to restore Savoy to his uncle, provided the latter surrendered Piedmont and allowed it to be annexed to the crown of France.

The duke, indignant at such a proposal, dismissed the messenger of his nephew, forbidding him to appear again in his presence.

Who had inspired François I. with this audacity of declaring war a fourth time on the Emperor?

It was because he had two new allies, Luther and Soliman, the Huguenots of Germany and the Saracens of Africa. Strange allies for the *most Christian* king, for the *eldest son of the Church!*

Singular thing! During this long struggle between François I. and Charles V. it was the one who is styled the *roi chevalier* that was constantly breaking his word. After losing everything *except honor* on the battlefield of Pavia, he inflicted on this same honor, which had remained untouched in spite of defeat, an ineffaceable stain by signing in prison what he had no intention of keeping.

And look at him now, this king whom historians ought to banish from history, as Christ chased the buyers and sellers from the Temple—look at him, this soldier knighted by Bayard and cursed by Saint-Vallier; as soon as he has broken his word, he seems hurled into insanity: he is the friend of the Turk and the heretic; he gives the right hand to Soliman and the left to Luther; he marches side by side with the son of Mahomet—he, a son of Saint-Louis. Therefore, God, after sending him defeat, the daughter of His anger, sends him the plague, the daughter of His vengeance.

All this does not prevent him being styled in books, at least in those of the historians, the *roi chevalier !*

It is true we poets call him the infamous king, a perjurer of his word toward his enemies, a perjurer of his word toward his friends, a perjurer of his word to his God.

This time, as soon as the answer of the Duke of Savoy was received, it was Nice that he threatened.

The Duke of Savoy left in Nice a brave Savoyard knight named Odinet de Montfort, and retired to Verceil, where he drew together the few forces he could still dispose of.

Emmanuel Philibert had solicited from his father the favor of remaining at Nice, and of making his first arms at once against Soliman and François I.; but the last heir of his house was too precious to the duke to permit of such a request being allowed.

It was not the same with Scianca-Ferro; permission was granted him, and he made good use of it.

Scarcely were the duke, his son, Leone, and their suite some leagues from Nice, when a fleet of two hundred sail was seen flying French and Turkish flags. It landed in the port of Villa Franca ten thousand Turks commanded by Khair-Eddin, and twelve thousand French commanded by the Duc d'Enghien.

The siege was terrible; the garrison defended itself desperately. Every one, citizen, soldier, and gentleman, performed prodigies of valor. A breach was made in the city in ten several places. They were entered by Turks and Frenchmen; then every street, every lane, every house, was defended. Fire kept pace with the besiegers. Odinet de Montfort retired into the castle, leaving to the enemy a city in ruins.

The next day, a herald summoned him to surrender; but he, shaking his head, answered:

"Friend, you make a mistake in proposing to me such baseness. My name is Montfort; my arms are *pales*, and my motto, *Il faut tenir.*"

Montfort was worthy of his motto, his arms, and his name. He held out until the arrival of the duke with four thousand Piedmontese, and of Alfonso of Avalos, on the part of the Emperor, with six thousand Spaniards, forced the Turks and French to raise the siege.

It was high festival for Duke Charles and his subjects the day he returned to Nice, ruined though the city was. It was also high festival for Emmanuel Philibert and his squire. Scianca-Ferro had gained the name given him by Charles III. When his foster-brother asked him how it felt striking real cuirasses and real bucklers, "Bah!" he answered, "it is not so difficult as splitting oaks; it is not so hard as breaking rocks."

"Oh, why was I not there!" murmured Emmanuel Philibert, without perceiving that Leone, clinging to his arm, had turned pale in thinking of the dangers Scianca-Ferro had already run, and of those Emmanuel might run one day.

It is true that some time after our poor page was fully reassured by the peace of Crespy, the result of the invasion of Provence by Charles V., as well as of the battle of Cérisoles.

Peace was signed on the 14th of October, 1544. It stipulated that Philippe d'Orléans, second son of François I., should marry in two years the daughter of the Emperor, and receive as dowry the duchy of Milan and the Low Countries; that, on his side, the King of France should renounce his claims to the kingdom of Naples, and restore to the Duke of Savoy what he had taken from him, except the fortresses of Pignerol and Montmélian, which would remain united to the French territory as places of security.

The treaty was to be executed in two years: that is to say, at the time of the marriage of the Duc d'Orléans with the daughter of the Emperor.

As we see, we have now arrived at the year 1545; the children had grown. Leone, the youngest of the three, was fourteen; Emmanuel was seventeen; Scianca-Ferro, the eldest, was six months more than Emmanuel.

What was passing in the heart of Leone, and why was the young man becoming sadder and sadder? Questions vainly put to each other by Scianca and Emmanuel; questions vainly put to Leone by Emmanuel.

And, indeed, it was strange. The more Leone advanced in years, the less the young page followed the example of his two companions. Emmanuel, to make his surname of Cardinalin quite forgotten, and the squire to deserve more and more his surname of Scianca-Ferro, passed their entire days in sham battles; the young lads, with sword or lance or axe ever in their hands, were rivals in address and strength. All that can be won by skill in the use of arms, Emmanuel had acquired; all the force and vigor God can give to human muscles, Scianca-Ferro had received from God.

During this time, Leone would stand pensive on some tower from which he could see the exercises of the two youths, and follow Emmanuel with his eyes; or if their excitement carried them too far away, he took a book, retired to some distant corner of the garden, and read.

The only thing Leone learned with joy—and doubtless because he saw in it a means of following Emmanuel—was to ride on horseback; but for some time, as his melancholy gradually increased, he renounced even this exercise.

One thing especially that astonished Emmanuel was that at the idea he was soon to become a rich and puissant prince, the countenance of Leone became more and more gloomy.

On a certain day, the duke received a letter from the Emperor Charles V., in which there was question of a marriage between Emmanuel Philibert and the daughter of his brother, King Ferdinand. Leone was present at the reading of this letter; he could not dissemble the effect it produced on him, and to the great astonishment of Duke Charles III. and of Scianca-Ferro, who sought in vain for the motives of such grief, he went out, sobbing wildly.

As soon as Duke Charles returned to his apartments, Emmanuel rushed after his page. The sentiment he experienced for Leone was strange, and in no way resembled that with which Scianca-Ferro inspired him. To save the life of Scianca-Ferro, he would have given his life; to spare the blood of his foster-brother, he would have given his own; but his life and his blood he would have given to arrest a tear trembling on the long dark eyelashes of Leone.

Therefore, having seen him weep, he wished to know the cause of this grief. For more than a year he had perceived the growing sorrow of the young page, and he had often asked the cause of such sadness; but Leone had immediately made an effort of self-control, had shaken his head, as if to chase away some gloomy thought, and replied with a smile:

"I am too happy, Monseigneur Emmanuel, and I am always afraid such happiness may not last!"

And Emmanuel in turn shook his head; but as he perceived that too much importunity only seemed to render Leone more unhappy, he contented himself with taking his hands in his own and gazing on him fixedly, as if to question him in every sense.

But Leone would slowly turn away his eyes, and gently withdraw his hands from Emmanuel.

And Emmanuel would then sadly seek Scianca-Ferro, who did not even think of asking what was the matter, who never took it into *his* head to grasp hands and question with a look, so different was the friendship uniting Emmanuel to Scianca-Ferro from that uniting Emmanuel to Leone.

But on that day Emmanuel vainly searched for the page for more than an hour in the castle and park; he did not find him. He questioned everybody; none had seen Leone. At last he addressed one of the grooms; according to the latter, Leone had entered the church, and must be there still.

Emmanuel ran to the church, took in at a glance the whole interior of the gloomy edifice, and saw Leone on his knees in the most retired corner of the darkest chapel.

He approached him near enough almost to touch him without the page, lost in meditation, even suspecting his presence. Then he made a step forward and touched his shoulder, pronouncing his name.

Leone started, and regarded Emmanuel with almost a scared expression.

"Pray what are you doing in this church at this hour, Leone?" asked Emmanuel, anxiously.

"I am asking God," said Leone, sadly, "to grant me the strength to execute the plan which I am contemplating."

"And what is this plan, child?" asked Emmanuel. "May I not know it?"

"On the contrary, monseigneur," replied Leone, "you shall be the first to know it."

"You swear it to me, Leone?"

"Alas, yes, monseigneur!" replied the young man, with a sad smile.

Emmanuel took his hand and tried to draw him out of the church; but Leone gently freed his hand, as he was accustomed doing for some time now, and, kneeling again, begged the young duke to leave him alone.

"By and by," he said; "just at present I want to be alone with God."

There was something so solemn and melancholy in the tones of the young man that Emmanuel did not venture to resist.

He left the church, but waited for Leone at the door.

Leone started on perceiving him, and yet he did not seem astonished to find him there.

"And shall I know this secret some day or other?" asked Emmanuel.

"To-morrow I hope to have strength enough to tell it to you, monseigneur," replied Leone.

"Where?"

"In this church."

"At what hour?"

"Come at the same hour as to-day."

"And in the meantime, Leone?" asked Emmanuel, entreatingly.

"In the meantime I hope that monseigneur will not force me to quit my chamber; I need solitude and reflection."

Emmanuel regarded the page with an inexpressible pang at the heart, and conducted him to the door of his chamber. Arrived there, Leone wished to take the hand of the prince and kiss it. Emmanuel, in turn, dropped his hand, threw his two arms around his comrade, and attempted to embrace him; but Leone gently repulsed him, disengaged himself, and with an accent of unutterable sweetness and melancholy said—

"To-morrow, monseigneur."

And he entered his room.

Emmanuel remained a moment motionless at the door. He heard Leone shooting the bolt.

The chill of the iron as he heard seemed to penetrate to the depths of his soul.

"My God!" he murmured quite low; "what is coming over me, and what is this I am feeling?"

"What the devil are you doing there?" said a rough voice behind him, while a vigorous hand was pressed on his shoulder.

Emmanuel heaved a sigh, took the arm of Scianca-Ferro, and drew him into the garden.

They sat down side by side on a bench.

Emmanuel related to Scianca-Ferro all that had just passed between him and Leone.

Scianca-Ferro reflected a moment, cast up his eyes, and bit his fist.

Then suddenly, "I bet I know what's the matter," he said.

"What is it then?"

"Leone is in love!"

It seemed to Emmanuel as if he had received a thrust through the heart.

"Impossible!" he stammered.

"And why impossible?" retorted Scianca-Ferro. "I am the same myself."

"You! And with whom?" asked Emmanuel.

"Eh, *parbleu!* with Gervaise, the daughter of the porter of the castle. She was terribly afraid during the siege, poor child, particularly when night came, and so to reassure her, I kept her with me."

Emmanuel made a motion with his shoulders to signify that he was very sure that Leone did not love the daughter of a porter.

Scianca-Ferro misinterpreted the gesture of Emmanuel, which he took for a mark of disdain.

"Ah, Master Cardinalin!" he said (in spite of the collar of the Golden Fleece, at certain moments Scianca-Ferro still gave this title to Emmanuel), "you needn't be quite so dainty. As for me, I declare to you, I prefer Gervaise to all the beautiful ladies of the court. And should there be a tournament, I am ready to wear her colors and defend her beauty against all comers!"

"I would pity those who would not be of your opinion, my dear Scianca-Ferro," replied Emmanuel.

"And you are right; because I would strike as hard for the daughter of a porter as for the daughter of a king."

Emmanuel rose, pressed Scianca-Ferro's hand, and returned to his apartments.

Decidedly, as he had said, Scianca-Ferro struck too hard

to comprehend what was passing in the heart of Emmanuel, and to divine what was passing in the soul of Leone.

As to Emmanuel, although endowed with a greater delicacy of feeling and a more exquisite susceptibility of spirit, he sought vainly in the solitude of his chamber and in the silence of the night, not only for what was passing in the soul of Leone, but for what was agitating his own heart.

He therefore awaited the morrow impatiently. The morning slipped by slowly, without Emmanuel seeing Leone. When the hour came, he walked trembling to the church, as if something of the highest importance was about to be decided in his life.

The treaty of Crespy, signed a year before, and which was to finally restore or take from him his states, had appeared to him of less gravity than the secret he was about to learn from Leone.

He found the young man on the same spot as on the evening before. Without doubt he had been a long time praying. Still, his face gave evidence of a resignation full of sadness.

Emmanuel went quickly up to him. Leone received him with a gentle, but melancholy smile.

"Well?" asked Emmanuel.

"Well, monseigneur," replied Leone, "I have a favor to beg of you."

"What is it, Leone?"

"You see my weakness and unfitness for all bodily exercises. In your almost royal future you require strong men like Scianca-Ferro, and not weak and timid children like me, monseigneur." Leone made an effort, and two big tears coursed down his cheeks. "Monseigneur, I beg of you the singular favor of allowing me to leave you."

Emmanuel took a step backward. His life, begun between Scianca-Ferro and Leone, had never presented itself to him in the future as deprived of either of these two friends.

"Leave me?" he said to Leone in amazement.

Leone did not reply, and bent his head.

"Leave me?" repeated Emmanuel, with an accent of the most poignant sorrow. "You leave me! me! impossible!"

"It is necessary," said Leone, in a voice almost unintelligible.

Emmanuel, like one who feels himself becoming mad, bore his hand to his forehead, looked at the altar, and let his two arms fall inert along his body.

For a few seconds, he questioned himself, then he questioned God, and, as he received no response either from earth or heaven, he fell back discouraged.

"Leave me!" he resumed for the third time, as if he could not grow accustomed to the word—"me, who found you dying, Leone; me, who received you as a messenger from Providence; me, who have always treated you as a brother! Oh!"

"It is for that very reason, monseigneur: it is because I owe you too much, and because in remaining near you I can make no return for what I owe you; it is because I wish to spend my whole life in prayer for my benefactor."

"Pray for me!" said Emmanuel, more and more astonished. "And where?"

"In some holy monastery, which seems a place much better suited for a poor orphan like me than that which I would occupy in a brilliant court such as yours is sure to be."

"My mother, my poor mother!" murmured Emmanuel, "what would you say, you who loved him so well, if you heard this?"

"In presence of that God who is listening to us," said Leone, placing his hand solemnly on the arm of the young prince—"in presence of that God who is listening to us, she would say that I am right."

There was such an accent of truth, such conviction of heart, if not of conscience, in the reply of Leone, that Emmanuel was shaken by it.

"Leone," he said, "do what you wish, my child; you

are free. I have tried to bind your heart; but I have never had the intention of binding your body. However, I ask you not to precipitate your resolution; take eight days, take—"

"Oh," said Leone, "if I do not set out on the moment when God gives me strength to leave you, I shall never be able to do so; and I tell you," continued the child, breaking into sobs, "I must depart."

"Depart! But why, why depart?"

To this question Leone replied by the same inflexible silence he had exhibited on two previous occasions—the first, when at the village of Oleggio the duchess had questioned him on his parents and his birth; the second, when at Genoa Emmanuel wished to know why he refused the diamond of Charles V.

He was about to insist on an answer when he heard a step in the church.

It was one of his father's servants, who announced that Duke Charles desired to see him on the instant.

Important news had just been received from France.

"You see, Leone," said Emmanuel to the child, "I must leave you now; I will see you again in the evening, and if you persist in your resolution, well, you shall be free, my child. You may leave me to-morrow, or even this evening, if you believe you ought to remain with me no longer."

Leone did not reply; he fell on his knees with a deep groan. It looked as if his heart were broken.

Emmanuel departed; but before leaving the church, he could not help turning his head two or three times to learn if the child felt as much pain in seeing him depart as he felt in departing.

Leone remained alone and prayed for another hour; then he grew calmer and returned to his chamber. In the absence of Emmanuel, his resolution, tottering in the presence of the young prince, became more firm, being strengthened by that angel with the heart of ice whom men call reason.

But once in his chamber, the idea that Emmanuel might

appear at any moment and make a final attempt to move him, disturbed the child.

At every noise he heard on the staircase, he started; the footsteps resounding in the corridor seemed, when passing before his door, to be treading on his heart.

Two hours glided past; a step was heard. Oh, this time Leone had no longer any doubt; he had recognized the step.

The door opened, and Emmanuel appeared. He was sad, and yet in his look there was a blending of joy with this sadness. "Well, Leone," he asked, after closing the door, "have you reflected?"

"Monseigneur," replied Leone, "when you left me, my reflections were already made."

"So that you persist in abandoning me?"

Leone had not the strength to reply; he contented himself with making a sign of the head in the affirmative.

"And this," continued Emmanuel, with a melancholy smile—"and this, because I am going to be a great prince and to have a brilliant court?"

Leone inclined his head anew.

"Well," said Emmanuel, with a certain bitterness, "on this point you may be reassured. I am to-day more miserable than I have ever been!"

Leone raised his head, and Emmanuel could see the amazement in his beautiful eyes shine through his tears.

"The second son of the King of France, the Duc d'Orléans, is dead," said Emmanuel, "so that the treaty of Crespy is broken."

"And—and?" asked Leone, questioning Emmanuel with every muscle of his face.

"And," returned Emmanuel, "as the Emperor Charles V., my uncle, will not give the duchy of Milan to my cousin François I., my cousin François I. will not restore his states to my father."

"But," asked Leone with an indescribable feeling of anguish, "that marriage with the daughter of Ferdinand, that

THE PAGE OF THE DUKE OF SAVOY 103

marriage proposed by the Emperor himself—that marriage will take place?"

"Ah! my poor Leone, the man whom the Emperor Charles V. wished as the husband of his niece was Count of Bresse, Duke of Savoy, and Prince of Piedmont; it was, in fine, a crowned husband, not poor Emmanuel Philibert, who out of all his states retains only the city of Nice, the valley of Aosta, and a few patches scattered here and there through Savoy and Piedmont."

"Oh!" cried Leone, with a feeling of joy he could not stifle. But, almost immediately recovering that powerful control over himself that threatened to escape him, "No matter, monseigneur; this must not change anything of what was arranged," he said.

"And so," asked Emmanuel, sadder and gloomier at this resolution of the child than he had been at the news of the loss of his states, "you quit me forever, Leone?"

"It is as necessary to-day as it was yesterday, Emmanuel."

"Yesterday, Leone, I was rich, I was powerful, I had a ducal crown on my head; to-day, I am poor, despoiled, and have nothing left but my sword. In leaving me yesterday you would be only cruel; leaving me to-day, you will be ungrateful. Adieu, Leone."

"Ungrateful!" exclaimed Leone; "O God! you hear him; he says I am ungrateful."

Then, as with bent brows and gloomy eye, the young prince was preparing to leave the chamber—

"Oh, Emmanuel!" cried Leone, "do not quit me thus; it would kill me!"

Emmanuel turned round; the arms of the child were stretched out to him. Leone was pale, tottering, almost fainting.

He rushed forward and supported him in his arms, and, carried away by the first impulse—an impulse he could not account for—he pressed his lips on the lips of his companion.

Leone uttered a cry as agonizing as if a red-hot iron had

touched them, fell backward, and fainted. The button of his doublet was pressing on his throat; Emmanuel opened it. Then, as the child was stifling in his arms, he tore it off, and at the same time to give him air opened all the buttons of his vest; but this time it was Emmanuel who uttered a cry, not of sorrow, but of surprise, astonishment, and joy.

Leone was a woman.

After returning to consciousness, Leone existed no longer; but Leona was the mistress of Emmanuel Philibert.

From that time there was no longer question for the poor child of separating from her lover, to whom now everything was clear without a word of explanation—sadness, solitude, and desire of flight. Perceiving that she loved Emmanuel Philibert, Leona had wished to be separated from him; but the moment the young man had taken possession of her love, Leona gave him her life.

In the eyes of every one else, the page continued to be a young man, and was called Leone. For Emmanuel Philibert alone, Leone was a beautiful young girl, and was called Leona.

As a prince, Emmanuel Philibert lost Bresse, Piedmont, and Savoy, with the exception of the valley of Aosta, and the cities of Nice and Verceil; but as a man he lost nothing, since God gave him Scianca-Ferro and Leona; that is to say, the two most magnificent presents in the gift of heaven that God can bestow on one of his elect—devotion and love.

X

THE THREE MESSAGES

LET us now tell in a few lines all that passed during the period of time elapsing between this period and the one we have reached at present.

Emmanuel Philibert had said to Leone that he had nothing left but his sword.

The league of the Protestants of Germany, raised by John Frederick, Elector of Saxony, who was disturbed by the successive encroachments of the Empire, had, on breaking out, given the young prince an opportunity of offering that sword to Charles V.

This time it was accepted.

The pretext was that, as long as the Emperor lived, his brother Ferdinand could not be King of the Romans.

The league was formed in the little town of Smalkalde, situated in the county of Henecery, and belonging to the Landgrave of Hesse; hence the name of *League of Smalkalde*, under which it is known.

Henry VIII. had a scruple, and kept apart from it; François I., on the contrary, entered into it with all his heart.

The thing was of old date; it dated from the 22d of December, 1530, the day of the first meeting.

Soliman was also in the league. In fact, he lent his aid to it by sending troops to besiege Messina in 1532; but Charles V. had marched against him with an army of ninety thousand foot-soldiers and thirty thousand cavalry, and forced him to raise the siege.

Then, the plague assisting him, he had destroyed the army of François I. in Italy, so that, on one side, had intervened the treaty of Cambrai, the 5th of August, 1529, and on the other the treaty of Nuremberg, the 23d of July, 1532, which had given a few moments of repose to Europe.

We know already how long treaties made with François I. lasted. The treaty of Nuremberg was broken, and the league of Smalkalde, which had had time to reunite all its forces, broke out.

The Emperor marched in person against the Smalkaldists. What was passing in Germany always seemed to affect more peculiarly what was passing elsewhere.

It was because Charles V. understood that since the decadence of the Papacy, the greatest power in this world was the Empire.

It was in these circumstances that Emmanuel Philibert

set out for Worms on the 27th of May, 1545, where the Emperor was staying. The young prince was, as usual, accompanied by Scianca-Ferro and Leone.

He was attended by forty gentlemen.

It was all the army his father could raise in his states and send to the Emperor—he who still bore the titles of Duke of Savoy, Chablais, and Aosta; Prince of Piedmont, Achaia, and the Morea; Count of Geneva, Nice, Asti, Bresse, and Romont; Baron of Vaud, Gex, and Faucigny; Lord of Verceil, Beaufort, Bugey, and Freibourg; Prince and Perpetual Vicar of the Holy Empire; Marquis of Italy and King of Cyprus.

Charles V. received his nephew most affectionately. He permitted him to bear the title of Majesty in his presence, on account of that kingdom of Cyprus to which his father laid claim.

Emmanuel Philibert repaid this kindly reception by performing prodigies of valor at the battles of Ingolstadt and Mühlberg.

The last ended the struggle. Ten of the forty gentlemen of Emmanuel Philibert were absent from the roll-call in the evening; they were dead or wounded.

As to Scianca-Ferro, recognizing the elector John Fredrick in the midst of the battle by his powerful Friesland horse, his gigantic figure, and the terrible blows which he struck, he had kept particularly close to him.

Certainly the young man would have won on that day the name of Scianca-Ferro, if it had not been given him already.

With a blow of his terrible battle-axe, he broke the right arm of the prince, then with the blade of the same weapon he cut his helmet and face at the same time; so that when the prisoner raised the mutilated visor of this same helmet in presence of the Emperor, he had to name himself. He was no longer recognizable; his face was one frightful wound.

François I. had died a month before. When dying, he

said to his son that all the misfortunes of France had come from his alliance with the Protestants and the Turks, and, recognizing that Charles V. had the Almighty God on his side, he recommended the future King of France to keep on good terms with him.

There was then an interval of peace, during which Emmanuel Philibert went to see his father at Verceil. The interview was tender and full of deep affection; doubtless the Duke of Savoy had a presentiment that he was embracing his son for the last time.

The recommendation of François I. to Henri II. did not leave a deep impression in the heart of the latter—a king without military genius, but with warlike instincts—and the war was renewed on account of the assassination of the Duke of Placentia, that Paul Louis Farnese of whom we have already spoken.

He was assassinated in Placentia in 1548, by Pallavicini, Landi, Anguisuola and Gonfalonieri, who immediately after the assassination placed the city in the hands of Ferdinand of Gonzague, the Milanese governor of Charles V.

On the other hand, Octavio Farnese, second son of Paul III., had taken possession of Parma, and, in order not to be forced to surrender it, had invoked the protection of Henri II.

Now during the life of Paul Louis even, Charles V. had never ceased to claim Parma and Placentia as forming parts of the duchy of Milan.

The reader will call to mind the differences he had on this subject with Paul III.

Nothing more was required to rekindle the war, which flamed up at the same time in Italy and the Low Countries.

It was in Flanders, as always, that Charles V. made his greatest efforts. It was then quite naturally that our eyes, on the lookout for Emmanuel Philibert, were turned toward the north at the beginning of this book.

We have told how, after the siege of Metz and the capture of Thérouanne and Hesdin, the Emperor, charging his nephew to rebuild the latter city, had named him commander-in-chief of his armies in Flanders and Governor of the Low Countries.

Then, as if to counterbalance this great honor, an ineffable sorrow struck the heart of Emmanuel Philibert. On the 17th of September, 1553, his father, the Duke of Savoy, died.

It is with this rank of commander-in-chief, and this sorrow which, if not denoted by his garb, as in the case of Hamlet, was not the less imprinted on his features, that we have seen him issuing from the imperial camp; and it is after enforcing his authority as Romulus enforced his that we see him return to it.

A messenger from Charles V. was waiting for him at the entrance to his tent; the Emperor desired to speak to him that very moment.

Emmanuel at once leaped from the saddle, threw the bridle to one of his men, nodded to his squire and page as a sign that he would meet them after his return, unbuckled his sword, and placed it under his arm, as he was accustomed to do when he walked, wishing at need to always have the hilt within reach of his hand, and then took his way to the tent of the modern Cæsar.

The sentry presented arms, and he entered, preceded by the messenger who was going to announce his arrival to the Emperor.

The field tent of the Emperor was divided into four compartments, without reckoning a kind of antechamber, or rather portico supported by four pillars.

These four compartments of the imperial tent served as a dining-room, parlor, bedchamber and office. Each of them had been furnished by the gift of a city, and adorned with the trophy of a victory.

The only trophy of the Emperor's bedchamber was the sword of François I. hanging at the head of his bed. The trophy was simple enough, the reader may well think; but it had more value in the eyes of Charles V., who carried it with him even into the monastery of Saint-Just, than all the trophies of the other three rooms united.

He who writes these lines has often, with a sad and melancholy look toward the past, held and drawn this sword, once held by François I., who surrendered it; by Charles V., who received it; and by Napoleon, who recovered it.

Strange nothingness of the things of this world!

Having become almost the sole dowry of a beautiful but fallen princess, it is to-day the property of a servant of Catherine II.

O François I.! O Charles V.! O Napoleon!

In the antechamber, although he barely crossed it, Emmanuel Philibert—with that glance of the born ruler of men that takes in everything in a second—remarked a man whose hands were tied behind his back, and who was guarded by four soldiers.

The man, thus bound, was clad like a peasant. As his head was uncovered, Emmanuel Philibert saw reason to conclude that neither his hair nor complexion were in harmony with his garb.

He thought it was a French spy they had just arrested, and that the Emperor had summoned him in connection with this spy.

Charles V. was in his cabinet; the duke was introduced as soon as he was announced.

Charles V., born along with the sixteenth century, was at this time a man of fifty-five years, not tall, but vigorous; his keen eyes sparkled under the eyebrows, but only when they were not dulled by pain. His hair was grizzled, but his beard, more thick than long, was of an ardent red.

He was lying on a sort of Turkish divan covered with Eastern stuffs that had been captured in the tent of Soliman before Vienna.

Within reach of his hand gleamed a trophy of kandjars and Arabian cimeters. He was muffled up in a long dressing-gown of black velvet. His visage was gloomy; and he appeared to be waiting impatiently for Emmanuel Philibert.

However, when the duke was announced, this expression of impatience disappeared on the instant, even as a cloud which darkens the brightness of the day disappears at the touch of the north wind.

During a reign of forty years, the Emperor had had time to learn to compose his countenance, and it must be said that none was more skilful in this art.

Still, at the first glance he cast on the Emperor, Emmanuel understood that he was about to converse with him on grave matters.

Charles V., as soon as he perceived his nephew, turned his head in his direction, and, making an effort to change his position, gave him a friendly greeting with head and hand.

Emmanuel Philibert bowed respectfully.

The Emperor opened the conversation in Italian. This sovereign, who regretted all his life not to know Greek and Latin, spoke equally well five living languages—Italian, Spanish, French, English and Flemish. "I learned Italian," he said, "to speak to the Pope; Spanish to speak to my mother Juana; English to speak to my aunt Catherine; Flemish to speak to my fellow-citizens and friends; in fine, French to speak to myself."

Whatever hurry he might be in to discuss affairs with those he summoned near him, the Emperor always began by saying a few words in their own language. "Well," he asked in Italian, "what news from the camp?"

"Sire," replied Emmanuel, employing the same language that Charles V. used, and which, for that matter, was his mother tongue, "news which your Majesty would soon learn, even if I did not bring it myself. This news is that, in order to have my title and authority respected, I have been forced to make a terrible example."

"A terrible example!" vaguely answered the Emperor, who had already become absorbed in his own thoughts; "and what was it?"

Emmanuel Philibert began the recital of what took place

between him and Count Waldeck; but important as was the narrative, it was evident the Emperor was only listening with his ears: his mind was elsewhere.

"Well?" said Charles V., for the third time, when Emmanuel Philibert had finished.

Plunged, as he was, in his own thoughts, he had in all probability not heard a single word of the report which his general had made him.

In fact, during all the time the narrative lasted, the Emperor, doubtless to hide his preoccupation, was looking at the fingers of his right hand, twisted and deformed by the gout.

That was the true enemy of Charles V.—a far deadlier enemy than Soliman or François I. or Henri II.!

The gout and Luther were the two enemies that troubled him incessantly; so he placed them both in the same rank.

"Ah! except for Luther and the gout," he would sometimes say, taking a fistful of his red beard as he descended from his horse, exhausted by some long march or some terrible battle—"except for Luther and the gout, how I should sleep to-night!"

There was a moment's silence between the narrative of Emmanuel Philibert and the resumption of the conversation by the Emperor.

At last, the latter, turning to his nephew—

"I, too, have news to give you, and bad news!"

"From where, august emperor?"

"From Rome."

"Is the Pope elected?"

"Yes."

"And his name?"

"Peter Caraffa. The one he replaces, Emmanuel, was just my own age, born the same year—Marcellus II. Poor Marcellus! Does not his death tell me to prepare to die?"

"Sire," said Emmanuel, "I do not think you ought to allow your mind to dwell on this event, or to judge the death of Marcellus from the standpoint of an ordinary death. Marcello Cervino, the cardinal, was healthy, robust, and might perhaps have lived a hundred years. Cardinal Marcello Cervino, become Pope Marcellus II., died in twenty days!"

"Yes, I know," replied Charles V., pensively; "he was also in too great a hurry to be pope. He had himself crowned with the tiara on Good Friday; that is to say, on the day on which our Lord was crowned with thorns. It brought him misfortune. So I am less preoccupied by his death than by the election of Paul IV."

"And yet, if I am not mistaken," replied Emmanuel, "Paul IV. is a Neapolitan; that is to say, a subject of your Majesty."

"Yes, undoubtedly. But I have always had bad reports of this cardinal, and while he was at the court of Spain I have had personal reasons to complain of him. Ah!" continued Charles V., with an expression of utter weariness, "I shall have to begin again with him the struggle I have sustained for twenty years with his predecessors, and I am at the end of my strength."

"Oh, sire!"

Charles V. fell into a kind of revery, from which he emerged almost immediately.

"For that matter," he added, as if speaking to himself, and with a sigh, "perhaps he will deceive me as the other popes have deceived me. They are always the very reverse of what they were as cardinals. I thought the Médicis Clement VII. a man of peaceful spirit, firm and constant; good! No sooner is he pope than I find I have been mistaken on all points; he is a restless, turbulent, variable spirit. On the other hand, I imagined Julius III. would neglect business for pleasure, and would be engrossed in diversions and amusements. *Peccato!* there never has been a more industrious and diligent pope, or one caring less for the joys of this world. What work he cut out for us, he and Cardinal Pole, in connection with the marriage of Philip and his cousin Mary Tudor! If we had not arrested that madman Pole at Augsburg, who knows if to-day the marriage would have been consummated? Ah, poor Marcellus!" said the Emperor, heaving a second sigh, still more expressive than the first, "it was not because you were crowned on Good Friday that you survived your enthroning only twenty days; it was because you were my friend!"

"Let us wait, august emperor," said Emmanuel Philibert: "your Majesty acknowledges that you have been deceived with regard to Clement VII. and Julius III.; perhaps you may also be deceived with regard to Paul IV."

"God grant it! but I doubt."

A noise was heard at the door.

"What is the matter?" demanded Charles V., impatiently. "I gave directions that I was to be disturbed by nobody. See, Emmanuel, what is wanted."

The duke raised the tapestry in front of the door, exchanged a question and answer with the persons in the neighboring compartment, and, turning toward the emperor—

"Sire," said he, "it is a courier from Spain, from Tordesillas."

"Let him enter; news of my good mother, no doubt."

The messenger appeared.

"Yes. Have you not news of my mother?" said Charles V., addressing the messenger in Spanish.

The messenger, without answering, tendered a letter to Emmanuel Philibert, who took it from his hand.

"Give it to me, Emmanuel; give it to me!" said the Emperor. "And she is well, is she not?"

The messenger continued to keep silence. Emmanuel, on his side, hesitated to give the letter to Charles V.: it had a black seal; Charles V. saw the seal, and shuddered.

"Ah!" he said, "you see the election of Paul IV. brings me misfortune already. Give it to me," he continued, holding out his hand to Emmanuel.

Emmanuel obeyed; to have delayed longer would have been puerile.

"August sovereign," said he, on handing over the letter, "remember, you are a man!"

"Yes," replied Charles V.; "that is what they used to say to the Roman generals who were honored with triumphs."

And, trembling, he opened the letter.

It contained only a few lines; yet to read it he had to return to it two or three times.

The tears hindered him from seeing; his eyes, worn and parched by ambition, were themselves astonished at this miracle; they had again found tears.

When he had finished, he handed the letter to Emmanuel Philibert, who took it from him, and fell back on the divan.

"Dead!" he said—"dead on the 13th of April, 1555, the very day Peter Caraffa was named pope! Ah! my son, did I not tell you this man would bring me misfortune?"

Emmanuel had cast his eyes over the letter. It was signed by the royal notary of Tordesillas; it, in fact, announced the death of Juana of Castile, mother of Charles V., better known in history by the name of Juana the Mad.

He remained a moment motionless in presence of this great sorrow, which he did not know how to deal with, for Charles V. adored his mother.

"Augustus," he murmured at last, "remember all you had the goodness to say to me when I also had the misfortune, two years ago, to lose my father."

"Yes, yes, such things are said," returned the Emperor, "good reasons are found for the consolation of others, and then, when our turn comes, we are powerless to console ourselves!"

"And so I do not console you, Augustus," said Emmanuel; "on the contrary, I say, Weep, weep, for you are only a man!"

"What a painful life was hers, Emmanuel!" said Charles V. "In 1496 she marries my father, Philip the Fair; she adored him! In 1506 he dies, poisoned from drinking a glass of water while playing tennis; she becomes mad with grief. For ten years she awaited the resurrection of her husband, which a Carthusian monk had promised her in order to console her; and for ten years she never left Tordesillas, except when, in 1516, she came to me at Villa-Viciosa, and with her own hands placed the crown of Spain on my head. Mad with the love which she had had for her husband, she only recovered her reason when she had to occupy herself with her son. Poor mother! All my reign will at least bear witness to the respect I had for her. Nothing of importance has been done in Spain for the last forty years without her advice on the matter being taken— not that she was always in a condition to give it; but it was my duty as a son to act thus, and I fulfilled it. Do you know that, though a Spaniard, and a good Spaniard at that, she came to Flanders for her *accouchement*, in order that I might be one day emperor in place of my grandfather Maximilian? Do you know that, although the best of mothers, she renounced the privilege of suckling me, lest, being nourished by her milk, I might be accused of being too Spanish? And, in fact, the two principal titles to which I owe the imperial crown are being a foster-child of Anne Sterel, and being a citizen of Ghent. Well, from before my birth, my mother had foreseen all this. And what can I do for her after her death—order for her a splendid funeral? She will have it. But, in truth, to be Emperor of Germany, King of Spain, Naples, Sicily, and the two Indias, to have an empire on which, according to my flatterers, the sun never sets, and to be able to do nothing for one's mother except to give her a splendid funeral! Ah, Emmanuel, the power of the most powerful man is very limited indeed!"

At this moment the hangings at the door of the tent were raised anew; and, through the opening, an officer was seen, all covered with dust, and seeming also to be the bearer of urgent news.

The expression on the Emperor's countenance was so sad that the usher, who had ventured to disregard the countersign in view of the importance of the news brought by the third messenger, and to enter the cabinet of Charles V., stopped short.

"Enter!" said Charles, in Flemish; "what is the matter?"

"Sire," said the messenger, "King Henri II. has opened a campaign at the head of three armies: the first, commanded by himself, having under his orders Connétable Montmorency; the second, commanded by Maréchal de Saint-André, and the third commanded by the Duc de Nevers."

"And what next?" asked the Emperor.

"Next, sire, the King of France has laid siege to Marienbourg, and taken it; he is now marching on Bouvines."

"And on what day did he lay siege to Marienbourg?" said Charles.

"On the 13th of April last, sire."

Charles V. turned round to Emmanuel Philibert.

"Well," he asked him in French, "what do you say of the date, Emmanuel?"

"A fatal date, indeed!" replied the latter.

"That is sufficient," said Charles V. to the messenger; "leave us."

Then, to the usher—

"Take as much care of that captain as if he brought us good news," said the emperor. "Go!"

This time Emmanuel Philibert did not wait for the Emperor to question him. Before even the hangings fell again, he began—

"Luckily," said he, "if we can do nothing, august emperor, against the election of Paul IV.; if we can do nothing against the death of your beloved mother—we can do something against the taking of Marienbourg."

"And what can we do?"

"Take it back again!"

"Yes, you may, not I, Emmanuel."

"Why not you?" said the Prince of Piedmont.

Charles V. raised himself from the divan, and, drawing himself up with difficulty, attempted to walk; but he could only take a few steps, limping.

He shook his head, and, turning to his nephew—

"See, look at my legs," he said: "they no longer sustain me now, either on foot or horseback; look at my hands; they can no longer hold a sword. There is a saying, Emmanuel, that he who can no longer hold a sword can no longer hold a sceptre."

"What are you saying, sire?" exclaimed Emmanuel, astounded.

"A thing of which I have often thought, and of which I shall think again. Emmanuel, everything warns me that it is time to leave my place to another: the surprise of Innspruck, from which I had to fly half-naked; the retreat of Metz, where I left the third of my army and the half of my reputation; yet, more than all that, look you, this disease which human strength cannot long resist; this disease which medicine cannot cure; this frightful, inexorable, cruel disease, which invades the body from the crown of the head to the soles of the feet, which contracts the nerves with intolerable pains, which penetrates the bones, freezes the marrow, and converts into solid chalk the beneficent oil spread through our joints to facilitate their movements; this disease, which mutilates a man limb by limb more cruelly, more surely, than does steel or fire or all the implements of war, and which breaks the strength and serenity of the soul under the tortures of matter—this disease is incessantly crying out to me: 'You have had enough of power, enough of sovereignty! Return into the nothingness of life before returning into the nothingness of the tomb! Charles, by the grace of God, Emperor of the Romans, Charles, King of Germany, Castile, Leon, Granada, Aragon, Naples, Sicily, Majorca, Sardinia, and the islands and Indias of both oceans, make way for another, for another!'"

Emmanuel wished to speak.

The Emperor arrested him by a gesture.

"And then, and then," continued Charles V., "there is another thing I had forgotten to tell you! As if the dissolution of this poor body was too slow for the wishes of my enemies, as if defeats and heresies and the gout were not sufficient, the poniard has come to play a part in the drama!"

"How, the poniard?" exclaimed Emmanuel.

The face of Charles V. was overcast.

"An attempt was made to assassinate me to-day," he said.

"An attempt to assassinate your Majesty?" cried Emmanuel, terrified.

"Why not?" replied the Emperor, with a smile. "Have you not just now reminded me that I was a man?"

"Oh!" cried Emmanuel, scarcely recovering from the emotion this intelligence had caused him; "and who is the wretch?"

"Ah! yes, indeed!" said the Emperor. "Who is the wretch? I hold the poniard, but not the hand!"

"In fact," said Emmanuel, "I just now saw a man bound in the antechamber—"

"That is the wretch, as you call him, Emmanuel. But who has employed him? The Turk? I do not believe so; Soliman is a loyal enemy. Henri II.? I do not even suspect him. Paul IV.? He has not been long enough elected; and then the popes—they generally prefer poison to the dagger: *Ecclesia abhorret a sanguine.* Octavio Farnese? He is too paltry a person to venture on attacking me—the imperial bird that Maurice did not dare to take, not being acquainted, he said, with a cage large enough to hold him. The Lutherans of Augsburg or the Calvinists of Geneva? I am altogether puzzled; and yet I should like to know— Listen, Emmanuel, this man has refused to answer my questions; take him into your tent and question him in your turn. Do with him whatever you please; I give him to you. But understand well—he must be made to speak. The nearer the enemy is to me, and the more powerful he is, the greater need I have to know him."

Then, after a moment's pause, he fixed his gaze on Emmanuel Philibert, who held his eyes pensively bent toward the ground.

"By the way," he said, "your cousin Philip has arrived at Brussels."

The transition was so abrupt that Emmanuel started. He raised his head, and his glance met that of the Emperor. This time he shuddered.

"Well?" he asked.

"Well," returned Charles, "I shall be happy to see my son again. Would you not say that he guesses the hour is come and the moment favorable for him to succeed me? But before I see him again, Emmanuel, I recommend my assassin to you."

"In an hour," replied Emmanuel, "your Majesty shall know all you desire to know."

And, bowing to the Emperor, who offered him his mutilated hand, Emmanuel Philibert withdrew, convinced that the thing of which Charles V. had spoken to him as if it were a mere casual remark introduced into the conversation, was, of all the events of the day, the one to which he attached the most importance.

XI

ODOARDO MARAVIGLIA

ON RETIRING, Emmanuel Philibert cast a fresh look on the prisoner, and this look confirmed him in his first idea; that is to say, that he was going to deal with a gentleman. He made a sign to the leader of the four soldiers to approach him.

"My friend," he said, "in five minutes you will, by order of the Emperor, conduct this man into my tent."

Emmanuel might have dispensed with naming Charles V.: it was known that the latter had delegated to him all his powers; and, in general, the soldiers, who worshipped him, would have obeyed him as they would have obeyed the Emperor himself.

"Your order shall be executed, your Highness," replied the sergeant.

The duke resumed the road to his lodgings.

The tent of Emmanuel was not, like that of the Emperor, a splendid pavilion, divided into four compartments; it was the tent of a soldier cut in two by a piece of mere canvas.

Scianca-Ferro was seated at the door.

"Remain where you are," said Emmanuel to him; "but take some weapon or other."

"Why?" asked Scianca-Ferro.

"A man is about to be brought hither who has attempted to assassinate the Emperor. I intend to question him without any witnesses. Look well at him when he enters; and, if he attempts to violate the pledge, which he will doubtless give, by trying to escape, stop him—but living, you understand? It is important that he live!"

"Then," said Scianca-Ferro, "I do not need weapons; my arms are sufficient."

"Do as you like; you are warned."

"Do not be disturbed about the matter," said Scianca-Ferro.

The prince entered his tent, and found Leone, or rather Leona, waiting for him. As he returned alone, and as the curtain of his tent fell behind him, Leona came to meet him with open arms.

"You are here at last, my love! My God! what a terrible scene was that at which we have been present! Alas! you were quite right in telling me that my emotion and paleness would lead one to take me for a woman."

"What would you have, Leona? These are ordinary scenes in the life of a soldier, and you ought to be accustomed to them by this time." Then, smiling, "Look at Scianca-Ferro, and take him for your model," he added.

"How can you utter such words as those with a smile,

Emmanuel? Scianca-Ferro is a man: he loves you as much as a man can love a man, as I well know; but I love you, Emmanuel, to a degree that cannot be expressed, as something without which one no longer lives! I love you as the flower loves the dew, as the bird loves the forest, as the dawn loves the sun. With you I live, exist, and love; without you I am no more!"

"My own darling," said Emmanuel, "yes, I know you are at the same time grace, devotion, and love; I know that you move beside me, but that it is really in me that you live, and so for you I have no mysteries or secrets."

"Why do you say this?"

"Because a man is about to be brought hither; because this man is a great criminal whom I wish to question; because he will perhaps make important revelations—who knows?—revelations that may compromise the highest personages. Pass to that side of the tent. Listen if you wish; whatever I hear will, I know, be heard by myself alone."

Leona shrugged her shoulders. "Except you," she said, "what is the rest of the world to me?"

And the young girl, sending a caress to her lover with her hand, disappeared behind the curtain.

It was time; the five minutes were passed, and, with the usual military punctuality, the sergeant arrived, conducting his prisoner.

Emmanuel received him seated, and half lost in the shadow. From the midst of this shadow he cast a third look, deeper and more prolonged, on the prisoner.

He was a young man of from thirty to thirty-five. His stature was so lofty and his face so distinguished that his disguise, as we have said, had not prevented Emmanuel Philibert from recognizing him as a gentleman.

"Leave the gentleman alone with me," said the prince to the sergeant.

The sergeant could only obey; he went out with his three men.

The prisoner fixed his keen and piercing eye on Emmanuel Philibert.

The latter rose, and went straight up to him. "Sir," said he, "those people did not know with whom they had to do, and so they have bound you. You are going to give me your word of honor not to attempt to escape, and I am going to untie your hands."

"I am a peasant, and not a gentleman," said the murderer; "I cannot, consequently, give you my word of honor as a gentleman."

"If you are a peasant, that word of honor does not bind you to anything. Give it to me, then, since it is the only pledge I require of you."

The prisoner did not answer.

"Then," said Emmanuel, "I will untie your hands without the word of honor. I do not fear to find myself alone with a man, even though that man had no honor to pledge!"

And the prince began untying the hands of the unknown.

The latter took a step backward. "Wait," he said; "on the faith of a gentleman, I shall not attempt to escape!"

"Come, now," said Emmanuel, smiling, "what the mischief! dogs, horses, and men know each other;" and he finished loosening the cord. "There! you are free; now let us talk."

The prisoner gazed coldly on his bruised hands, and let them fall by his side. "Talk?" he repeated, with irony; "and of what?"

"Why," replied Emmanuel Philibert, "of the cause that led you to this crime."

"I have said nothing," replied the unknown, "and I have nothing to say."

"You have said nothing to the Emperor, whom you wished to kill, that is conceivable; you said nothing to the soldiers who arrested you, that I can easily understand; but to me, a gentleman who treats you, not as a vulgar assassin, but as a gentleman—to me you will tell everything."

"For what good?"

"For what good? I am about to tell you: because I do not regard you as a man paid by some coward who has placed your arm at the end of his own, not daring to strike himself. For what good? Because you must not be hanged as some thief or lurking assassin, but decapitated as a noble and a lord."

"They have threatened to torture me to make me speak," said the prisoner; "let them do it!"

"Torture would be a useless cruelty; you would undergo it and you would not speak; you would be mutilated, and not vanquished; you would keep your secret and leave the shame to your tormentors. No, that is not what I want; I want you to speak to me, a gentleman and a prince, as you would speak to a priest. And if you judge it unsafe to speak to me, it is because you are one of those wretches with whom I did not wish to confound you; it is because you have acted under the influence of a base passion you dare not avow; it is because—"

The prisoner drew himself up to his full height, and, interrupting, said:

"My name is Odoardo Maraviglia, monsieur! Revive your recollections, and stop insulting me."

At this name of Odoardo Maraviglia, Emmanuel thought he heard a stifled cry in the other compartment of the tent; what he was sure of was that the canvas that divided it trembled, as if something had set it in motion.

On his part, Emmanuel felt something vibrate strongly in his memory at the sound of that name. In fact, that name had served as a pretext for the war which had deprived him of his states.

"Odoardo Maraviglia!" he said. "Are you the son of Francesco Maraviglia, the French ambassador at Milan?"

"I am his son."

Emmanuel concentrated his thoughts on the distant recollections of his boyhood; he found that name among them, but it threw no light on the present situation.

"Your name," he said, "is surely the name of a gentleman; but it does not recall any memory connected with the crime of which you are accused."

Odoardo smiled disdainfully.

"Ask the most august emperor," said he, "if there is the same obscurity in his memory that there is in yours."

"Excuse me, sir," returned Emmanuel; "at the time when Comte Francesco de Maraviglia disappeared I was still a child; I was hardly eight years old. It is not astonishing, then, that I was ignorant of a disappearance which, as I think I can recall, remained a mystery for everybody."

"Well, monseigneur, I am about to throw some light on this mystery. You know what a wretched prince was the last Sforza, eternally wavering between François I. and Charles V., according as the genius of victory favored the one or the other. My father, Francesco Maraviglia, was appointed envoy extraordinary to him by François I. This was in 1534. The Emperor was occupied in Africa; the Duke of Saxony, the ally of François, had just made peace with the King of the Romans; Clement VII., another ally of France, had just excommunicated Henry VIII., King of England. Everything turned to the detriment of the Emperor in Italy. Sforza, who still owed four hundred thousand ducats, turned, like every one else, and intrusted all his political fortunes to the envoy extraordinary of King François I. It was a great triumph. Francesco Maraviglia had the imprudence to boast of it. The words he spoke crossed the seas, and startled Charles V. in presence of the Turks. Alas! fortune is fickle. Two months after, Clement VII., who was the strength of the French in Italy, died; Tunis was taken by Charles V., and the Emperor, with his victorious army, landed in Italy. An expiatory victim was necessary. Francesco Maraviglia was marked by fate to be that victim. In a quarrel between the servants of Comte Maraviglia and some of the rabble of Milan, two of the latter happened to be slain. The duke only wanted a pretext for keeping his promise to the august emperor. The man who for a year had been more powerful in Milan than the duke himself was arrested as a vulgar malefactor, and conducted to the citadel. My mother was present; she had with her my sister, a child four years old. I was in Paris, at the Louvre; I was one of the pages of François I. The count was torn from the arms of my mother; he was dragged away without the poor woman being told what he was charged with, or where he was being taken. Eight days passed, during which, despite all their efforts, the countess could discover nothing as to the fate of her husband. Maraviglia was known to be immensely rich; his wife was able to purchase his liberty at his weight in gold. One night a man knocked at the door of my mother's palace; it was opened for him; he asked to speak to the countess without witnesses. Everything was of importance under the circumstances. Through the agency of friends and Frenchmen my mother spread a report through the city that she would give five hundred ducats to whoever would tell her where my father was. Probably this man, who desired to speak to her alone, was bringing news of the count, and, fearing betrayal, wished, by excluding witnesses, to insure secrecy.

"She was not mistaken; this man was one of the jailers of the fortress of Milan, where my father was imprisoned. Not only did he come to tell where my father was, but he brought a letter from him. On recognizing her husband's handwriting, she counted out the five hundred ducats.

"The letter of my father announced his arrest, and that he had been placed in solitary confinement, but did not express any keen anxiety as to the result. My mother, in her reply, told her husband to dispose of her; her life and fortune were his. Five days passed. In the middle of the night the same man knocked at the palace; it was opened, and he was immediately introduced to the countess. The situation of the prisoner had, in the meantime, been aggravated. He was placed in another dungeon, and his confinement was made more rigidly secret.

" 'His life,' said the jailer, 'was in peril.'

"Did this man want to extract some large sum from the countess, or was he telling the truth? Either of these two hypotheses might be correct. But fear induced my mother to adopt the latter. Moreover, she questioned the jailer, and his replies, while giving evidence of cupidity, also bore the impress of frankness.

"She gave him the same sum as on the first occasion, and told him at all hazards to form some plan for the count's escape. As soon as such a plan was arranged, he would receive a sum of five thousand ducats; and, once the count was out of danger, twenty thousand more would be handed over to him.

"It was a fortune! The jailer left the countess, promising to think over what he had just heard. The countess, on her side, made inquiries into the situation; she had friends near the duke; she knew through them that the situation was even worse than it had been described by the jailer. It was intended to prosecute the count as a spy. She awaited impatiently the visit of the jailer; she did not even know his name; and, even though she knew it, would she not ruin the jailer and ruin herself, if she were rash enough to inquire after him?

"However, one thing reassured her somewhat: there was to be a prosecution. What accusation could they bring against my father? The death of these two Milanese? It was an affair between domestics and peasants, with which a gentleman, an ambassador, could have nothing to do. But some voices said, quite low, that there would be no prosecution; and these voices were the most sinister of all, for they let it be understood that the count would not the less surely be condemned for all that. At last, my mother was startled one night by the noise of the knocker on the door; she was beginning to recognize the manner in which her nocturnal visitor knocked; she awaited him on the threshold of her bedchamber. He addressed her with even more mystery than usual; he had found a means of escape, and was come to propose it to the countess. This was the plan he adopted.

"The dungeon of the prisoner was separated from the lodging of the jailer by a single gallery, opening into the dungeon by means of an iron door barred at the top. The jailer had the key of this second dungeon as well as of the first. He proposed to bore through the wall behind his bed, at a spot concealed from every eye. Through this opening he would enter the empty cell, and from there pass into the count's dungeon. The fetters of the count knocked off, he could pass from his dungeon into the neighboring cell, and then into the jailer's room.

"There he would find a ladder of ropes, by the aid of which he would descend into the fosse, at the darkest and most solitary part of the wall; a carriage would wait for the count a hundred yards from the fosse, and would carry him out of the duke's states with all the speed of two horses. The plan was good; the countess accepted it, but, fearing some deception might be practiced on her with regard to the count, and she might be told he was saved while still a captive, she required to be present at this flight. The jailer objected the difficulty of introducing her into the fortress; but by a single word the countess removed this difficulty. She had obtained permission for herself and her daughter to see her husband—a permission she had not yet availed herself of, and could therefore still make use of it. On the day appointed for the count's flight, she would enter the fortress at nightfall; she would see the count; then, on leaving him, instead of quitting the fortress, she would enter the jailer's room. There she would await the moment for the prisoner's flight. The jailer, who would depart with the count, would receive from the latter the sum agreed on. The carriage awaiting them was to contain a hundred thousand ducats.

"The jailer was sincere in his offers; he accepted. The flight was arranged for the day after the next day. Before leaving, the jailer received his five thousand ducats, and indicated the place where the carriage was to be stationed. The care of this carriage was confided by the countess to one of her servants, a man of tried fidelity.

"But, pardon, monseigneur," said Odoardo, interrupting himself. "I forget I am speaking to a stranger, and that all these details, full of emotion and life for me, are indifferent to my listener."

"You are mistaken, sir," said Emmanuel; "I desire, on the contrary, to make appeal to your memory, in order that I myself may be able to share in all your recollections. I am listening."

Odoardo continued:

"The two days passed in all the anguish that precedes the execution of such a project. One thing, however, tranquillized the countess: it was that the jailer had such an overpowering interest in the success of the enterprise; a hundred years' fidelity would not give this man the reward to be obtained by a quarter of an hour's treason. Ten times the countess asked herself why she had not decided on making the attempt at the end of twenty-four hours instead of at the end of forty-eight. It seemed as if the last twenty-four hours would never end, or would lead to some catastrophe that would upset the plan, however well conceived and ingenious it might be. The time swept by, measured by the hand of eternity. The hours struck with their ordinary impassibility. At last that one arrived that was to tell her the moment had come to enter the prison. In presence of the countess, the carriage was laden with all the objects necessary for the flight of the count, in order that he might not be forced to stop on the route; two horses had been led beyond Pavia, so that he could make about thirty leagues without any delay. At eleven o'clock the horses would be harnessed to the carriage, which at midnight would be at the spot agreed upon.

"Once out of danger, the fugitive would take steps to warn the countess, and the latter would join her husband, wherever he might be. The hour struck. Face to face with the moment of execution, the countess now thought it had come very soon. She took her little daughter by the hand, and directed her course toward the prison. One fear agitated her during the journey: it was that as the permit was dated eight days back, she might be refused entrance to the prison.

"The countess was mistaken; she was introduced, without any difficulty, to the prisoner. The reports she heard were not exaggerated; and the manner in which a man of the count's rank was treated showed there could be no illusion on the fate that awaited him. The ambassador of France had a chain on his foot, as if he were a vile felon. The interview would have been very painful, if escape had not been imminent and certain. During this interview all that was not yet arranged was finally settled.

"The count was resolved on everything; he knew he had no quarter to expect; the Emperor had positively insisted on his death—"

Emmanuel Philibert made a movement.

"Are you sure of what you say, sir?" he asked severely. "Do you know this is a grave accusation you are making against so great a prince as the Emperor Charles V.?"

"Does your Highness order me to stop, or permit me to continue?"

"Continue! but why not answer my question?"

"Because the progress of my narrative will, I fancy, render that question useless."

"Continue, then, sir," said Emmanuel Philibert.

XII

WHAT PASSED IN THE DUNGEON OF THE FORTRESS OF MILAN ON THE NIGHT OF THE 14TH AND 15TH OF NOVEMBER, 1534

"A FEW minutes after nine," returned Odoardo, "the jailer came to warn the countess that it was time to withdraw. The sentries were about to be changed, and it was well the sentinel who had seen her enter should see her leave. The separation was cruel; and yet in three hours they would see each other again, never more to be separated. The child uttered piteous cries, and refused to abandon her father. The countess had almost to tear her from his arms. They passed the sentinel again, and plunged into the darkest depths of the courtyard. From the place where they were they gained, with infinite precautions, and without being seen, the house of the jailer. Once there, the countess and her daughter were shut up in a cabinet, and bidden not to utter a single word or make a single movement, as an inspector might at any moment enter the jailer's residence. The countess and her child kept themselves dumb and motionless. One hazardous movement, one whispered word, might deprive a father and husband of life.

"The three hours that still remained till midnight appeared as long to the countess as the forty-eight hours that had slipped by. At last the jailer opened the door.

" 'Come!' he said, in a low voice—a voice so low that the countess and her daughter guessed what this man intended to say, rather than what he said.

"The mother had not wished to leave her child, in order that the father, on escaping, might give her a last kiss. Besides, there are moments when, for an empire, one would not separate from those one loves.

"Did she know what was about to happen, this poor mother who was fighting for the life of her husband with his executioners? Might she also not be forced to fly, either with her husband, or on her own account? And if she had to fly, could she part with her child?

"The jailer pushed the bed aside; an opening two and a half feet high and two feet wide had been made in the wall behind.

"It was more than was needed for all the prisoners in the fortress to escape, one after another. Preceded by the jailer, the mother and child entered the first dungeon. After their passage, the wife of the jailer replaced the bed, in which a boy of four years was sleeping. The jailer, as I have said, had the key of the first dungeon; he opened the door of it, having first taken good care to oil the lock and the bolts, and found himself in the dungeon of the count. The latter had received, an hour before, a file with which to cut through his chain; but, unaccustomed to such labor, and, besides, fearing to be heard by the sentry, who was walking in the corridor, he was hardly half through the work. The jailer took the file in his turn; and, while the count clasped his wife and child in his arms, began filing the chain. Suddenly he lifted his head, and remained listening, with one knee on the ground, his body resting on the hand that held the file, and the other hand extended in the direction of the door. The count wished to question him.

" 'Silence!' he said; 'something unusual is passing in the fortress!'

" 'Oh, my God!' murmured the countess, frightened.

" 'Silence!' repeated the jailer.

"Every one was silent; they held their breath as if they would never breathe again. These four individuals resembled a group of bronze, representing all the shades of fear, from astonishment to terror. A slow and deep noise was heard, increasing as it approached. It was that of several persons in line of march. By the measured footfall of the steps it might be gathered that among these persons was a certain number of soldiers.

" 'Come!' said the jailer, taking the countess and the child each by an arm, and dragging them with him, 'come! It is doubtless some night visit, some round of the governor. But, in any case, you must not be seen. As soon as the visitors have quitted the dungeon of the count, if, indeed, they enter it, we can resume the work where we left off.'

"The countess and her daughter opposed a weak resistance. Besides, the prisoner himself pushed them toward the door. They passed out of it, followed by the jailer, who closed it after them. As I have told your Highness, there was in the second dungeon a grated door, opening into the first, and through which, thanks to the darkness and the closeness of the bars, one could see everything without being seen.

"The countess held her daughter in her arms. The mother and child, hardly breathing, glued their faces to the bars to see what was going to happen.

"The hope they had for a moment entertained, that the business of the new-comers was not with the count, was soon dissipated. The procession halted at the door of the dungeon, and the key was heard grating in the lock. At the spectacle presented to her eyes the countess could hardly refrain from a cry of terror; it was evident the jailer guessed as much.

" 'Not a word, madame; not a syllable! not a gesture, whatever happens! or—'

"He thought for a moment what means he should adopt to impose silence on the countess; then, drawing a thin, sharp blade from his breast—

" 'Or I poniard your child!' he said.

" 'Wretch!' stammered the countess.

" 'Oh!' he replied, 'each one here must think of his own life; and that of a poor jailer is, in the eyes of the poor jailer, of as much value as that of a noble countess!'

"The countess placed her hand on the mouth of the child in order to silence the child. As to herself, after the threat of the jailer, she was sure she would not let a sound escape.

"This is what the countess saw from the other side of the door, and what had torn from her the cry stifled by the jailer.

"First, two men, clad in black, and having each a torch in his hand; behind them, a man bearing a parchment unfolded, from which hung a big red seal; behind this man, another man, masked, and muffled in a brown robe; behind the man masked, a priest. They entered, one by one, into the dungeon without the countess betraying her emotion by a word or by a gesture; and, moreover, when they entered, the poor woman saw, outlined in the shadow of the corridor, a group still more sinister! Facing the door was a man wearing a costume half black, half red, his two hands resting on the hilt of a long broad naked sword. Behind him were six Brothers of Mercy, clad in black-hooded cloaks, with openings for the eyes only, and bearing a bier on their shoulders. Finally, beyond them were seen the mustaches of a dozen soldiers drawn up against the wall. The two men holding the torches, the man holding a parchment, the man masked, and the priest entered, as I have said, into the dungeon. Then the door was shut, leaving outside the executioner, the Brothers of Mercy, and the soldiers.

"The count was standing, leaning against the gloomy prison-wall, from which loomed out his pale features. His eye sought, behind the bars of the door, the direction of the frightened eyes he could not see, but which he guessed were glued to those bars. Those spectral visitors, mute and unlooked for though they were, left him no doubt as to the fate that awaited him. Besides, if he had had the good fortune to have reason for doubting, his doubt would not have been of long duration.

"The two men bearing torches placed themselves, the one on his right, the other on his left; the masked man and the priest stayed near the door; the man holding the parchment advanced.

"'Count,' he asked, 'do you believe that you are fit to meet God?'

"'As fit as one can be,' replied the count, in a calm voice, 'who has nothing to reproach himself with.'

"'So much the better!' replied the man with the parchment; 'for you are condemned, and I am come to read your sentence of death.'

"'Pronounced by what tribunal?' asked the count, ironically.

"'By the all-powerful justice of the duke.'

"'On what accusation?'

" 'On that of the most august emperor, Charles V.'

" 'It is well. I am ready to hear the sentence.'

" 'On your knees, count! It is on his knees that a man about to die should hear the sentence that condemns him.'

" 'When he is guilty, but not when he is innocent.'

" 'Count, you are not beyond the common law: on your knees! or we shall be constrained to employ force.'

" 'Try!' said the count.

" 'Let him stand,' said the masked man; 'let him cross himself only, in order to place himself under the protection of the Lord!'

"The count started at the sound of this voice.

" 'Duke Sforza,' he said, turning toward the masked man, 'I thank you.'

" 'Oh, it is the duke,' murmured the countess; 'perhaps I might prevail on him to pardon.'

" 'Silence, madame, if you value the life of your child!' said the jailer, in a whisper.

"The countess gave utterance to a groan which was heard by the count, and made him start. He hazarded a gesture with his hand, which meant 'Courage!' then, as the masked man had invited him, he said aloud, making the sign of the cross—

" 'In the name of the Father, and of the Son, and of the Holy Ghost.'

" '*Amen!*' murmured those present.

"Thereupon the man with the parchment began to read the sentence. It was rendered in the name of Duke Francesco Maria Sforza, at the request of the Emperor Charles V., and it condemned Francesco Maraviglia, agent of the King of France, to be executed at night, in a dungeon, as a *traitor, spy, and betrayer of state secrets.*

"A second groan reached the ear of the count—a groan so faint that he alone was able, not to perceive, but to divine it.

"He turned his gaze toward the spot from which this doleful sound came.

"'Unjust as is the sentence of the duke,' he said, 'I receive it without trouble and without anger. However, as the man who cannot defend his life ought to defend his honor, I appeal from the sentence of the duke.'

"'And to whom?' asked the masked man.

"'To my king and master, François I., in the first place, and then to the future and to God!—to God, in whose hands are all men, and particularly princes, kings, and emperors.'

"'Is it the only tribunal to which you appeal?' said the masked man.

"'Yes, and I summon you to appear before that tribunal, Duke Francesco Maria Sforza!'

"'And pray when?' retorted the masked man.

"'In the same time that Jacques de Molay, Grand Master of the Templars, assigned to his judge; that is to say, in a year and a day. To-day is the 15th of November, 1534; on the 16th of November, 1535, then— Do you hear me, Duke Francesco Maria Sforza?'

"And he stretched forth his hand toward the masked man to emphasize the menace and the summons. But for the mask hiding the face of the duke, his paleness would have been visible to all; for it was he, beyond all doubt, who was present at the agony of his victim. For a moment it was the condemned who triumphed, and the judge who trembled before him.

"'It is well,' said the duke; 'you have a quarter of an hour to pass with this holy man before undergoing your sentence.'

"And he pointed to the priest.

"'Try to finish in a quarter of an hour, for you shall not have a minute longer.'

"Then, turning to the man of God—

"'Father,' he said, 'do your duty.'

"And he left, with the two torch-bearers and the man with the parchment.

"But he left the door wide open behind him, in order that his eyes and the eyes of the soldiers might be able to see the interior of the dungeon, and follow all the movements of the condemned, whom he had only quitted through respect for the rite of compassion and so as not to hear the voice of the penitent.

"Another sigh passed through the bars, and touched gently the palpitating heart of the condemned. The countess had hoped that the door might be shut on him and the priest, and—who knows?—perhaps by supplication and tears, the sight of a wife on her knees praying for her husband, of a child praying for her father, might prevail on the man of God to consent to turn aside his head, and let the count escape.

"It was the last hope of my poor mother; it failed her—"

Emmanuel Philibert started. Sometimes he forgot that this recital was made by a son who was relating the last moments of his father. It seemed to him as if he was reading the pages of some terrible legend.

Then, on a sudden, a word recalled him to reality, and made him comprehend that the recital did not issue from the pen of a cold historian, but fell from the lips of a son, a living chronicle of the agony of his father.

"Yes, it was the last hope of my poor mother; it failed her!" repeated Odoardo, pausing a moment in his narration, on seeing the movement of Emmanuel. "For," he continued, "on the other side of the door, lighted by the two torches and by the glare of the smoky lamps of the corridor, the dismal spectacle was still there, terrible as a vision, deadly as reality. The priest alone remained near the count, as I have told you. The count, without disturbing himself as to from whom this last consoler came, knelt before him. Then began the confession—a strange confession, in which the man about to die did not seem to think of himself, but to be preoccupied only with others; in which the words said to the priest were really addressed to the wife and child, and ascended to God only after having passed through the hearts of a mother and a daughter! My sister alone, if she still lives, could recount the tears with which this confession was received; for I was not there. I, a merry lad, was playing, laughing, singing, perhaps, ignorant of what was passing within three hundred leagues of me, at the very moment when my father, at the threshold of death, was speaking of his absent son to my weeping mother and sister!"

Oppressed by this memory, Odoardo stopped an instant; then he resumed, stifling a sigh:

"The quarter of an hour was soon passed. The masked man, with a watch in his hand, followed the face of priest and penitent; but when the fifteen minutes had elapsed—

" 'Count,' he said, 'the time allotted you to remain among the living has expired. The priest has finished his task; it is for the executioner now to do his.'

"The priest gave the count absolution, and rose. Then, pointing to the crucifix, he retired backward toward the door, and as the priest retired, the executioner advanced. The count remained on his knees. 'Have you any last petition to address to Duke Sforza or to Charles V. ?'

" 'I have no petition to address to any one but God,' replied the count.

" 'Then you are ready ?' asked the same man.

" 'You see it, since I am on my knees.'

"And, in fact, the count was on his knees, his face turned toward the bars of that gloomy door through which his wife and child were looking at him. His mouth, which seemed to continue to pray, sent them words of love, which was still a last prayer.

" 'If you do not wish my hand to sully you, count,' said a voice behind the victim, 'pull down the collar of your shirt. You are a gentleman, and I have no right to touch you except with the blade of my sword.'

"The count, without answering, pulled his shirt down to his shoulders, and remained with the neck bare.

" 'Good and Gracious Lord!' said the count, 'Almighty and Merciful God, into Thy hands I commend my spirit!'

"He had scarcely said the words when the sword of the

executioner flamed and hissed in the darkness, like a flash of lightning, and the head of the victim fell from his shoulders, rolling, as if with a last impulse of love, to the foot of the grated door. A hoarse, muffled cry was heard at the same time, and also the noise of a body falling backward.

"But the bystanders believed this cry was the last sound uttered by the victim; the noise they thought was made by his body falling on the flagstone of the dungeon—

"Excuse me, monseigneur," said Odoardo, stopping; "but if you wish to hear the rest I must have a glass of water, for I feel faint."

And, in fact, Emmanuel Philibert saw that the narrator of this terrible history was pale and tottering. He ran forward to support him, placed him on a pile of cushions, and gave him the glass of water he asked for.

The sweat was running down the forehead of the prince, and, soldier though he was, accustomed to fields of battle, he seemed as near fainting as he whom he was succoring.

At the end of ten minutes Odoardo recovered.

"Would you know more, monseigneur?" he asked.

"I wish to know everything, sir," said Emmanuel; "such narratives as yours are great lessons for princes who are some day to reign."

"Be it so," answered the young man; "besides, the most terrible part is finished."

He wiped the perspiration from his forehead with his hand, and perhaps, also, his eyes, wet with tears at the same time, and continued:

"When my mother recovered her senses, everything had vanished like a vision, and she might have believed she had had a bad dream, if she had not found herself lying on the bed of the jailer. Such terrible orders had been given by her to my sister not to cry, for fear her sobs might be heard, that, although the poor child believed she had lost both father and mother, she regarded the latter with wide, scared eyes, from which the tears were flowing; but these tears continued to flow from the eyes of the child as silently for the mother as they did for the father. The jailer was no longer there; there remained only his wife. She took pity on the countess, and made her put on one of her garments; she dressed my sister in a suit of her son's, and at daybreak she set out with them and guided them on the road to Novara; then she gave two ducats to the countess, and recommended her to God.

"My poor mother seemed pursued by a terrible vision. She did not dream either of returning to the palace and taking some money out of it, nor of finding the carriage in which the count was to escape; she was mad with terror. Her only care was to fly, to cross the frontier, to quit the territories of the Duke of Milan. She disappeared with her child in the neighborhood of Novara, and nothing further was heard of her. What has become of my mother? What has become of my sister? I am utterly ignorant of their fate! The news of the death of my father reached Paris. It was the king himself who informed me of it, at the same time telling me I should never want his protection, and that he was about to exact vengeance for the assassination of the count by war.

"I asked the king's permission to accompany him. Fortune, at the beginning, favored the arms of France. We crossed the states of your father, of which the king took possession; then we arrived at Milan.

"Duke Sforza had taken refuge with Paul III. at Rome.

"An inquiry was made into the murder of my father; but it was impossible to find any one who had taken a share in this murder, or had been present at it. Three days after the execution the executioner suddenly died. The name of the usher who read the sentence was unknown. The jailer had taken flight with his wife and son.

"Thus, in spite of all inquiries, I could not even discover the spot where the body of my father rested. Twenty years had elapsed since those useless inquiries when I received a letter dated from Avignon.

"A man, who merely signed his initials, invited me to

come at once to Avignon if I wished to gain reliable information on the fate of my father, Comte Francesco de Maraviglia. He gave me the name and address of a priest whose mission it would be to conduct me to him if I accepted the invitation.

"The letter offered me that which was the desire of my whole life; I set out on the very instant. I went straight to the priest; the priest was prepared. He led me to the writer. It was the jailer of the fortress of Milan. Seeing my father dead, and knowing the spot where the carriage was waiting with a hundred thousand ducats, the evil spirit tempted him. He had placed my mother on his bed, recommending her to his wife; then he let himself down by means of a rope-ladder, crept up behind the coachman, who was waiting for my father, saying that he came from the latter, stabbed him, and, after throwing his body into the fosse, continued on his way, taking the carriage with him.

"Once over the frontier, he took post-horses, gained Avignon, sold the carriage, and, as no one ever claimed its contents, he appropriated the hundred thousand ducats. He then wrote to his wife and son to join him.

"But the hand of God was on this man. His wife died first; next, after wasting away for ten years, the son joined the mother; at last, he felt that his own turn would soon come for rendering an account to God of what he had done during his passage through this world. It was this summons from on high that made him repent and think of me. You understand, therefore, what was his object in wishing to see me.

"It was to confess everything to me, and to ask my pardon, not for the death of my father, with which he had no concern, but for the murder of the coachman and the robbery of the hundred thousand ducats. As to the man assassinated, there was no remedy for the crime; the man was dead.

"But as to the hundred thousand ducats, he had purchased with them a castle and a magnificent property at Ville-neuve-lez-Avignon, on the revenues of which he lived.

"I began by making him relate to me all the details of the death of my father, not once, but ten times. For that matter, the night had appeared so terrible to him that no incident escaped him, and he recalled the slightest details of the sinister event as if it had passed the evening before. Unfortunately, he knew nothing of my mother and sister except what his wife had told him, who lost sight of them on the road to Novara. They must have perished of hunger and fatigue!

"I was rich, and had no need of this increase of fortune; but a day might arrive when my mother and sister would reappear. Not wishing to dishonor this man by a public declaration of his crime, I had him make a gift of this castle and estate to the Comtesse de Maraviglia and her daughter. Then, as far as in me lay, and as God gave me power, I pardoned him.

"But there my mercy ended. Francesco Maria Sforza died in 1535, a year and a day after the summons given him by my father to appear before the tribunal of God. I had nothing further, therefore, to do with him; he was punished for his weakness, if not for his crime.

"But there remained the Emperor Charles V.—the Emperor at the pinnacle of his power, at the summit of his glory, at the height of his prosperity! It was he who had remained unpunished; it was he I resolved to strike.

"You will say that the men who bear the crown and sceptre are to be judged only by God; but sometimes God seems to forget.

"It is for men then to remember. I remembered—that is all. But I was ignorant that the Emperor wore, under his clothes, a coat of mail. He, too, remembered! I am Odoardo Maraviglia, and I wished to slay the Emperor, because he had my father assassinated by night, and caused my mother and sister to die of hunger and fatigue!

"I have spoken. Now, monseigneur, you know the truth. I wished to kill; I deserve to be killed; but I am a gentleman, and I demand the death of a gentleman."

Emmanuel Philibert bowed his head in token of assent.

"It is just," he said, "and your demand shall be granted. Do you desire to be free up to the moment of execution? By *being free*, I mean not being bound."

"What must I do for this?"

"Give me your word of honor not to escape."

"You have it already."

"Renew it to me, then."

"I renew it; only make haste. The crime is public; the confession is complete. What is the use of making me wait?"

"It is not for me to fix the hour of the death of a man. It must be according to the good pleasure of the Emperor Charles V."

Then, summoning the sergeant—

"Conduct this gentleman to a private tent," said Emmanuel, "and let him want for nothing! A single sentinel will suffice to guard him: I have his parole as a gentleman. Go!"

The sergeant left, taking the prisoner with him. Emmanuel Philibert followed him with his eyes until he was some distance from his tent. Then, as he thought he heard a feeble sound behind him, he turned.

Leona was standing on the threshold of the second compartment, the tapestry of which had fallen behind her.

It was the noise made by this tapestry falling which had attracted the attention of Emmanuel Philibert.

Leona had her hands clasped; her face bore the trace of the tears she had no doubt shed at the recital of the prisoner.

"What do you want?" asked the prince.

"I want to say to you," she said—"I want to say to you that this man must not die!"

The countenance of Emmanuel became overcast.

"Leona," said Emmanuel, "you have not reflected on what you ask. This man has committed a horrible crime, if not in fact, at least in intention."

"No matter," replied Leona, throwing her arms around the prince's neck; "I repeat to you, this man must not die!"

"The Emperor will decide his lot, Leona. The only thing I can do is to report everything to the Emperor."

"And I tell you, though the Emperor condemned this young man to a death of shame, you would still obtain his pardon, would you not, Emmanuel?"

"Leona, you believe I have a power over the Emperor I do not really possess. The imperial justice must follow its course. If it condemns—"

"Even if it condemned, still must Odoardo Maraviglia live; you hear me? He must live, my dearest Emmanuel!"

"And why, pray?"

"Because," replied Leona—"because he is my brother!"

Emmanuel uttered a cry of amazement.

That woman dying of hunger and fatigue on the bank of the Sesia, that child obstinately keeping the secret of her birth and sex, that page refusing the diamond of Charles V. —all was explained by those four words which had just escaped from Leona in reference to Odoardo Maraviglia, "He is my brother!"

XIII

THE DEMON OF THE SOUTH

AT THE very time the scene we have related was passing under the tent of Emmanuel Philibert, a great event, announced by flourishes of trumpets and hurrying of soldiers, was creating excitement in the imperial camp.

A little troop of horsemen had been distinguished coming from the direction of Brussels; couriers had been sent forward to meet this troop, and had returned galloping and making great signs of joy. They announced that the leader of the cavalcade was no less a person than the only son of the most august emperor, Philip, Prince of Spain, King of Naples, and husband of the Queen of England.

Amid the flourishes of trumpets and the cheers of the first who perceived the prince, all left their tents and hurried to greet the new-comer.

Philip was mounted on a handsome white steed, which he managed gracefully enough. He was clad in violet mantle and black tunic—the two mourning colors of kings; his breeches were violet also, and he had on immense boots of buffalo leather, and wore a little black cap, such as was the fashion at the period, adorned with a silken band and a black plume.

Round his neck was the collar of the Golden Fleece. He was then a man of twenty-eight years, of middle height, rather fat than lean, with cheeks somewhat puffed, a blond beard, close, thin lips that rarely smiled, a straight nose, and eyes that trembled under their lashes like those of hares. Although he was handsome rather than ugly, the *ensemble* of his physiognomy had nothing sympathetic; and it might be easily seen that under that brow, wrinkled before its time, were harbored gloomy rather than pleasant thoughts.

The Emperor had a great affection for him. As he had loved his mother, he loved his son. But whenever a caress drew the two hearts together, he felt that the prince's was enveloped in a sheeting of ice which no embrace could ever melt.

Sometimes, when he was long without seeing his son, when he could no longer try to penetrate with his eyes the troubled and shifting look of the young prince, he would anxiously meditate in what direction this darksome miner, eternally occupied with underground intrigues, was burrowing in the interests of his ambition. Was it against their common enemies? Was it against himself? And with this doubt in his heart, he would let some of those terrible words escape which Emmanuel Philibert had heard that very morning with reference to the prisoner.

The birth of the young prince had been as gloomy as his life was to be. There are gloomy dawns which are reflections of the entire day. The Emperor received the news of his birth, which took place on Tuesday, the 31st of May, 1527, at the same time as that of the death of the Connétable de Bourbon, the sack of Rome, and the captivity of Clement VII. All rejoicings were forbidden at this birth, for fear it might form a contrast with the universal mourning of Christendom.

Only a year after, the royal heir was recognized as Prince of Spain. Then there were grand festivals; but the child who as a man was to cause the shedding of so many tears—the child did nothing but weep during these festivals.

He had just reached his sixteenth year, when the Emperor, wishing to make trial of him in war, ordered him to compel the French, commanded by the Dauphin, to raise the siege of Perpignan; but in order that he might not run the risk of any check in this enterprise, he was accompanied by six grandees of Spain, fourteen barons, eight hundred gentlemen, two thousand cavalry, and five thousand infantry.

Against such a reinforcement of fresh troops no headway could be made. The French raised the siege, and the Infante of Spain began his military career with a victory.

But after the report he ordered to be laid before him of this campaign, Charles V. easily understood that the instincts of his son were not warlike. He reserved, therefore, to himself the risks of war and the uncertain fortunes of battles, leaving to the heir of his power the study of politics, for which he seemed to have a natural bent.

At sixteen, the young prince had made such progress in this great art of government that Charles V. did not hesitate to name him governor of all the kingdoms of Spain.

In 1544, he married Doña Maria of Portugal, his cousin-german, born in the same year as himself, and even in the very hour.

He had a son, Don Carlos, the hero of a lamentable history, and of two or three tragedies. This son was born in 1545.

In fine, in 1548, Philip left Barcelona for the purpose of visiting Italy in the midst of a frightful storm, which had scattered the fleet of Doria, and forced it to return for the moment into port; with a contrary wind, he attempted the voyage again, landed at Genoa, from Genoa proceeded to Milan, explored the battlefield of Pavia, required to be shown the spot where François I. surrendered his sword, and measured with his eyes the depth of the ditch in which the French monarchy was near being buried; then, taciturn and silent as ever, he quitted Milan, crossed central Italy, and joined the Emperor at Worms. Then Charles V., Flemish by birth and heart, presented him to his fellow-countrymen of Namur and Brussels.

At Namur, Emmanuel Philibert received him, and did him the honors of the city. The two cousins embraced each other tenderly at their meeting, and afterward Emmanuel gave him the spectacle of a little war, in which, it may be well conceived, Philip did not take any part.

The festivals were not less sumptuous at Brussels than at Namur. Seven hundred princes, barons, and gentlemen received outside the gates the heir of the greatest monarchy in the world. Then when this heir had been fully recognized and seen, his father sent him back to Spain.

Emmanuel Philibert accompanied him to Genoa. It was during this journey that the Prince of Savoy saw his father for the last time.

Three years after the return of Philip into Spain, King Edward VI. of England died, leaving the crown to his sister Mary, daughter of Catherine, that aunt whom the Emperor loved so much that he learned English, he said, for no other reason except to speak to her.

The new queen was pressed to choose a husband. She

was forty-six years old; consequently, she had little time to lose. Charles V. proposed his son Philip.

Philip had lost that charming Doña Maria, who had lived only the age of the flowers. Four days after the birth of Don Carlos, the women of the queen, curious to see a magnificent auto-da-fé, left the new mother alone in front of a table covered with fruits. The sick woman had been forbidden to eat of those fruits. A daughter of Eve on all points, the poor princess disregarded the injunction. She rose, bit with her beautiful young teeth, not into an apple, but into a melon, and in twenty-four hours was dead.

Nothing, therefore, prevented Don Philip from marrying Mary Tudor, from uniting England and Spain, and stifling France between the island of the North and the peninsula of the South.

It was the grand aim of the union.

Philip had two rivals for the hand of his cousin. They were Cardinal Pole, a cardinal without being a priest—son of George, Duke of Clarence, brother of Edward IV., consequently, cousin to the queen in nearly the same degree of relationship as Philip; and the Earl of Courtenay, nephew of Henry VIII., consequently, as nearly related as the two others to Mary.

Charles V. began by making sure of the support of Mary herself; and having gained this support through the influence of Father Henry, her confessor, he did not hesitate to act.

The Princess Mary was an ardent Catholic. The title of "Bloody Mary," given to her by successive English historians, is a proof of it.

The Emperor began then by banishing from her presence the Earl of Courtenay, a young man of thirty-two, handsome as an angel and brave as a Courtenay. He accused him of being a zealous protector of heresy; and, in fact, Mary regarded the two of her ministers who were most favorable to this marriage as strongly tainted with that false religion of which her father had made himself the Pope, in order to have no further connection with the *bishops of Rome*, as he called them.

This point having been well fixed in the mind of the queen, Courtenay was no longer to be feared.

Remained Cardinal Pole, perhaps less brave than Courtenay, but as handsome as he, and assuredly more of a statesman, raised as he had been in the school of the popes.

Cardinal Pole was so much the more to be feared that, before being crowned, Mary Tudor, with or without intention, had written to Pope Julius III. to send Cardinal Pole to her as apostolic legate in order that the latter might labor with her in the holy task of re-establishing their religion. Luckily for Charles V., the Pope, who knew what Pole had to suffer under Henry VIII., and what dangers he had encountered, hesitated sending all at once, in the midst of the fermentation that reigned in England, a prelate of his distinction. He despatched, therefore, first, John Francis Commendon, master of the chamber, to act near Mary; but the queen wanted Pole, and not Commendon. She dismissed the latter, begging him to hasten the arrival of the cardinal.

Pole started; but the Emperor had his spies at Rome. He was informed of this departure; and as the legate *a atere* was to cross Germany, and pass by Innspruck, Charles V. ordered Mendoza, who commanded a body of cavalry in this city, to arrest Cardinal Pole on his passage, on the ground that he was too nearly related to the queen to give her disinterested advice in the matter of her marriage with Don Philip.

Mendoza was the kind of captain needed by princes in such circumstances. He had ears only for the word of command. His orders were to arrest Cardinal Pole; he arrested him and kept him prisoner until the articles of the marriage contract between Philip of Spain and Mary of England were signed.

These articles being signed, he was released. Pole took it as a man of good sense should, and filled the office of legate *a latere* not only to Mary, but to Philip.

One of the articles declared that Mary Tudor, Queen of England, could only marry a king; this did not embarrass Charles V.; he made his son Philip king of Naples.

This success somewhat consoled the Emperor, saddened by the two checks he had experienced: the one at Innspruck, where, surprised in the night by Duke Maurice, he had fled so precipitately that he forgot he had put on his baldrick and forgotten his sword; the other before Metz, the siege of which he had been forced to raise, abandoning, in the slush and mud caused by a thaw, his cannon, war material, and a third of his army.

"Oh," he cried, "fortune is then returning to me at last!"

Finally, on the 24th of July, 1554—that is to say, nine months before the period at which we are arrived—the very day of the feast of Saint-James, protector of Spain, Mary of England was united to Philip of Spain. She who might be called the *Tigress of the North* was united to him who was to be the *Demon of the South*. Philip set out from Spain accompanied by twenty-two vessels of war, carrying six thousand men; but before entering Hampton port, he dismissed all these, having decided to approach England with only the ships which Queen Mary sent to meet him. These numbered eighteen. They were preceded by the largest vessel ever built in England, and which was launched for this occasion.

The vessels advanced to meet the prince a distance of three leagues from the shore; and there, amid discharges of artillery and rolling of drums and flourishes of clarions, Philip passed from his own ship into that supplied by his betrothed.

He was followed by sixty gentlemen, twelve being grandees of Spain; among them, the Duke of Medina-Cœli and Ruy Gomez de Silva had each forty pages and valets. "In fine, it was reckoned a marvellous thing, and what was never before seen," says Gregorio Leti, the historian of Charles V., "that these sixty lords had among them twelve hundred and thirty pages and attendants." The marriage was celebrated at Windsor. Those who wish to know how Queen Mary met her husband, what robe she wore, what jewels adorned her, what was the form of the amphitheatre surmounted by two thrones which awaited the two spouses; those who wish to penetrate further still, and learn the manner in which Mass was celebrated, the manner in which their Majesties sat down to table, in fine, that in which "they arose *so adroitly* from table, that although there were before them a quantity of lords and ladies, they disappeared through a secret door, and withdrew into their chamber"—will find these details and many others in the historian we have just quoted.

As to ourselves, interesting and picturesque as those details are, they would lead us too far, and we shall return to the King of England and Naples, Philip II., who, after nine months of marriage, appeared again on the Continent, and at the moment when he was least expected, arrived, as we have said, at the barriers of the camp, saluted by the rolling of drums, the flourishes of trumpets, and by the cheers of the German and Spanish soldiers who joined his train.

Charles V. had been one of the first to be informed of the unexpected arrival of his son; and glad that Philip had no motive (so it appeared, at least) for concealing his presence from him in Flanders, since he was come to find him in his camp, he made an effort, and, supported by the arms of one of his officers, he dragged himself to the door of his tent.

He was hardly there when he perceived Don Philip advancing toward him, amid shouts, drums and trumpets, as if he were already master and lord.

"Well, well," murmured Charles V., "it is the will of God!" But as soon as Philip perceived his father, he brought his horse to a standstill, and leaped to the ground; then approaching, with his arms stretched out and head uncovered and bent, he threw himself at the feet of the Emperor.

This humility chased every bad thought from the mind of Charles V. He raised Philip, pressed him in his arms, and, turning toward those who formed the train of the prince—

"Thanks, gentlemen," he said, "for having divined the joy the presence of my beloved son was to cause, and for having announced it beforehand by your cheers and hurrahs." Then to his son, "Don Philip," he said, "it is nearly five years since we have seen each other; come, we have many things to converse about."

And saluting all this crowd, soldiers and officers assembled before his tent, he leaned on the arm of his son, and returned to the pavilion amid cries a thousand times repeated of "Long live the King of England!" and "Long live the Emperor of Germany!" and "Long live Don Philip!" and "Long live Charles V.!"

In fact, as the Emperor had presupposed, Philip had very many things to say to him. And yet, after Charles V. was seated on the divan, and Philip, refusing the honor of sitting beside his father, had taken a chair, there was a moment's silence.

It was Charles V. who first broke this silence, which Philip had kept perhaps through respect for his father.

"My son," said the Emperor, "nothing but your dear presence could dissipate the bad impression produced on me by the ill news received to-day."

"The most fatal news of all was already known to me, as you can see by my garb, my father," answered Philip; "we have had the misfortune to lose, you a mother, I a grandmother."

"You have learned this news in Belgium, have you not, my son?"

Philip bowed.

"In England, sire, our communications with Spain are quite direct, while the courier your Majesty has received has been obliged to come here from Genoa by land; this must have delayed him."

"Yes, it must be as you say," said Charles V.; "but apart from this motive of sorrow, my son, I have another subject for anxiety."

"Does your Majesty wish to speak of the election of Paul IV., and of the league he has proposed to the King of France—a league which must be signed at this hour?"

Charles V. regarded Don Philip with astonishment.

"My son," said he, "is it also an English vessel which has made you as well informed as you are on this point? The passage, however, from Civita Vecchia to Portsmouth is long."

"No, sire, the news has come to us from France; hence it happens that I know it before you. The passages of the Alps and Tyrol are still encumbered with snows, and have delayed your messenger; while ours came straight from Ostia to Marseilles, from Marseilles to Boulogne, and from Boulogne to London."

Charles V. frowned. He had long believed it was his right to be informed of every grave event that happened in the world; and here was his son, who knew before him, not only the death of Queen Juana and the election of Paul IV., but announced to him a thing of which he was ignorant; namely, the league signed between Henri II. and the new Pope.

But Philip did not appear to perceive the astonishment of his father.

"For that matter," he continued, "all measures were so well taken by Caraffa and his partisans that the treaty was sent to the King of France during the conclave. This explains the boldness with which, after taking Marienbourg, Henri II. marched on Bouvines and on Dinant, with the aim, no doubt, of cutting off your retreat."

"Oh, oh!" exclaimed Charles, "has he advanced as far as you say, and am I threatened with a new surprise like that of Innspruck?"

"No," said Philip, "for I hope your Majesty will not refuse to conclude a truce with Henri II."

"By my soul!" cried the Emperor, "I should be very foolish if I refused it, and even if I did not propose it."

"Sire," said Philip, "such a truce proposed by you would render the King of France too proud. And so Queen Mary and I have had the idea of devoting ourselves to this task in the interest of your dignity."

"And you are come to ask from me authority to act? Be it so: act; lose no time; send the most skilful ambassadors to France—they can never arrive too soon."

"It is what we have thought of, sire; and we have sent, reserving to your Majesty full liberty to repudiate us, Cardinal Pole to King Henri to ask a truce."

Charles shook his head.

"He will not arrive in time," he said; "and Henri will be in Brussels before Pole has landed at Calais."

"Consequently Pole has gone by Ostend, and has joined the King of France at Dinant."

"However able a negotiator he may be," said Charles V., with a sigh, "I doubt of his success in such a negotiation."

"I am then very happy to announce to your Majesty that he has succeeded," said Philip. "The King of France accepts, if not a truce, at least a suspension of arms, during which the conditions of a truce will be regulated. The monastery of Vocelles, near Cambrai, has been selected by him as the place where the conferences are to be held, and Cardinal Pole, on coming to Brussels to announce to me the result of his mission, told me he did not believe there would be any difficulty in coming to an arrangement."

Charles V. regarded Philip with a certain admiration; the latter, in the most humble fashion imaginable, had just announced to him the happy issue of a negotiation which he had regarded as impossible.

"What will be the duration of this truce?" he said.

"Real or conventional?"

"Conventional."

"Five years, sire."

"And real?"

"As long as it shall please God."

"And how long do you believe, Don Philip, that its continuance is likely to be pleasing to God?"

"Why," said the King of England, with an imperceptible smile, "just the time necessary for you to draw from Spain a reinforcement of ten thousand Spaniards and for me to send you ten thousand Englishmen from England."

"My son," said Charles V., "this truce was my most ardent desire; and as it is you who have made it, I promise you that it shall be you who will keep it or break it according to your good pleasure."

"I do not understand what my august emperor means," said Philip, whose self-control could not prevent him from darting from his eyes a flash of hope and covetousness.

He had just got a glimpse, almost within reach of his hand, of the sceptre of Spain and the Low Countries, and—who knows?—perhaps of the imperial crown.

Eight days after, a truce was signed in these terms:

"There shall be a truce for five years, as well on sea as on land, to be equally enjoyed by all the people, states, kingdoms, and provinces of the Emperor, the King of France, and King Philip.

"During all this space of time of five years, there shall be a suspension of hostilities, and, however, each of these potentates shall keep whatever he has taken in the course of the war.

"His Holiness Paul IV. is comprehended in this truce."

Philip himself presented this treaty to the Emperor, who cast an almost frightened glance on the impassive countenance of his son.

All that was wanting to the treaty was the signature of Charles V.

Charles V. signed.

Then, when with infinite difficulty he had traced the seven letters of his name—

"Sire," said he, giving for the first time this title to his son, "return to London, and be ready to meet me at Brussels on my first summons."

XIV

IN WHICH CHARLES V. KEEPS THE PROMISE MADE TO HIS SON DON PHILIP

ON FRIDAY the 25th of October, 1555, there were great crowds in the streets of the city of Brussels, not only of the people of the capital of southern Brabant, but of the other Flemish states of the Emperor Charles V.

All this multitude was pressing toward the royal palace, which no longer exists, but which then towered over the city from the summit of Caudenberg.

The occasion of this excitement was that a great assembly, the cause of which was yet unknown, had been convoked by the Emperor, and, having been adjourned once before, was to be held to-day.

For this reason, the interior of the grand hall had been adorned and hung with tapestry on the eastern side—that is to say, in the direction of the barriers—and a sort of scaffold had been there constructed, covered with magnificent carpets and surmounted by a dais with the imperial arms, protecting three armchairs, empty for the time, but evidently destined to be soon occupied: that in the centre by the Emperor, that on the right by Don Philip, who had arrived the evening before, and that on the left by Charles V.'s sister, Mary of Austria, Queen Dowager of Hungary.

Benches were arranged parallel to these three chairs, and formed with them a kind of hemicycle.

Other seats were placed in front of the platform, arranged like the benches in a theatre.

King Philip, Queen Mary, Queen Eleonore, widow of François I., Maximilian, King of Bohemia, Christina,

Duchesse de Lorraine, had taken possession of their apartments at the palace. Charles alone continued to inhabit what he called his little house in the park.

At four in the afternoon he left this little house, mounted on a mule, whose gentle pace made him suffer less than any other mode of locomotion. As to going on foot, it was impossible to dream of it: the attacks of the gout had redoubled in violence; and the Emperor was not sure even that he could walk from the threshold of the door to the scaffold of the grand hall, or that he would not have to be carried during that short passage. Kings and princes followed the mule of the Emperor on foot.

The Emperor was clad in the imperial cope, all of cloth of gold, over which fell the grand cordon of the Golden Fleece. He had the crown on his head; but the sceptre, which his hand had no longer the strength to bear, was carried before him on a cushion of red velvet.

The persons who were to occupy the benches placed on both sides of the armchairs and in front of the platform had been introduced previously into the hall.

There were, on the right of the armchairs, the knights of the Golden Fleece, seated on a tapestried bench.

On the bench on the left, also tapestried, were the princes, the grandees of Spain, and the lords.

Behind them, on other benches not tapestried, were the three councils—the council of state, the privy council, and the council of finance.

Finally, on other benches placed in front, were, first, the states of Brabant, then the states of Flanders, then the other states according to their rank.

The galleries around the hall had been packed with spectators since morning.

The Emperor entered at a quarter past four; he was leaning on the shoulder of William of Orange, surnamed later on *The Taciturn*.

Beside William of Orange walked Emmanuel Philibert, accompanied by his squire and page.

On the other side, in front of kings and princes, some steps to the right of the Emperor, appeared a man of from thirty to thirty-five years, unknown to every one, and who seemed as much astonished at finding himself there as the spectators seemed to be at his presence on the occasion.

It was Odoardo Maraviglia, drawn from his prison, clad in a magnificent garb, and led here without knowing where he was going or what was wanted with him.

On the appearance of the Emperor and his august suite, every one rose.

The Emperor advanced to the front of the platform, walking with great difficulty, supported though he was. It was evident that great courage, and especially great habitual endurance, were needed to prevent him from uttering a groan at every step he took.

He sat down, having King Philip on his right and Queen Mary on his left.

Then on a sign from him, each did the same, except on the one side, the Prince of Orange, Emmanuel Philibert, and the two persons forming his suite, and on the other, Odoardo Maraviglia, who, free, and dressed, as we have said, in a magnificent costume, was looking at the spectacle with astonished eyes.

When everybody was seated, the Emperor made a sign to Councillor Philibert Brussellius to open the proceedings.

Every one was in a state of anxious expectation. The countenance of Philip alone remained calm and impassive. His eye seemed to see nothing; it could be hardly guessed if the blood circulated under that pale and inanimate skin. The orator explained in a few words that the kings, princes, grandees of Spain, knights of the Golden Fleece, and the members of the states of Flanders present in the hall, had been convoked to assist at the abdication of the Emperor Charles V. in favor of his son Don Philip, who, starting from this moment, succeeded him in his titles of King of Castile, Leon, Granada, Navarre, Aragon, Naples, Sicily, Majorca, the isles, Indias, and lands of the Pacific and

Atlantic Oceans, and in those of Archduke of Austria, Duke of Burgundy, Lothier, Brabant, Luisbourg, Luxemburg, and Quelières; of Count of Flanders, Artois, and Burgundy; of Palatine of Hainault, Zeland, Holland, Feurette, Haguenau, Namur, and Zutphen; in fine, of those of Prince of Zuane, Marquis of the Holy Empire, Lord of Frise, Salmi, Malines, and of the cities and countries of Utrecht, Overyssel, and Groeningen.

The imperial crown was reserved for Ferdinand, already King of the Romans.

At this reservation, a livid pallor overspread the face of Don Philip, and a slight trembling sent a shiver through the muscles of his cheeks.

This abdication, at which all held their breath in astonishment, was attributed by the orator to the Emperor's desire to revisit Spain, which he had not seen since twelve years, and particularly to the sufferings he experienced from the gout—sufferings increased by the rigorous climate of Flanders and Germany. He finished by praying, in the name of the Emperor, the states of Flanders to take in good part this cession which he made of them to his son Don Philip.

After concluding the discourse with a peroration in which he called upon God to have the august Emperor always under his safeguard and protection, Philibert Brussellius was silent, and resumed his seat.

Then the Emperor rose in his turn; he was pale, and the perspiration of suffering bedewed his countenance. He wished to speak, and held in his hand a paper on which he had written his discourse, in case his memory failed him.

At the first sign shown by him of his intention to speak, the confused murmurs which had run through the hall at the close of the discourse of Councillor Brussellius ceased as if by enchantment; and weak as the Emperor's voice was, the moment he opened his mouth, a single word of what he said was not lost. It is true that as he progressed in his speech, and as he recalled his toils, his dangers, his great deeds, and his plans, his voice rose, his gestures had a larger sweep, his eyes became singularly animated, and his accent had some of those solemn intonations often heard in the last words of the dying.

"Dear friends," he said,[1] "you have just heard the motives which have led me to decide on resigning the sceptre and the crown into the hands of my son. Let me add some words which will make clearer to your eyes my resolution and my thought. Dear friends, several of those who are listening to me to-day must remember that it is just forty years ago on the 5th of January last, since my grandfather, the Emperor Maximilian, of glorious memory, released me from his guardianship, and in this very hall, at this very hour, when I reckoned hardly fifteen years, made me master of all my rights. In the following year, King Ferdinand the Catholic, my maternal grandfather, being dead, I was crowned, being then only sixteen years old.

"My mother was alive; but, though living and though still young, her mind, as you know, was so much affected by the death of her husband that she did not feel in a condition to rule by herself the kingdoms of her father and mother, and it became necessary for me, at seventeen years, to begin my journeys across the seas by setting out in order to take possession of the kingdom of Spain. Finally, when my grandfather, the Emperor Maximilian, died, thirty-six years ago—I was nineteen then—I ventured to become a candidate for the imperial crown he had worn, not from the desire of ruling over a larger number of countries, but in order to watch more efficaciously over the safety of Germany, of my other realms, and particularly of my beloved Flanders.

"It was with this object I undertook and accomplished

---

[1] We have made no alteration in the discourse of the Emperor, which we borrow from a work published in 1830 at Brussels, by the learned conservator of the archives of the kingdom, M. L. P. Gachard.

so many journeys; count them, and you will be yourselves astonished at their number and extent.

"I have passed nine times into upper Germany, six times into Spain, seven times into Italy, ten times into Belgium, four times into France, twice into England, and twice into Africa, which makes in all forty voyages or expeditions. Besides these forty voyages or expeditions, I have made journeys to visit islands and provinces brought under my sway.

"For the latter purpose, I have traversed the Mediterranean eight times and the Western Sea three times, which I am making ready to cross to-day for the last time.

"I pass under silence my journey through France, which I made from Spain to the Low Countries—a journey rendered necessary, as you know, by grave motives.[1]

"I have been forced, on account of these numerous and long absences, to place at the head of the government of these provinces, madame, my good sister, the queen here present. Now I know, and the different orders of the state know as well as I, how she has acquitted herself of these functions.

"I have, at the same time I made these journeys, carried on many wars; all these enterprises have been undertaken or accepted against my will; and what afflicts me to-day on bidding you farewell, my dear friends, is not to be able to leave you a peace more stable, an assurance of more certain tranquillity. . . . All these things have not been done, as you may well think, without protracted toils and great fatigue; and the heaviness of that fatigue, the burden of those toils, can be measured by seeing my paleness and my feebleness. Consequently, let no one believe me so ignorant of myself as not, when comparing the responsibilities thrust upon me by events with the strength granted me by God, to have comprehended my insufficiency for the mission given me.

---

[1] The revolt of the people of Ghent.

THE PAGE OF THE DUKE OF SAVOY 161

"But it seems to me that, on account of the mental state of my mother and the tender age of my son, it would have been a crime to lay down the burden before the proper hour, however heavy it might be, which Providence, in giving me the crown and sceptre, had imposed on my head and on my arm.

"However, when I last quitted Flanders to go into Germany, I had already the project of accomplishing the purpose which I execute to-day; but, seeing the miserable condition of affairs, feeling that I had still a remnant of strength, moved by the disturbances which agitated the Christian republic, attacked at the same time by the Lutherans and the Turks, I believed it my duty to put off the time for repose, and to sacrifice to my subjects whatever remained to me of strength and existence. I was nearly attaining my aim, however, when the German princes and the King of France, in violation of their pledged word, flung me back into the midst of troubles and battles. The former attacked my person, and almost succeeded in making me a prisoner in Innspruck; the latter took possession of Metz, which belonged to the domain of the Empire. I hastened to besiege it myself with a numerous army. I was conquered and my army destroyed; but it was not by men, it was by the elements. To counterbalance the loss of Metz, I wrested Thérouanne and Hesdin from the French. I did more: I met the King of France at Valenciennes, and forced him to withdraw, doing all I could at the battle of Renty, in despair of not being able to do more.

"But to-day, besides the insufficiency which I have recognized in myself, the disease with which I am afflicted is become more acute, and prostrates me.

"Happily, at the very moment God takes from me a mother, he gives me a son of an age to govern. Now that my strength fails me and that death is approaching, I do not care to prefer the love and passion for sovereignty to the good and to the repose of my subjects. Instead of an infirm old man who has already seen descend into the tomb the best part of himself, I give you a vigorous prince, who must be acceptable to you on account of his flourishing youth and virtue. Swear then to him that fidelity and affection which you have sworn to me, and which you have so loyally kept. Take care especially that the heresies which are gliding in among you do not disturb the fraternity that ought to unite you; and if you see them putting forth any roots, hasten to extirpate them, to tear them out of the soil, and cast them afar.

"And now, to say a last word about myself, to all I have already spoken, I will add that I have fallen into many faults, whether through ignorance in my youth, or pride in my maturity, or through other weaknesses inherent in human nature. Nevertheless, I declare here that I have not done knowingly or voluntarily injury or violence to any one whatever, or that when violence or injury has been done, and I have learned of it, I have always made reparation, as, in the face of all, I am going to do now with regard to one of the persons here present, whom I beg to receive that reparation with patience and mercy."

Then, turning to Philip, who at the close of the discourse had thrown himself at his feet—

"My son," said he, "if merely by my death you had entered into the possession of so many realms and provinces, I should still merit something from you for having left you a heritage so rich and so largely augmented by my labors. But since this great succession does not come to you to-day by my death, but only by my will; since your father has desired to die before his body descended to the tomb, to enable you to enjoy during his life the benefit of his succession—I ask you, and I have the right to ask you, to bestow on the welfare of your subjects all that which you rightly seem to owe to me for having enabled you to enjoy the satisfaction of ruling before your time.

"Other kings rejoice at the thought of giving life to their children and bequeathing to them kingdoms; but I have wished to wrest from death the glory of making you this present, believing that I receive a twofold joy in seeing you both live and reign through me. Few will be found to imitate my example, as, indeed, I have found few such examples in past ages that it would be well to imitate; but at least mine will be praised when it is seen that you deserve the experiment should be made in your case; and you will obtain this advantage, my son, if you preserve that wisdom which has distinguished you up to now; if you have continually in your soul the fear of the Sovereign Master of all things; if you undertake the defence of the Catholic religion and the protection of justice and the laws, which are the greatest strength and the best supports of empires. In fine, it remains to me now to wish in your favor such good fortune in your children that you may transfer to them your empire and your power freely, and without being thereto constrained otherwise than I am."

On saying these words, whether that they were in reality the end of the discourse, or that the discourse was interrupted by emotion, the voice of Charles V. stuck in his throat; and, laying his hand on the head of his kneeling son, he remained for an instant motionless and dumb, the tears in his eyes coursing abundantly and silently down his cheeks.

Then after a minute of this silence, more eloquent still than the discourse he had just pronounced, as if his strength was failing him, he stretched his hand to his sister; while Don Philip, rising from his knees, passed his arm around his body to support him.

Thereupon, Queen Mary drew from her pocket a crystal flagon containing a rose-colored liquid, and poured the contents into a little golden cup which she presented to the Emperor.

While the Emperor was drinking, all in the assembly gave free course to their emotion. There were few hearts among those present, whether their rank brought them near to the throne or kept them far from it, that were not touched, few eyes that were not obscured by tears.

And indeed it was a great spectacle given to the world, that of this sovereign, warrior, and Cæsar, who, after forty years of such power as few men had ever received from Providence, descended voluntarily from the throne, and, weary in body and crushed in spirit, proclaimed with a loud voice the nothingness of human greatness in presence of the successor to whom he abandoned it.

But a spectacle greater still was to come—the one just promised by the Emperor—it was that of a man publicly acknowledging a fault committed, and asking pardon of him to whom the wrong had been done.

The Emperor understood that this was expected of him; and, mustering all his strength, he gently pushed his son away from him.

It was seen that he was going to speak a second time, and there was silence.

"Dear friends," resumed the Emperor, "I promised just now a public reparation to a man I had offended. Be ye all witnesses, therefore, that after boasting of what I have done well, I have accused myself of what I have done ill."

Then, turning to the unknown man in the magnificent costume, whom every one had already remarked—

"Odoardo Maraviglia," he said in a firm voice, "approach."

The young man to whom this formal invitation was addressed grew pale, and, tottering, approached Charles V.

"Count," said the Emperor, "I have done you serious wrong, whether voluntarily or involuntarily, in the person of your father, who suffered a cruel death in the prisons of Milan. Often has this act been presented to me veiled by uncertainty. To-day it appears to me like a spectre clad in the winding-sheet of remorse. Comte Maraviglia, here, in the face of, beneath the eyes of, men and of God, at the moment when about to lay aside the imperial mantle, which for thirty-six years has weighed upon my shoulders, I humble myself before you, and pray you not only to grant me pardon, but further to ask it for me of the Lord, who will perhaps sooner grant it to the petitions of the victim than to the supplications of the murderer."

Odoardo Maraviglia uttered a cry and fell on his knees.

"Magnificent Emperor," he said, "it is not without reason that the world has given you the name of august. Oh, yes, yes! I pardon you in the name of my father and in my own name! Yes; God will pardon you. But from whom shall I seek that pardon, august Emperor, which I no longer grant myself?"

Then, rising, "Gentlemen," said Maraviglia, turning toward the assembly—"gentlemen, you behold in me a man who tried to assassinate the Emperor, and whom the Emperor has not only pardoned, but of whom he has asked pardon."

"King Don Philip," he added, bending before him who from that moment was to be called Philip II., "the murderer places himself in your hands."

"My son," said Charles V., whose strength was failing him for the second time, "I recommend to you this man; let his life be sacred to you!"

And he fell back almost fainting on his armchair.

"Ah, my dear Emmanuel!" said the page of the Duke of Savoy, who managed to reach the prince on account of the commotion occasioned by the Emperor's faintness, "how good you are! how great! how I recognize you in what has passed!"

And before Emmanuel Philibert could prevent it, Leone-Leona had kissed his hands almost with as much respect as love.

The ceremony, a moment interrupted by the unforeseen accident we have related, which was not the least affecting of the scenes of that solemn day, was about to resume its course; for, in order that the abdication might be complete, after Charles V. had given, it was necessary that Philip should accept.

Philip, who had made a sign of assent to the recommendation of the Emperor, again bowed humbly before him, and in Spanish—a language which many of the audience did not speak, but which almost all understood—he said in a voice marked for the first time perhaps by a shade of emotion:

"I have not deserved, most invincible Emperor and my very good father, I could never have believed that I should deserve, a paternal love so great that there assuredly has never been anything like it in the world, never, at least, one that has produced such effects that it at once covers me with confusion, when I view the little merit which I have, and fills me with gratitude and respect in presence of your greatness. But since it has pleased you to treat me so tenderly and generously as a consequence of your august goodness, exercise the same goodness, my very dear father, by continuing in the belief that every effort shall be made on my part to have your decision in my favor universally approved and accepted, as I intend governing in such a manner as to convince the states of the affection I have always entertained for them."

At the conclusion of these words, he kissed the hand of his father several times; while the latter, pressing him to his breast, said—

"I wish you, my son, the most precious blessings of Heaven and its divine aid."

Then Don Philip kissed the hand of his father for the last time, wiped a tear from his eyes which probably was not there, rose, turned toward the states, saluted them, and, with his hat in his hand—the same attitude in which all were except the Emperor, who was covered and seated—he pronounced in French the following words:

"Gentlemen, I would that I could speak better the language of this country, in order that you might the better understand the good affection and favor I bear you. But as I do not know it as well as would be necessary for my purpose, I will ask the Bishop of Arras to act in my name."

At the same time, Antoine Perrenot de Grandville, who was afterward cardinal, took his stand as interpreter of the sentiments of the prince. He eulogized the zeal of Don Philip for the good of his subjects, and expressed the resolution he had adopted of conforming exactly to the good and wise instructions the Emperor had given him.

Then Queen Mary, the Emperor's sister, governess for twenty-six years of the provinces of the Low Countries, rose in turn, and in a few words resigned into the hands of her nephew the regency which she had received from her brother.

After this, Philip swore to maintain the rights and privileges of his subjects, and all the members of the assembly, princes, grandees of Spain, knights of the Golden Fleece, deputies of the states either in their own name or in the name of those they represented, swore obedience to him.

This double oath pronounced, Charles V. rose, placed Don Philip on his throne, put the crown on his head, and said in a loud voice—

"Grant, O Lord, that this crown be not for your elect a crown of thorns!"

Then he made a step toward the door.

Immediately Don Philip, the Prince of Orange, Emmanuel Philibert, and all the princes and lords rushed forward to support the Emperor; but he made a sign to Maraviglia, who approached, hesitating, for he could not comprehend what the Emperor wanted with him.

The Emperor wished to have no other support in retiring than that afforded by Maraviglia, for whose father's death he was responsible, and who, in retaliation for the bloody deed, had tried to slay him.

But, as the second arm of the Emperor fell inert by his side—

"Sire," said Emmanuel Philibert, "allow my page Leone to be the second support on which your Majesty may lean; and the honor you do him, I shall consider done to myself."

And he pushed Leone toward the Emperor.

Charles V. looked at the page and recognized him.

"Ah, ah!" he said raising his arm, in order that the

latter might present his shoulder, "it is the young man of the diamond. You want to be reconciled to me, then, fair page?"

Then, looking at his hand, on the little finger of which only he had, on account of his cruel sufferings, been able to wear a gold ring—

"You lost something by waiting, fair page," he continued; "instead of the diamond, you will have only this simple ring. It is true it has my seal on it, which perhaps may be a compensation."

And drawing it from his little finger, he put it on the thumb of Leone, the thumb of that delicate hand being the only finger large enough to hold it.

Then he left the hall under the eyes and amid the acclamations of the assembly—eyes that would have been still more curious, acclamations that would have been still more enthusiastic, if the spectators had been able to guess that this monarch who was descending from a throne, that this Christian who was marching toward solitude, that this sinner who was bent under the weight of pardon, was advancing to a tomb in the near future, leaning not only on the son, but on the daughter of that unhappy Francesco Maraviglia, who was done to death by his orders, one gloomy night in September, in a dungeon of the fortress of Milan.

It was repentance sustained by prayer; that is to say, if we are to believe the words of Jesus Christ, the most agreeable spectacle here below to the eyes of the Lord.

But, on reaching the gate of the solitary street where his mule awaited him, the Emperor decided that neither of these young people should take a step further, and he dismissed Odoardo to his new lord, Don Philip and Leone to his old master, Emmanuel Philibert.

Then without other guard or suite than the groom who held the bridle of his peaceful steed, he took his way to his little house in the park; so that none who saw him riding along in the darkness even guessed that this humble pilgrim was the same man whose abdication was at that very hour the sole talk of Brussels, and soon to be the talk of the whole world.

Charles V., on arriving at the gate of this little house, on whose site the palace of the House of Representatives stands to-day, found it open.

The groom, therefore, had only to push one of the wings aside to admit the rider, the mule, and himself.

Then, having on the order of the Emperor brought the mule as close as possible to the door of the house, in order that the passage to the parlor might be as short as possible, he received his master in his arms, and placed him on the threshold.

The door was open, as the gate had been.

The Emperor paid no attention to this circumstance, plunged as he was in reflections which it is more easy for our readers to imagine than for us to relate.

Supported on one side by his staff, which he found in the same place he had left it, behind the door, on the other by his servant, he gained the parlor, which was hung with thick warm tapestry, furnished with thick carpets, and had a blazing fire in the immense chimney.

The parlor was lighted only by the glare of the flame, which was coiling greedily around the brands while devouring them.

He stretched himself on the sofa; and, having dismissed the groom, he recalled each of the phases of that life crowded with the events of a whole half-century; and what a half-century!—that in which lived Henry VIII., Maximilian, Clement VII., François I., Soliman and Luther. He forced his memory to recross the road he had travelled, sailing up the stream of his years, like a traveller who, toward the close of his life, would sail up the river with flowery and perfumed banks which he descended in his youth.

The journey was immense, magnificent, marvellous; it was made through the adoration of courtiers, the acclamations of the world, and the genuflections of the multitudes who ran to greet this gigantic fortune on its passage.

Suddenly, in the midst of this dream, which was less that of a man than of a god, one of the brands on the hearth burst, and one fragment fell in the ashes, while the other rolled on the carpet, from which a thick smoke immediately began to rise.

This incident, commonplace though it was, and perhaps for that very reason, brought the Emperor back to reality.

"Ho!" he called, "ho! who is on service here? Some one come quick!"

There was no answer.

"Is there nobody in the antechambers?" cried the ex-Emperor, growing impatient and striking the floor with his stick.

This second call met with no more reply than the first.

"Let some one come, I say, and fix this fire, and let him make haste!" said Charles V., now more impatient than ever.

Same silence.

"Oh!" said he, dragging himself from one piece of furniture to another, in order to reach the chimney, "if Providence had wished to inspire me with repentance for what I have done, the lesson has come very soon."

And then he himself, after many painful efforts, succeeded in regulating the fire with his own hands which could scarcely hold the tongs from pain.

All, from princes to valets, were busy around the new king, Don Philip.

The Emperor kicked back the last cinders smoking on the carpet, when a step was heard in the antechamber, and a human form appeared framed by the door and outlined in the shadow.

"At last!" murmured the Emperor.

"Sire," said the new-comer, who saw that Charles V. was mistaken as to his identity, "I ask pardon of your Majesty for thus presenting myself before you; but, having found all the doors open, and seeing nobody in the antechambers to announce me, I have ventured to announce myself."

"Announce yourself, then, sir," replied Charles, who was quickly learning, as we see, his apprenticeship as a private individual. "Come, who are you?"

"Sire," replied the unknown, in the most respectful tone, and bowing to the very ground, "I am Gaspard de Chatillon, Sire of Coligny, Admiral of France, and envoy extraordinary from his Majesty King Henri II."

"Monsieur envoy extraordinary of his Majesty King Henri II.," said Charles, smiling with a certain bitterness, "you have mistaken the door; it is no longer with me that you have business, it is with King Philip II., my successor to the throne of Naples since nine months, and to the throne of Spain and the Indias since twenty minutes."

"Sire," said Coligny, in the same respectful tone and bowing a second time, "whatever change may have occurred in the fortunes of Don Philip since nine months or since twenty minutes, you are always for me the elect of Germany, the very great, very holy, and very august Emperor Charles V.; and as it is to your Majesty that the letter of my sovereign is addressed, permit me to place it in your Majesty's hands."

"In that case, monsieur, help me to light these tapers," said Charles V., "for the accession of my son Don Philip has taken away from me even my last lackey."

And the Emperor, aided by the admiral, lighted the tapers in the candelabra, in order to be able to read the letter addressed to him by Henri II., and perhaps also, moved by some curiosity to see the man who for three years had been such a doughty adversary of his.

Gaspard de Chatillon, Sire of Coligny, was, at the period we have reached, a man of thirty-eight or thirty-nine years, with piercing eyes, a martial presence, and a tall and well-built figure. Being of a loyal and intrepid heart, he was held in great esteem by François I. and Henri II., as he was also to be by François II.

Immense as was the massacre of the 24th of August, 1572, there was needed, to render the miserable assassination of such a man possible, the hereditary hatred of Henri, Duc de Guise, joined to the hypocrisy of Catherine de Médicis and the weakness of Charles IX.

This hatred, which was beginning to separate the illustrious admiral from his old friend François de Guise at the very time we are introducing him to the reader, had its birth on the battlefield of Renty. In their youth, these two great captains, whose genius united would have wrought such marvels, had been intimate friends; there were no labors, no pleasures, no exercises which they did not share. In their studies of antiquity, they proposed as models for themselves not only the men who have left fine examples of courage, but also those who have left fine examples of fraternity.

This mutual affection went so far that "they wore," says Brantôme, "the same ornaments and the same livery." When King Henri II. sent a messenger to Charles V., and this messenger was not the Connétable de Montmorency, it could only be the Amiral de Coligny or the Duc de Guise.

The Emperor regarded the admiral with a certain admiration. It was impossible, we are assured by contemporary historians, to see any man who gave one a better idea of a great captain.

But, at this very same moment, it occurred to Charles that Coligny had been sent to Brussels, not precisely to give him the letter he held in his hand, but rather to report to the court of France what had taken place in the palace of Brussels on that famous day of the 25th of October, 1555. So the first question the Emperor put to Coligny, when a long gaze at the countenance of Coligny had allowed him to satisfy his curiosity, was the following:

"When did you arrive, M. l'Amiral?"

"This morning, sire," replied Coligny.

"And you bring me—"

"This letter from his Majesty King Henri II."

And he presented the letter to the Emperor.

The Emperor took it, and made some vain attempts to

break the seal, to such a degree were his hands tortured and twisted by the gout.

Then the admiral offered to render him this service.

Charles V. handed him the letter, laughing.

"Am I not, in truth, M. l'Amiral," he said, "a nice cavalier for running and breaking a lance—I who can no longer even break a seal?"

The admiral returned the letter opened to Charles V.

"No, no," said the Emperor, "read it yourself; my sight is as bad as my hand. I think, then, you will acknowledge that I have done well to resign everything, force and power, into the hands of one younger and more adroit."

The Emperor emphasized the last word.

The admiral did not answer, but began reading the letter.

During the reading, Charles V., who pretended to see no longer, was devouring Coligny with his eagle glance.

The message was quite simple—a letter announcing to the Emperor the final completion of the truce; the preliminaries had been arranged five or six months before.

The letter read, Coligny took from his jerkin the parchments signed by the plenipotentiaries, and sealed with the royal seal of France.

It was the exchange made for the corresponding papers sent previously by Charles V. to Henri II., signed by the Spanish, German and English plenipotentiaries, and sealed with the seal of the Empire.

The Emperor cast his eyes over these political contracts; and as if he divined that a year would hardly pass before they were broken, he threw them on a large table covered with a black cloth, and took the admiral's arm to help him to his seat.

"M. l'Amiral," said he, "is it not a miracle of Providence that I, weak and retired from the world, should to-day be supported by an arm that was once very nearly overturning me at the height of my power."

"Oh, sire!" replied the admiral, "only one man could have overturned Charles V., and that was Charles V. himself; and if it has been the lot of us poor pygmies to struggle against a giant, it was because God wished in a surpassing manner to prove to the world our weakness and your power."

Charles V. smiled. It was evident the compliment did not displease him coming from a man like the admiral.

However, sitting down and making a sign to Coligny to be seated also—

"Enough," he said, "enough, admiral. I am no longer emperor, I am no longer king, I am no longer prince; I must have nothing to do now with flattery. Let us change the conversation. How is my brother Henri?"

"Wonderfully well, sire," replied Coligny, obeying the invitation to be seated when repeated for the third time.

"Ah, how glad I am of that!" said Charles; "so glad that my heart dances with joy, and not without cause, for I hold it great honor to have sprung, on the maternal side, from that lily that bears and supports the most celebrated crown in the world. But," he continued, affecting to lead back the conversation to the commonplaces of life, "I have been sometimes told nevertheless that this well-beloved brother of mine was getting gray; and yet it seems to me not three days ago since he was in Spain, a youngster without a hair on his face. Ah, twenty years, however, have slipped by since then!"

And Charles V. heaved a sigh, as the mere fact of these words escaping his lips opened up the vast horizon of the past.

"It is true, sire," returned Coligny, in reply to the question of the Emperor, "that his Majesty King Henri is beginning to count gray hairs, but by twos and threes at the most. Now, are not many people, younger than he is, grayheaded?"

"Oh, what you say is quite true!" replied the Emperor. "And now, as I have questioned you on the gray hairs of my brother Henri, I must tell you the history of my own. I was almost the same age, thirty-six or thirty-seven scarcely; it was on my return from Goulette and arrival in Naples. You know the beauty of that admirable city of Naples, M. l'Amiral, and the beauty and grace of the dames who dwell there."

Coligny bowed smiling.

"I am a man," continued Charles; "I wished to merit their favor like others. So, on the day of my arrival, I summoned my barber to curl and perfume me. This man presented me a glass, that I might follow the operations as he went along. It was long since I had looked at myself; I had been too busy making war on the Turks, the allies of my good brother François I. Suddenly I cried out, 'I say, barber, what is that, my friend?' 'Sire,' he answered, 'it is two or three white hairs.' Now, I must tell you the flatterer lied; it was not two or three, but, on the contrary, a dozen. 'Quick! quick! master barber,' I jerked out, 'pull them out; don't leave a single one.' He did so; but do you know what happened? Some time after, on looking in the glass again, I found that for every one he had plucked out, ten had returned. So that, if I had plucked these out, too, in less than a year I should have been as white as a swan. Tell my brother Henri, M. l'Amiral, to guard his three white hairs preciously, and not allow them to be plucked out, even by the fair hands of Madame de Valentinois."

"I will not fail, sire," replied Coligny, laughing.

"And talking of Madame de Valentinois," continued Charles, showing by the transition that he was not a stranger to the scandals of the court of Henri II., "what news have you, M. l'Amiral, of your dear uncle, the great constable?"

"Excellent," replied the admiral, "although his head is quite white."

"Yes," said Charles, "his head is white; but he is like the leeks, with a white head and the rest of the body green. And except this was the case, he would not be such a favorite as he is with the great ladies of the court. But, ah, by the way—for I do not like letting you go without having news of everybody—how is the daughter of our old friend François I.?"

And Charles emphasized with a smile these three words *our old friend.*

"Does your Majesty mean Madame Marguerite of France?"

"She is still called the fourth Grace, the tenth Muse, is she not?"

"Always, sire; and she deserves the title more and more every day, by the protection she grants to our great geniuses, such as MM. de l'Hôpital, Ronsard and Dorat."

"Eh!" said Charles V., "it looks as if our brother Henri II. was jealous of his royal neighbors, and was determined to keep this beautiful pearl for himself alone: I hear nothing said of the marriage of Madame Marguerite, and she must be" (Charles appeared to be making a calculation) "very nearly thirty-two."

"Yes, sire, but she hardly looks twenty; she is fresher and lovelier every day!"

"It is the privilege of roses to bud and bloom anew every spring," returned Charles. "But, speaking of lords and roses, tell me, my dear Coligny, tell me how our young Queen of Scotland is getting along at the court of France? Could I not help you in arranging matters with my daughter-in-law of England?"

"Oh, sire, there is no hurry," replied Coligny; "and your Majesty, who knows so well the age of our princesses, must be aware that the Queen of Scotland is hardly thirteen years old. Now she is—I do not think I am revealing a secret in confiding this to your Majesty—she is to wed the Dauphin François, and the marriage cannot take place for a year or two."

"Stay a moment; stay a moment, my dear admiral. I am trying to recall something," said Charles V. "I think there is somewhere in my memory a reminiscence which may serve as a warning to my brother Henri II., although it is based merely on cabalistic science. Ah! I have it. But first, can you tell me what has become of a young lord named Gabriel de Lorges, Comte de Montgommery?"

"Certainly: he is at the court of the king, with whom he is a great favorite, and is a captain in the Scotch Guard."

"A great favorite! indeed!" said Charles, pensively.

"Have you anything to say against this young lord?" asked Coligny, respectfully.

"No. But I have a story to tell you; listen."

"I am listening, sire."

"When I was crossing France, with the permission of my brother François I., in order to chastise the revolt of my well-beloved fellow-countrymen and subjects of Ghent, the King of France paid me—as you may remember, although your beard had hardly sprouted at the time—the King of France paid me all kinds of honor. He sent the dauphin with a multitude of young lords and pages to meet me at Fontainebleau. It is as well to tell you, my dear admiral, that I had no fancy for a journey through France, and, but for stern necessity, would have preferred another route. Everything had been done to make me distrust the loyalty of King François I., and I do not mind confessing that I myself sometimes was afraid (very groundlessly, as the event proved) that my brother of France might take advantage of the occasion and retaliate for the treaty of Madrid. I had brought with me, then (just as if human science could outweigh the purposes of God), a very able man, a renowned astrologer, who, by the inspection of the faces of people, judged at once whether a man venturing among such people was in danger of his life or liberty."

The admiral smiled.

"Wait, and you shall see. We were then on the road from Orléans to Fontainebleau, when suddenly we saw a great *cortège* approach us. It was, as I told you, the Dauphin of France with a crowd of lords and pages. At first, in the distance, seeing only the dust which enveloped the horses, we believed it was a troop of men-at-arms, and we halted. But soon, through the gray cloud formed by this dust, we saw satin and velvet shining, and gold sparkling. Evidently this troop, so far from being hostile, was an escort of honor. We proceeded, therefore, on our way, full of confidence in the word of King François I. The cavalcades soon met, and the dauphin, advancing, complimented me in the name of his father. The compliment was so gracious and so calculated to set at rest—oh! not my suspicions. God, to whom I am about to consecrate my life, is my witness that never for a moment did I suspect my good brother!—the compliment, I repeat, was so gracious that I wished to embrace the young prince on the spot. Now, while I was holding him in my arms, for, I believe, a good minute, the two troops mingled together; and the young lords and pages in the suite of the dauphin, curious to observe me, doubtless because of some little noise that I have made in the world, clustered around me, approaching as near as they could. Then I noticed that my astrologer, an Italian from Milan, named Angelo Policastro, had made his way through them on horseback, and taken a position on my left. This seemed to me audacious —the notion of such a man mingling with such a fine and rich nobility."

" 'Oh, Signor Angelo,' I said, 'what are you doing there?'

" 'Sire,' he replied, 'I am in my place.'

" 'No matter! keep a little further back, Signor Angelo.'

" 'I cannot, I must not, my august lord,' he answered.

"Thereupon I suspected something had occurred likely to disturb the harmony of my journey; so, fearing he might obey my first injunction—

" 'Remain, then, Signor Angelo,' I said; 'remain, since you are here with a good intention. Only when we enter the castle, you will tell me why you have taken up such a position, will you not?'

" 'Oh, sire, I shall not fail, the thing being my duty; but turn your head to the left, and observe that blond young man who is near me, and who wears the hair long.'

"I looked from the corner of my eye; the young man was the more remarkable, and it was the easier singling him out that he looked like a foreigner, an Englishman, and was the only one who wore his hair long.

"'Well, I see him,' I answered.

"'That is enough,' said the astrologer—'for the moment, at least; later on I shall speak to your Majesty.'

"In truth, I had hardly entered the castle and withdrawn to my apartments to change my toilet, when Signor Angelo followed me.

"'Well,' I asked, 'what have you to tell me about this young man?'

"'Have you noticed, sire, the furrow this young man has between the eyebrows, although so young?'

"'No, faith,' I replied; 'not having examined him so nearly as you.'

"'Well, that furrow is what we men of the cabala call the *line of death*. Sire, that young man will kill a king!'

"'A king or an emperor?' I asked.

"'I cannot say, sire; but he will strike a head wearing a crown.'

"'Ah, ah! you have no means of knowing if this head will be mine?'

"'Yes, sire; but for this I shall need a lock of his hair.'

"'Good! a lock of his hair—how will you get it?'

"'I do not know, but I must have it.'

"I began to reflect. At this moment the gardener's daughter entered, carrying a basket of flowers which she came to arrange in the vases on the mantelpiece and in those on the consoles. When she had finished, I took her by the hand, and drew her toward me. Then, taking two new gold maximilians from my pocket, I gave them to her. She thanked me.

"'And now,' I said, kissing her on the forehead, 'would you like to earn ten times as many?'

She cast down her eyes and blushed.

"'Oh!' said I to her, "'it is not that—there is no question of that—'

"'Of what, then, lord Emperor?' she asked.

"'Come here,' I said, leading her to the window, and pointing to the blond young man who was amusing himself running the quintaine in the court; 'you see that young lord?'

"'Yes, I see him.'

"'What do you think of him?'

"'He is very handsome and splendidly dressed.'

"'Well, bring me a lock of his hair to-morrow morning, and, instead of two gold Maximilians, you shall have twenty!'

"'But how can I get the hair of this young man?' she asked, regarding me naïvely.

"'Oh! upon my word, my fair girl, I have nothing to do with that; it is for you to find the way. All that I can do is to give you a Bible.'

"'A Bible?'

"Yes; that you may see what means Delilah adopted to cut the hair of Samson.'

"The young girl blushed again, but it seemed as if the information was sufficient; for she went away at once, pensive and smiling, and the next day she returned, with a lock of hair gleaming like gold. Ah! the most simple woman is more cunning than the craftiest of us all, M. l'Amiral!"

"Does your Majesty not intend finishing the story?"

"Oh, certainly. I sent the lock of hair to Signor Angelo, who made his cabalistic experiments on it, and said it was not I, but a prince bearing the *fleur-de-lis* in his coat of arms, whom the horoscope threatened. Well, my dear Coligny, the blond young man with the line of death between the eyebrows, the Seigneur de Lorges, Comte de Montgommery, captain in the Scotch Guard of my brother Henri—"

"What! Your Majesty suspects—?"

"Oh," said Charles, rising to indicate that the audience

was over, "I suspect nothing. God forbid! I only repeat to you, word for word, as a thing that might be useful to my brother Henri, the horoscope of Signor Angelo Policastro; and I advise his Majesty to pay good attention to this line that happens to be between the two eyebrows of his captain of the Scotch Guard, which is called the line of death, reminding him that it specially threatens a prince bearing the *fleur-de-lis* in his coat of arms."

"Sire," said Coligny, "his Majesty shall be informed of the friendly warning you have given him."

"And that you may not forget it, my dear Coligny, accept this," said Charles, throwing round the neck of the ambassador the magnificent gold chain he was himself wearing, from which hung that diamond star called the *star of the west*, in honor of the western possessions of the kings of Spain.

Coligny wished to receive the gift on his knees; but Charles would not allow this mark of respect, and, holding him in his arms, he kissed him on both cheeks.

At the door, Coligny encountered Emmanuel Philibert, who, as soon as the ceremony was over, or rather, a little before, left everything to offer his homage at the feet of that Emperor who was now greater in his eyes than before he abdicated his greatness.

The two captains saluted each other courteously; both had met on the field of battle, and their mutual esteem was on a level with their courage; that is to say, lofty and grand.

"Your Majesty," said Coligny, "has nothing else to say to me for the king my master?"

"No, nothing." Then, looking at Emmanuel Philibert, he smiled.

"Unless, my dear admiral, that, if our health permits us, we devote some attention to the task of finding a husband for Madame Marguerite of France."

Then, leaning on the arm of Emmanuel—

"Come, my dear Emmanuel," he said, returning to the parlor, "it seems an age since I saw you!"

XV

AFTER THE ABDICATION

FOR those of our readers who wish to see the issue of every occurrence and the philosophy of every event, we have decided to write the present chapter, which perhaps may interfere for a moment with the march of our action, but which will allow the eye, resting for a while on the Emperor Charles, to follow the fortunes of that illustrious sovereign, concealed, though they were, by the obscurity of his new life from the day of his abdication to that of his death; that is to say, from the 25th of October, 1555, to the 21st of September, 1558.

After the conqueror of François I. has been laid in the sepulchre, whither his rival has preceded him by nine years, we shall return to the living, to combats and festivals, to scenes in which love and hatred play their several parts; in fine, to all those immense and confused murmurs which cradle the dead, waiting in the depths of their tombs for the eternal resurrection.

The different political affairs which Charles V. had to regulate in the Low Countries, and the abdication of the Empire in favor of his brother Ferdinand—an abdication which followed that of his hereditary states in favor of his son Don Philip—still kept him nearly a year in Brussels; so that it was only in the first days of September, 1556, that he could quit that city and set out for Ghent, escorted by all the grandees, nobles, ambassadors, magistrates, captains, and officers in Belgium.

King Philip had expressly desired to conduct his father to the place of embarkation; that is to say, to Flessingen, which the Emperor reached in his litter, accompanied by the two queens, his sisters, with their ladies, King Philip with his court, and Emmanuel Philibert with his two inseparable companions, Leone and Scianca-Ferro.

The adieus were long and sad: not only was a man who had held the world clasped in his two arms separating from his sisters, from his son, from a grateful and devoted nephew, but he was, moreover, separating from the world, from life almost, his intention being to retire into a monastery immediately on his arrival in Spain.

Consequently, the ex-emperor wished to have these adieus over on the eve of his departure, saying that if they were to take place on the morrow, at the moment he was going to embark, he would never have the courage to set his foot on board the vessel.

The first person Charles V. took leave of—because, perhaps, in his heart he loved him least—was Don Philip. After receiving his father's kiss, the King of Spain knelt and asked his blessing.

Charles V. gave it to him with that majesty which never deserted him under any circumstances, and recommended him to keep peace with the Allied Powers, particularly with France, if it were possible.

Don Philip promised his father to comply with his wishes, expressing a doubt, however, as to the possibility of peace with France, but asseverating that he would nevertheless keep, on his side, the truce faithfully, as long as his cousin Henri II. did not break it.

After this Charles embraced Emmanuel Philibert, holding him a long time in his arms, as if he could not bring himself to separate from him.

'Finally, calling Don Philip, with tears in his eyes and in his voice, he said:

"My dear son, I have given you many things—I have given you Naples, Flanders, the two Indias; for your sake, indeed, I have despoiled myself of all I possessed. But keep this well in your mind: neither Naples and its palaces, nor the Low Countries and their commerce, nor the two Indias and their mines of gold, silver, and precious stones are worth the treasure I give you in bequeathing to you your cousin Emmanuel Philibert—a man equally prompt to plan and execute, a good statesman, and a great captain. I recommend you to treat him, therefore, not as a subject, but as a brother; and even then he will be scarcely treated by you according to his merits."

Emmanuel Philibert tried to kiss the knees of his uncle, but the latter held him in his arms; then, gently pushing him from his arms into those of Don Philip—

"Go," he said; "go! it is a shame for men to groan and weep thus on account of a short separation in this world! Let us manage, by good deeds and the virtues of a Christian life, to make sure of our union in a happier world; that is the essential point!"

And, making a sign with his hand to the two young men to depart, he remained with his back turned until they were outside of the apartment, and then went to take leave of his sisters.

Don Philip and Emmanuel Philibert mounted their horses and started at once for Brussels.

As to the ex-emperor, he embarked the next day, 10th of September, 1556, on a vessel "truly royal in size and adornment," says Gregorio Leti, historian of Charles V.; but it was hardly outside the harbor when it was saluted by an English ship. This ship carried the Earl of Arundel, sent to her father-in-law by Queen Mary, to beg him not to pass so near the coasts of Great Britain without paying her a visit.

But at this invitation Charles merely shrugged his shoulders, and, in a tone not wholly free from bitterness, he said—

"Eh! what pleasure could so great a queen take in seeing herself the daughter-in-law of a private gentlemen?"

In spite of this reply, the Earl of Arundel persisted, with so many courteous supplications and respectful prayers that Charles V. could no longer defend himself from such importunity, and at last said—

"My lord, everything will depend on the winds."

The two queens had embarked with their brother. Sixty ships escorted the imperial vessel; and, seeing that, although the winds were far from being unfavorable, the Emperor passed Yarmouth, London, and Portsmouth without stopping, the Earl of Arundel insisted no further. He placed himself respectfully in the suite of the imperial vessel, and followed it into Loredo, a port of Biscay, where Charles was received by the Grand Constable of Castile.

But he had no sooner touched that land of Spain, over which he had so gloriously reigned, than he knelt down, before listening to a word of the discourse the grand constable had prepared; and, kissing the soil of that realm which had become now a kind of second birthplace, he said:

"I salute thee with all reverence, oh common mother! and, as I came forth from the womb of my mother to receive so many treasures, I wish now also to return naked into thy bosom, my very dear mother! And if it was then a duty of nature, it is to-day an effect of grace upon my will."

He had not finished this prayer, when the wind began to swell, and such a violent tempest arose that all the fleet which had accompanied him perished in the harbor, not excepting even the imperial vessel, which was laden with treasure and with the magnificent gifts brought by the Emperor from Belgium and Germany as gifts to the churches of Spain —which gave occasion to a saying by one of the personages of the suite of Charles V. that the vessel, foreseeing that never again would such glory ennoble it, had sunk into the sea in order to show at once its respect, regret, and sorrow.

It was just as well, perhaps, that inanimate things should give such proofs of respect, regret, and sorrow to Charles V., for men were very cold in presence of his changed fortunes. At Burgos, for example, the Emperor crossed the city without any deputation meeting him, and without the citizens even giving themselves the trouble to run to their doors to look at him passing. Which seeing, the Emperor shook his head, murmuring—

"In truth, the inhabitants of Burgos must have been listening to me when I said at Loredo that I was returning naked into Spain!"

The same day, however, a noble lord named Don Bartolomeo Miranda having come to visit him, and having said to him—

"It is to-day exactly a year, sire, since your Imperial Majesty abandoned the world to devote yourself entirely to the service of God—"

"Yes," said Charles; "and it is to-day exactly a year since I have repented of it!"

Charles V. recalled the sad and solitary evening of his abdication when the coals fell upon the carpet, and he had no one to help in regulating the fire but Admiral Coligny.

From Burgos the Emperor travelled to Valladolid, which was then the capital of Spain. Half an hour from the city, he met a procession. It consisted of nobles and lords, led by his grandson Don Carlos, then eleven years old.

The child managed his steed admirably, and rode on the left of the Emperor's litter. It was the first time he saw his grandfather, and the latter regarded him with an earnestness that would have disconcerted any one but the young prince. Don Carlos did not even lower his eyes, contenting himself with taking off his cap respectfully every time the Emperor's eyes were fixed upon him. He replaced it on his head when Charles turned away his eyes.

As a consequence, the Emperor no sooner entered his apartments than he sent for him, in order to have a nearer view of him, and to converse with him.

The boy presented himself, respectful in manner, but without any embarrassment.

"And so it was you, my grandson, who came to meet me," said Charles.

"It was my duty," replied the boy, "as I am your subject in a twofold manner; for you are my grandfather and my emperor."

"Ah, indeed!" exclaimed Charles, astonished at finding so much coolness in a child of such tender years.

"Besides, even if it was not my duty to meet your Imperial Majesty, I should have done so through curiosity."

"And why so?"

"Because I have often heard that you were an illustrious emperor, and that you have done great things."

"Ah, truly!" said Charles V., who was amused by the strange disposition of the child; "and would you like me to relate those great things to you?"

"It would be a keen pleasure and an immense honor for me," replied the young prince.

"Well, sit down there."

"With the permission of your Majesty, I shall listen standing," said the child.

Then Charles V. related all his wars with François I., the Turks and the Protestants.

Don Carlos listened with the greatest attention, and when his grandfather had finished, showing that the recital was no novelty for him, he exclaimed—

"Oh, yes, that is how it all happened."

"But," returned the Emperor, "you do not, my fair grandson, tell me what you think of my adventures, or whether you believe I have conducted myself as a brave man."

"Oh!" said the young prince, "I am well enough satisfied with what you have done; there is one thing, though, I cannot pardon you."

"Upon my word!" said the astonished Emperor; "and, pray, what is it?"

"Your flight from Innspruck one night, half naked, before Duke Maurice."

"But I could not help it, I swear to you," answered the Emperor, laughing. "He surprised me, and I had nothing to protect me but the house I was living in."

"Still, I would not have fled," said Don Carlos.

"What! you would not have fled?"

"No."

"But it was necessary to fly, since I had no means of resistance."

"I would not have fled," repeated the young prince.

"Should I have allowed myself to be taken, then? That would have been a great imprudence, for which I should have been blamed still more."

"No matter! I would not have fled," repeated the child for the third time.

"Tell me, then, what you would have done on such an occasion; and, to help you to an answer, what would you do at the present moment if I set thirty pages, say, at your heels?"

"I would not fly," the child contented himself with answering.

The Emperor frowned, and, summoning the governor of the young prince—

"Sir," he said, "take my grandson with you: I congratulate you on the education you are giving him; if he continues, he will be the greatest warrior of our family!"

The same evening, he said to Queen Eleonore, his sister, whom he was leaving at Valladolid:

"I fear, sister, Don Philip is not fortunate in his son Don Carlos; his manners and disposition at such an early age do not please me. I cannot imagine what he is likely to be when he is twenty-five. Study the words and actions of this child, then, and when you write to me, tell me sincerely what you think on the subject."

Two days afterward Charles entered Palencia, and on the ensuing day Queen Eleonore wrote:

"My brother, if the manners of Don Carlos have displeased you after seeing him only on one day, they have much more displeased me after seeing him on three."

This little man, who would not have fled from Innspruck, was the same Don Carlos who was put to death by his father, Philip II., twelve years later, under the pretext that he conspired with the rebels in the Low Countries.

At Valladolid the Emperor had dismissed his entire court, with the exception of twelve domestics and twelve horses, reserving for his own use only a few rare and precious articles of furniture, and distributing all the rest among the gentlemen who had accompanied him; then he had bade farewell to the two queens, and set out for Palencia.

Palencia was eighteen miles from the monastery of Saint-Just, belonging to the order of Hieronimites, which the Emperor had selected for his retreat, and where he had sent, during the preceding year, an architect to build six rooms for him on the ground floor, four exactly like the cells of the monks, and two a little bigger. The artist was also to lay out a garden, on a plan designed by Charles himself.

This garden was the charming feature of the imperial retreat; it was watered on two sides by a little rivulet, limpid and murmuring, and planted with orange, lemon and cedar trees, whose branches shaded and perfumed the windows of the illustrious recluse.

In 1542 he had visited this same monastery of Saint-Just, and, on leaving, said—

"A real place of retreat for a second Diocletian."

The Emperor took possession of his apartments in the monastery of Saint-Just on the 24th of February, 1557. It was the anniversary of his birth, and that day had always been a fortunate day for him.

"I wish," he said, on crossing the threshold, "to be born again for heaven on the same day on which I was born for earth."

Out of the twelve horses he had kept, he sent away eleven; he used the one he retained for riding occasionally in the delicious valley of Serandilla, distant only a mile, and which is called the Paradise of Estremadura.

Starting from that moment, he kept up little communication with the world, receiving only rare visits from his old courtiers, and, once or twice a year, letters from King Philip, the Emperor Ferdinand, and the two queens, his sisters; his only distraction was the rides we have mentioned, the dinners he gave now and then to the gentlemen who visited him and whom he retained until evening, saying, "My friends, remain with me and live the religious life," and the pleasure he took in attending to the little birds of every species he kept in cages.

This life lasted a year; but, at the end of the year, it seemed still too worldly for the august solitary, and on the anniversary of his birth, the day, also, it will be remembered, of his entrance into the monastery, he said to the Archbishop of Toledo, who had come to pay him a visit of ceremony:

"My lord, I have lived fifty-seven years for the world, and a year for my intimate friends and servants in this lonely spot; now I wish to give to the Lord the few months I have still to live." And, in consequence, while thanking the prelate for his visit, he begged him not to take the trouble of coming again, except he called him for his soul's sake.

In fact, from the 25th of February, 1558, the Emperor lived almost as austerely as the monks, eating with them, inflicting the discipline on himself, going regularly to the services, and not allowing himself any other distraction than that of having Masses said for the innumerable quantity of soldiers, sailors, officers and captains who had died in his service in the different battles waged by himself or by his orders in the four quarters of the globe.

He had special Masses said in the name of the generals, councillors, ambassadors and ministers—he had a perfectly exact register of the anniversary of their deaths—at private altars erected for the purpose; so that it might be said that, just as he had formerly placed his glory in reigning over the living, he now placed it in reigning over the dead.

At last, growing tired, toward the beginning of the July of this same year, 1558, of assisting at the funerals of others,

Charles V. resolved to assist at his own. However, it took some time to accustom him to this rather odd idea; he was afraid he would be taxed with pride and singularity in giving way to this desire; but at last it became irresistible, and he disclosed his intention to a monk of the same monastery, named Father John Regola.

It was with trembling that Charles ventured on this confidence, fearing the monk might throw some obstacle in the way of the execution of his plan; but the monk, on the contrary, to the great joy of the Emperor, answered that, although it would be an extraordinary and unprecedented act, he saw no harm in it, and considered it even pious and exemplary.

Nevertheless, this approval by a simple monk did not seem to the Emperor sufficient in such a grave circumstance; then Father Regola offered to take the opinion of the Archbishop of Toledo.

Charles thought the advice good, and the monk, being appointed ambassador to the archbishop, set out on a mule, and with an escort, to get the desired permission.

Never in the days of Charles V.'s power had the return of a messenger, however important the message, been awaited with such impatience as was this one.

At last, at the end of a fortnight, the monk reappeared; the reply was favorable; the archbishop regarded the desire of the Emperor as very holy and very Christian.

On the next day, which was a genuine festival, preparations were made to render the funeral ceremony worthy of the great Emperor who was about to be buried alive.

The first thing undertaken was the construction of a magnificent mausoleum in the centre of the church; Father Vargas, who was an engineer and sculptor, made a design that was satisfactory to the Emperor, except in some details which he retouched.

The design being approved, master joiners and painters were summoned from Palencia, who for five weeks employed twenty men each day in building this mausoleum.

At the end of the five weeks, thanks to the activity inspired by the presence of the Emperor, the mausoleum was finished. It was forty feet long, thirty broad and fifty high; around it were galleries mounted by several staircases; there might be seen a series of pictures representing the most illustrious emperors of the House of Austria, and the principal battles of Charles V. himself. In fine, on the top was laid the bier, without a lid, having on its left Fame, and on its right Immortality.

Everything being completed, the morning of the 24th of August was fixed for this fictitious funeral.

At five o'clock, just an hour and a half after sunrise, four hundred immense tapers painted black were placed, lighted, on the sarcophagus, around which the domestics of the Emperor were arranged, dressed in mourning, bareheaded, each with a torch in his hand. At seven, Charles entered, clad in a long mourning robe, having on his right and left a monk garbed like himself. He sat down on a seat prepared for him in front of the altar, having also a torch in his hand. There, without a movement, his torch resting on the ground, he listened, living, to all the chants sung for the departed, from the Requiem to the *Requiescat*, while six monks of different orders said six Low Masses at the side altars of the church.

Then, at a given moment, he went, escorted by two monks, and bowed before the high altar. Kneeling at the feet of the prior, he said:

"I ask and supplicate Thee, O arbiter and sovereign of our life and of our death, that, just as the priest takes from my hands with his this torch which I offer him in all humility, Thou mayest deign to receive my soul, which I commend to Thy divine clemency, and take it, when it is Thy will, into the bosom of Thy infinite goodness and mercy!"

Then the prior placed the taper in a silver chandelier of great size, which the counterfeit departed had presented to the monastery for this grand occasion.

After this Charles rose, and, always accompanied by the

two monks, who followed him as his shadow, he went and took his seat.

The Mass over, the Emperor judged that there remained something for him to do, and that they had forgotten the most important part of the ceremony: he then had a flagstone in the choir raised, and ordered a black velvet covering to be spread over the bottom of the ditch which had been excavated in accordance with his wishes, and a pillow to be also laid. Then, assisted by two monks, he descended into the ditch, stretched himself on his back, with his hands crossed over his breast and his eyes closed, counterfeiting death as well as he could.

Immediately the officiating priest intoned the "De Profundis Clamavi," and while the choir was chanting it, all those monks clad in black, all those gentlemen and servants in mourning, with torches in their hands, shedding tears, defiled around the deceased, each in turn sprinkling holy water and wishing eternal rest to his soul.

The number carrying holy water was so large that the ceremony lasted more than two hours: consequently, the Emperor was quite deluged with the holy water, which pierced through his black robe; this, joined to the cold and biting wind which blew on him up from the mortuary cellars of the abbey through the crevices in the stone, had such an effect on the Emperor that he was shivering frightfully when, after all had left the church except himself and his two monks, he regained his cell. So that, feeling himself quaking all over—

"I do not know, my good Fathers," he said, "if it was worth while, in truth, for me to get up again."

In fact, after entering his cell, Charles V. had to take to his bed, and, once in bed, he never did get up again; so that in less than a month after the counterfeit ceremony, the real ceremony was celebrated, and all that had been prepared for the fictitious death served for the true one.

It was on the 21st of September, 1558, that the Emperor Charles V. rendered the last sigh in the arms of the Archbishop of Toledo, who was fortunately at Palencia, and whom the dying man sent for, for the last time, according to the promise he had made, six months before, to summon him at the hour of death.

He had lived fifty-seven years, seven months, and twenty-one days; he had reigned forty-four years, governed the empire thirty-eight, and as he had been born on the festival of one apostle, Saint-Mathias, so he died on the festival of another apostle, Saint-Matthew; namely, on the 21st of September.

Father Strada relates, in his "History of Flanders," that on the very night of the death of Charles V., a lily flowered in the garden of the monastery of Saint-Just; of which fact the monks having been informed, this lily was exposed on the high altar as an evident proof of the *whiteness* of the soul of Charles V.

History is a beautiful thing! And that is the reason why, not considering ourselves worthy to be a historian, we have become a romancer.

SECOND PART

I

THE COURT OF FRANCE

A LITTLE more than a year after the abdication of Charles V. at Brussels, about the period when the ex-emperor was isolating himself from the world in the monastery of Saint-Just, at the moment when, from the heights of Saint-Germain, the harvests of the plain could be seen yellowing in the distance, and just as the last days of July were rolling their clouds of flame in a sky of azure, a brilliant cavalcade was issuing forth from the old chateau and advancing into the park, whose fine tall trees were beginning to take on those warm hues which the painter loves.

A brilliant cavalcade, if ever there was one! for it was composed of King Henri II., his sister, Madame Marguerite of France, his mistress, the beautiful Duchesse de Valentinois, his daughter, Elisabeth de Valois, the young Queen of Scotland, Mary Stuart, and the principal lords and ladies who, at this time, made the ornament and glory of the House of Valois—a house that succeeded to the throne in the person of François I., who died, as we have said, on the 31st of May, 1547.

Moreover, over one of the highest balconies of the chateau leaned Queen Catherine de Médicis, resting on an iron railing wrought as delicately as lacework, with the two young princes who were to be afterward Charles IX. and Henri III., but now, respectively, seven and six years old; and little Marguerite, five years of age, and destined to be Queen of Navarre. All three, as we may see, were too young to accompany their father to the hunt which was in preparation.

As for Queen Catherine, she had made a slight indisposition the pretext for not forming one of the hunting party; and as Queen Catherine was one of those women who never do anything without a reason, we may be very sure she had, if not a real indisposition, at least a reason for being indisposed.

All the personages we have named being required to take a very active part in the story we have undertaken to relate, the reader will permit us, before taking up the broken thread of events, to place before his eyes a physical and moral picture of these personages.

Let us begin with Henri II., who was riding in advance, having on his right Madame Marguerite, his sister, and on his left the Duchesse de Valentinois.

He was at this time a handsome, haughty chevalier of thirty-nine years, with black eyebrows, black eyes, black beard, a swarthy complexion, aquiline nose, and fine white teeth; not so tall, not so muscular as his father, but with a form admirably proportioned, which was above the middle height; fond of war to that degree that, when he had not one in his own states or in those of his neighbors, he wished to have the semblance of one in his court and in the midst of his pleasures.

And so, even in times of peace, King Henri II.—having barely that tincture of letters necessary for the dispensation of honorable rewards to poets, his opinions on whom were ready made, being all received from his sister Marguerite, his mistress, the fair Diane, or his charming little ward, Mary Stuart—so, even in times of peace, we repeat, King Henri II. was the least idle man in his realm. Here is how he divided his days:

His mornings and evenings—that is to say, the hours after rising and before retiring—were devoted to business; two hours in the morning were usually sufficient for the purpose. Then he heard Mass very piously; for he was a good Catholic, as he proved when he declared he would like to see Jean Dubourg, counsellor to the Parliament, burned with his own eyes—a pleasure he could not have, however, as he died six months before the poor Huguenot was sent to the stake. He dined at noon, after which he paid a visit, accompanied by the lords and ladies of his court, to Queen Catherine, with whom he found, as Brantome tells us, a crowd of *human goddesses*, one lovelier than the other. Then, while he entertained the queen, or madame his sister, or the little queen dauphiness, Mary Stuart, or his eldest daughters, each lord and gentleman did the same as the king, chatting with the lady who pleased him best. This lasted nearly two hours; then the king passed to his exercises. During summer these exercises were tennis.

Henri II. was passionately fond of tennis; not that he was a very skilful player, but he played second or tierce; that is to say, he always selected, in harmony with his adventurous character, the most dangerous or most difficult posts; so he was the best *second* and the best *tierce* in his kingdom, to use the language of the period. Moreover, it was he who always defrayed the expenses of the game, whether he won or lost: if he won, he abandoned the winnings to his partners; if the latter lost, he paid for them.

The stakes were usually from five to six hundred crowns, and not, as in the case of the kings his successors, four thousand, six thousand, ten thousand crowns. "But," says Brantome, "the payments were made at once, while in our day you are obliged to submit to any number of honorable compositions."

The other exercises of the king held a secondary place in his esteem, but in them he was very adroit also.

If it was winter, and there was a hard frost, the court set out for Fontainebleau, and there was sliding either on the avenues of the park or on the ponds. When the snow had been excessive, bastions were erected, and there was a battle of snowballs; finally, if it rained instead of snowing, they scattered among the halls on the ground-floors, and practiced fencing.

M. de Boucard had been the victim of this latter exercise. The king, when dauphin, happened, while fencing with him, to destroy one of his eyes—*an accident for which he politely begged his pardon*, says the author from whom we borrow these details.

The ladies of the court were present at all these exercises, summer and winter, the opinion of the king being that their presence spoiled nothing, and gave a grace to many things.

In the evening, after supper, they returned to the queen; and when there was no ball—an amusement, for that matter, rare enough at the time—two hours were spent in conversation. The poets and men of letters were introduced; namely, MM. Ronsard, Dorat, and Muret—*as clever Limousins as ever munched a turnip*, says Brantome—and MM. Danesius and Amyot, the tutors of Prince François and Prince Charles, respectively; and then there was between those illustrious jousters assaults of science and poesy which much delighted the ladies.

One thing—when by some chance it was thought of—cast a veil of mourning over this noble court; it was an unfortunate prediction made on the day of King Henri's accession to the throne.

A soothsayer, summoned to the chateau to draw his nativity, had announced, in presence of the Connétable Montmorency, that the king would die in single combat. Thereupon, the latter, quite joyous because such a death was promised him, turned to the constable, saying—

"Do you hear, gossip, what this man promises me?"

The constable, believing the king frightened at the prediction, answered with his customary brutality:

"What, sire! would you believe these rascals, who are nothing but liars and babblers? Let me fling the prediction in the fire, and him along with it, to teach such knaves not to humbug us with such trickery!"

But the king answered, "By no means, gossip; it sometimes happens, on the contrary, that these people tell the truth. And, besides, the prediction is not a bad one, in my opinion. I would rather die that death than any other, provided, of course, that I fall beneath the stroke of a brave and valiant gentleman, and that my glory remain intact."

And, instead of flinging the prediction and the astrologer into the fire, he munificently rewarded the latter, and gave the prediction into the keeping of M. de l'Aubespine, one of his good counsellors, whom he specially employed in diplomatic affairs.

This prediction was again discussed for a moment when M. de Chatillon returned from Brussels; for it will be remembered that Charles V., in the little house in the park, had requested the admiral to warn his fair cousin Henri that his captain of the Scotch Guard, Gabriel de Lorges, Comte de Montgomery, had between the eyes a fatal sign presaging the death of one of the princes of the *fleur-de-lis*.

But, reflecting on the matter, King Henri II. saw the little probability there was of a duel between him and his captain of the Guards, and, after classing the first prophecy among things possible and deserving attention, he classed the second among things impossible deserving no attention at all; so that, instead of separating from Gabriel de Lorges, as would perhaps have done a prince less timid, he, on the contrary, redoubled his favor and familiarity toward him.

We have said that Madame Marguerite of France, daughter of François I., was riding on the king's right.

Let us turn our attention, for a moment, to this princess, one of the most accomplished of the age, and more closely connected with our subject than any other.

The Princess Marguerite of France was born on the 5th of June, 1523, in that same chateau of Saint-Germain through whose door we have just passed; hence it follows that, at the moment we make her pass under the eyes of the reader, she was thirty-three years and nine months old.

How was it that so great and fair a princess remained so long without a spouse? For this there were two reasons: the first she had told aloud and before all; the second she did dare, perhaps, to whisper to herself.

When she was quite a young girl, François I. desired to marry her to M. de Vendome, first prince of the blood; but she, proud even to disdain, replied that she would never marry a man who must some day be the subject of the king her brother.

This was the reason she gave aloud for remaining single, and not falling from her rank as a princess of France.

Let us now look at the reason she whispered to herself, and which was probably the true cause of her refusal.

At the time of the interview at Nice between Pope Paul III. and François I., the Queen of Navarre, by order of the king, visited the late Duke of Savoy in the castle of Nice, accompanied by her niece, Madame Marguerite. Now, the old duke thought the young princess charming, and spoke of a marriage between her and Emmanuel Philibert. The two children saw each other; but Emmanuel, entirely devoted to the exercises of his age, to his affection for Leona, and his friendship for Scianca-Ferro, hardly noticed the young princess. It was not the same with her; the image of the young prince had made a strong impression upon her heart, and when negotiations were broken off, and war was resumed between the King of France and the Duke of Savoy, she suffered from real despair—a childish despair to which no one paid any attention, and which, for a long time, fed with her tears, had changed to a gentle melancholy, encouraged by that vague hope which never deserts tender and believing hearts.

Twenty years had vanished since that epoch; and now, under one pretext or another, Marguerite refused the hand of every suitor proposed to her.

While waiting for the chances of fate or the decrees of Providence to second her secret wishes, she had grown, had advanced in years, and was now a charming princess, full of grace, pleasantness, and tender compassion, with beautiful blond hair, the color of golden ears of corn, chestnut eyes, the nose a little pronounced, thick lips, and a complexion of a lovely white tinged with rose.

We have said that on the other side of the king rode Diane de Poitiers, Comtesse de Brézé, daughter of that Sieur de Saint-Vallier who, as an accomplice of the Connétable de Bourbon, had been condemned to be beheaded on the Grève, and who, when kneeling under the sword of the executioner, had been pardoned—if the thing can be called a pardon—and had his sentence commuted to perpetual imprisonment "within four walls, the floor and roof both built of stone, and with one little window only, through which he was to receive whatever he ate and drank."

Everything connected with Diane was mystery and marvel. She was born in 1499, and had, at the period we are describing, reached the age of fifty-eight years; yet, by her apparent youth and real beauty, she threw the fairest and youngest princesses of the court into the shade; so that the king loved her before all and above all.

Some of the mysterious and marvellous things told of the fair Diane, who had been created Duchesse de Valentinois by Henri II. in 1548, were the following:

In the first place, she was most undoubtedly descended from the fairy Mélusine, and the king's love and her wonderfully preserved beauty were both results of this descent. Diane de Poitiers inherited from her ancestress, the great sorceress, the double secret, a secret rare and magical, of being always beautiful and always beloved.

Diane, it was stated, owed this eternal beauty to soups composed of potable gold. We know what an important ingredient was potable gold in the chemical preparations of the Middle Ages.

This love without end was due to a magical ring the king had received from her, and which had the virtue of binding his love to her as long as he wore it.

The last report attained particular credit, for Madame

de Nemours used to relate, to all who cared to listen, the anecdote we are about to relate in our turn.

The king having fallen sick, Queen Catherine de Médicis said to Madame de Nemours:

"My dear duchess, the king has a great affection for you. Go to his chamber, sit near the bed, and, while talking with him, try to take from the third finger of the left hand the ring he wears on it; it is a talisman given him by Madame de Valentinois to make him love her."

Now, nobody in the court felt any very deep affection for Madame de Valentinois, not that she was ill-natured, but the young did not like her because she was so obstinate in continuing young, and the old women detested her because she would not become old. Madame de Nemours willingly took charge of the commission; and, having made her way into the king's chamber, and sat down near the bed, she succeeded in sportively drawing the ring from Henri's finger, he himself being quite ignorant of its virtue. But the ring was scarcely off the sick man's finger when he begged Madame de Nemours to whistle for his *valet de chambre*. We know that, up to the time of Madame de Maintenon, who invented bells, the gold or silver whistle was used by kings, princes, and great lords for summoning their people. The sick man then had begged Madame de Nemours to whistle for his *valet de chambre*, who, having entered immediately, received the king's order to close his doors to all comers.

"Even to Madame de Valentinois?" asked the astonished valet.

"To Madame de Valentinois as to others," answered the king, sharply; "the order admits no exception."

A quarter of an hour afterward Madame de Valentinois presented herself at the king's door, and was refused admittance.

She returned at the end of an hour: same refusal. Finally, at the end of two hours, in spite of a third refusal, she forced the door, entered, marched straight up to the king, took his hand, perceived that the ring was missing, made him confess what had passed, and insisted on Henri's getting the ring back from Madame de Nemours. The king's order to surrender the precious jewel was so peremptory that Madame de Nemours, who had not yet delivered it to Catherine de Médicis, grew frightened at the consequences, and sent it back. The ring once again on the king's finger, the fairy resumed all her power, which, indeed, since that day had gone on increasing.

In spite of the grave authorities who relate the history—and note well that for the potable gold we have no less a witness than Brantome, while to the truth of the affair of the ring, we have the solemn affirmations of De Thou and Pasquier—we are tempted to believe that the beauty of Diane de Poitiers was unconnected with the miraculous, a beauty which was to have its counterpart a hundred years later in the case of Ninon de Lenclos; and we are disposed to accept, as the only and true magic used by her, that contained in the receipt she gave to any one for the asking; namely, a *bath of spring water* in all weathers, even the coldest. Besides, every morning she rose with the lark, rode for two hours, and on her return went to bed again, where she stayed till noon, reading, or chatting with her women.

But this has not been all: everything in connection with the fair Diane has been a subject of controversy, and the gravest historians would seem, in her regard, to have forgotten this first condition of history, which is to always have the proof standing behind the accusation.

Mézeray relates—and we are not sorry to catch Mézeray in a blunder—that François I. granted the pardon of Jean de Poitiers, father of Diane, only after he had deprived the daughter *of the most valuable thing she possessed.* Now this took place in 1523; Diane, born in 1499, was twenty-four at the time, and had been married to Louis de Brézé for ten years. We do not say that François I., a monarch chary in exacting his dues, did not impose certain conditions on the fair Diane; but it was not, as Mézeray says, on a young girl of fourteen that he imposed these conditions, and unless we want to caluminate poor M. de Brézé, to whom his widow raised that magnificent monument still admired in Rouen, we cannot imagine he allowed the king to deprive a woman of twenty-four of the most valuable thing she possessed at fourteen.

All we have written has, for that matter, only one object: to prove to our fair readers that the history written by romancers is far superior to the history written by historians; in the first place, because it is truer, and in the second, because it is more amusing.

To make a long story short, Diane, though at this period twenty-six years a widow and twenty-one years King Henri's mistress, had, in spite of the fact that she was fully fifty-eight, the smoothest and loveliest complexion that could be seen, curly hair of the most bewitching black, a form of admirable symmetry, and a faultless neck and throat.

This was the opinion of old Connétable Montmorency, who, notwithstanding his sixty-four years, claimed to enjoy quite peculiar privileges in the case of the beautiful duchess —privileges which would have rendered the king very jealous, if it were not an admitted fact that it is always the people interested in being the first to know a thing who know it last, and sometimes never know it at all.

We ask pardon for this long historico-critical digression; but if any woman in that graceful, lettered and gallant court deserved the trouble of it, surely it was she who made her royal lover wear her colors as a widow—black and white— and adopt the crescent for an escutcheon inspired by her fine pagan name of Diane, with these words for a motto: *Donec totum impleat orbem!*

We have said that behind King Henri II., having on his right Madame Marguerite of France, and on his left the Duchesse de Valentinois, came the Dauphin François, having on his right his sister Elisabeth, and on his left his betrothed, Mary Stuart.

The dauphin was fourteen, Elisabeth thirteen, Mary Stuart thirteen—forty years in all.

The dauphin was a weak and sickly child, with pale complexion and chestnut hair. His eyes were dull and expressionless, except when they looked upon Mary Stuart; for then they became animated, and had an expression of desire which turned the child into a young man. Moreover, he was little inclined toward the violent exercises in which his father delighted, and seemed the prey of an incessant languor, the cause of which was vainly sought for by his physicians. They would have found it, perhaps, according to the pamphlets of the time, in the chapter of Suetonius's "Twelve Cæsars," where he relates the rides of Nero in a litter with his mother, Agrippina. Still, let us hasten to say it, Catherine de Médicis, both as a Catholic and a foreigner, was hated by one party, and we should not believe, without careful scrutiny, everything related in the pasquinades, ribald songs, and satires of the times, almost all products of the Calvinistic press. The premature deaths of the young princes, François and Charles, to whom their mother preferred Henri, contributed not a little to give credit to all these malicious rumors which have traversed the ages, and have come down to us, wearing an aspect of almost historic authenticity.

The Princess Elisabeth, although a year younger than the dauphin, was much more of a young woman than he was of a young man. Her birth had been at once a private joy and a public happiness; for, at the very moment she appeared in the world, peace was signed between François I. and Henry VIII. Thus, she who by her marriage was to bring about peace with Spain, by her birth brought about peace with England. Besides, her father, Henri II., held her in such esteem for her beauty and character that, having married her younger sister, Madame Claude, to the Duc de Lorraine, he replied to some one who was remonstrating with him on the wrong this marriage did the elder: "My daughter Elisabeth is not one of those who are satisfied with a duchy for dowry; she needs a kingdom, and not one of the minor kingdoms either, but one of the grandest and noblest, so grand and noble is she herself in everything!"

She won the kingdom promised her, and with it misfortune and death.

Alas! a better fate was not awaiting that lovely Mary who rode on the left of the dauphin, her betrothed!

There are misfortunes which have such a reverberation that they have awakened an echo through the whole world, and which, having attracted to their objects the gaze of their contemporaries, still attract to them the eyes of posterity whenever the utterance of some name recalls them.

Such are the misfortunes—misfortunes somewhat deserved, perhaps—of the fair Mary. They have so far surpassed the ordinary measure that the faults, even crimes, of the guilty queen have disappeared in presence of the exaggeration of the chastisement.

But, all the same, the little Queen of Scotland followed joyously her path in a life saddened at its beginning by the death of her father, the chivalrous James V.; her mother wore for her that Scottish crown of thorns, which, according to the words of her father, "came with a lass and would go with a lass!" On the 20th of August, 1548, she arrived at Morlaix, and for the first time touched the soil of France, where her happiest days were passed. She brought with her that garland of Scotch roses called the Four Marys, who were of the same age, born in the same year and month as herself, and who were named Mary Fleming, Mary Seaton, Mary Livingstone and Mary Beaton. She was at this time an adorable child, and, as she grew, became an adorable young girl. Her uncles, the Guises, who believed they saw in her the realization of all their ambitious projects, and who, not content with extending their sway over France, dreamed of extending it by her means over Scotland, perhaps over England, made her the object of their ardent worship. Thus the Cardinal de Lorraine wrote to his sister, Marie de Guise:

"Your daughter has increased, and is every day increasing in goodness, beauty, and virtue; the king spends his time conversing with her, and she addresses him in words as good and wise as would a woman of twenty-five years of age."

But it was now the bud of this impassioned rose that was opening to love and pleasure. Not knowing how to do anything which did not please her, she did, on the contrary, with ardor, everything that pleased her: did she dance, it was until she fell exhausted; did she ride, it was at a gallop, and until the best steed was worn out; did she attend a concert, the music sent through her electric thrills.

Sparkling with precious stones, flattered, caressed, and adored, she was, at the age of thirteen, one of the marvels of that court of Valois, so full of marvels. Catherine de Médicis, who was not specially fond of her son, said, "Our little Scottish queen has only to smile to turn all French heads."

Ronsard said:

> Midst the lilies of Spring her fair body was born,
> Of whose whiteness a copy the lily alone is,
> And the bloom on her red cheeks laughèd to scorn
> The roses tinged with the blood of Adonis.
> The darts in her eyes were Love's own darts,
> And the heavenly Graces, with zeal and fervor,
> Imparted to her all that heaven imparts
> And left their abodes from a craving to serve her.

And of all these charming flatteries, the royal child could comprehend the delicate shades: prose and verse had no secrets from her. She spoke Greek, Latin, Italian, English, Spanish and French; and while poetry and science made for her a crown, the other arts had her protection. The court was constantly changing its place of residence; and so she was led with it from Saint-Germain to Chambord, from Chambord to Fontainebleau, from Fontainebleau to the Louvre. There she grew more fascinating every day beneath the ceilings of Primatice, in the midst of the canvases of Titian, the frescoes of Rosso, the masterpieces of Leonardo da Vinci, the statues of Germain Pilon, the sculptures of Jean Goujon, the monuments, porticoes, chapels of Philibert Delorme; so that any one seeing her so poetic, so charming, so perfect among all those marvels of genius, would be tempted to believe that she was not a visible creation belonging to humanity, but rather some metamorphosis, like that of Galatea, some Venus detached from the canvas, some Hebe descended from the pedestal.

And now, as we lack the pencil of the painter, we can only try, with the pen of the romancer, to give an idea of that intoxicating loveliness.

She was, we have said, about fourteen years old. Her complexion was a blending of the lily, the peach, and the rose, with a little more of the lily, perhaps, than of all the rest. Her forehead was high and rounded in the upper part, and seemed the fitting seat of lofty dignity, being at once—strange mixture—full of gentleness, intelligence and daring. One felt that the will inclosed by that forehead, if directed toward love and pleasure, would leap beyond ordinary passions, and when its voluptuous and despotic instincts should need satisfaction, would not hesitate even at crime. Her nose, fine and delicate, yet firm, was aquiline, like those of the Guises. Her ear was small, and with the convolutions of a shell of mother of pearl, irised with rose under the palpitating temple. Her brown eyes, of that tint which wavers between chestnut and violet, were of a humid transparency, and, however full of flame, under chestnut lashes and eyebrows designed with an antique purity. In fine, two charming curves formed a mouth with purple lips, tremulous and half-opened, which, in smiling, seemed to spread joy around her, and which surmounted a vigorous chin, white, rounded, and lost in contours which insensibly united with an undulating, velvety neck like that of a swan.

Such was the young girl whom Ronsard and Du Bellay named their *tenth Muse;* such was the head destined thirty-one years later to rest on the block of Fotheringay, and to be separated from the body by the axe of Elizabeth's executioner.

Alas! if a magician came and told all that crowd, gazing upon the brilliant cavalcade, plunging under the great trees of the park of Saint-Germain, the fate that awaited these kings and princes and princesses, these great lords and great ladies, is there a woollen jacket or a drugget gown that would have changed its lot for that of these fine gentlemen in silks and velvets, or of these fair dames with corsages embroidered with pearls and gold-brocaded petticoats?

Let us allow them to wander under the gloomy vaults of chestnut and beech, and return to the chateau of Saint-Germain, where we have said that Catherine de Médicis remained, under pretext of a slight indisposition.

II

THE KING'S HUNT

HARDLY had the pages and equerries, forming the last ranks of the *cortège*, disappeared in the depths of the coppices which succeed the great trees, and which, at this period, made a sort of girdle to the park of Saint-Germain, before Catherine withdrew from the balcony, leading Charles and Henri with her, and then, sending the elder away to his professor, and the younger to his woman attendants, she remained alone with the little Marguerite, still too young for people to trouble themselves about what she might see or hear.

When Catherine's two sons were gone, her confidential *valet de chambre* entered, and announced that the two persons she expected were at her orders, in her cabinet.

She rose immediately, hesitated an instant to consider whether she would not dismiss the young princess, as she had dismissed the young princes, but, doubtless judging her presence of little danger, she took her by the hand, and proceeded toward her cabinet.

Catherine de Médicis was at this time a woman of thirty-eight years, of a fine and generous presence, and of great majesty. Her dark eyes were almost always half closed, except when she felt it necessary to read to the bottom of the hearts of her enemies; then their look had the twofold brilliancy and the twofold keenness of two blades drawn from their scabbards, and plunged at the same time into the same breast, where they remained buried until its most secret recesses were explored.

She had suffered much, and had smiled much to hide her sufferings. At first, during the ten years of her marriage—which were barren, and during which it was twenty times debated whether she should not be repudiated, and a new spouse given to the dauphin—her husband's love protected her and struggled obstinately against the most terrible of all reasons—a state reason. Finally, in 1544, after being married eleven years, she gave birth to Prince François.

But her husband had already become the lover of Diane de Poitiers nine years before.

Perhaps if she had been a happy mother and a fruitful spouse from the beginning of her marriage, she would, as woman and queen, have struggled against the fair duchess; but her barrenness reduced her to a lower rank than that of a mistress.

Instead of struggling, she yielded, and by her humility earned the protection of her rival.

Moreover, all these brave lords, all these brilliant warriors who had no esteem for any nobility that had not its root in blood, and was not a flower gathered on the field of battle, made little case of the commercial race of the Médicis. They played on the name and on the coat of arms: her ancestors were doctors, *medici;* their arms were not cannon-balls, but pills, they said.

Mary Stuart, who caressed with her pretty hand the

Duchesse de Valentinois, sometimes used the same hand as a claw to scratch Catherine.

"Are you coming with us to see the Florentine tradeswoman?" she said to Connétable de Montmorency.

Catherine drank all these insults to the dregs: she was waiting. What was she waiting for? She did not know herself for certain. Henri II. was of the same age as she, and his health promised him a long life. No matter; she waited with the obstinacy of genius, which, feeling and appreciating its own value, understands that God makes nothing useless, and therefore the future held something in store for her.

At this time she belonged to the party of the Guises. The character of Henri was weak, and he could never be sole master: now he was master with the constable, and the Guises were in disgrace; now he was master with the Guises, and it was the constable who was out in the cold.

And so the following quatrain had been made on Henri II.

> Sire, if you let yourself be too much governed,
> And kneaded, melted, this and that way turned,
> As Charles and Diane both alike require, 'tis *cire* (wax)
> You are, and surely no more *sire*.

We know who Diane was; as to Charles, he was the Cardinal de Lorraine.

And, indeed, the family of Lorraine was a proud and noble family. One day came Duc Claude to render homage to François I. at the Louvre. He was accompanied by his six sons, and King François said to him, "My cousin, I hold you for a very fortunate man to see yourself renewed before dying in such a fair and wealthy posterity."

These words were true: Duc Claude, at his death, left behind him the richest, ablest, and most ambitious family in the kingdom. These six brothers, presented to François by their father, possessed a revenue of about eight hundred thousand livres; that is to say, more than four millions, according to the value of money at present.

First came the eldest, he who was called Duc François *le Balafré;* the great Duc de Guise, in fact. His position at court was that of a prince of the blood. He had a chaplain, eight secretaries, twenty pages, eighty officers, kennels whose tenants were only inferior to the greyhounds of the king, "the royal pedigree," as the term then was; stables filled with Arabian horses brought from Africa, Turkey, and Spain; gerfalcons and falcons beyond price, sent him by Soliman and all the infidel princes, who presented them to him as tokens of their respect for his fame. The King of Navarre wrote to him to announce the birth of his son, afterward Henri IV. The Connétable de Montmorency, the haughtiest baron of his age, in writing to him, began his letter with *Monseigneur,* and ended with *Your very humble and obedient servant,* while he, on the other hand, addressed him as, *M. le Connétable* and *Your very good friend;* which, for that matter, was far from being true, the House of Guise and the House of Montmorency being at eternal feud.

It is necessary to read the chronicles of the time, either placed before our view by the aristocratic pen of Brantome, or registered hour by hour in the journal of the Grand Audiencier Pierre de l'Estoille, to form an idea of the power of this privileged race, as much at home in the streets as on the field of battle, as eagerly listened to in the stalls of the markets as in the cabinets of the Louvre, Windsor, and the Vatican, especially when it spoke through the lips of Duc François. Just only look at the cuirass in the Musée d'Artillery, which the eldest of the Guises wore at the siege of Metz, and you will see there the trace of five balls, three of which would certainly have been mortal if they had not been deadened against the rampart of steel.

Consequently, it was a joy for the population of Paris when he issued forth from the Hotel de Guise, and when, far better known and more popular than the king himself, mounted on *Fleur-de-lis* or *Mouton*—they were his two favorite steeds—with his pourpoint and breeches of crimson silk, his velvet mantle, his cap surmounted by a plume of the same color, and followed by four hundred gentlemen, he traversed the streets of the capital. All flocked to see him on his passage, some breaking off branches and others plucking flowers and casting branches and flowers under his horse's feet, while crying—

"Long live our Duke!"

And he, standing up on his spurs, as he did on the field of battle, in order to see further and invite danger to himself, or leaning down to the right and left, with a courteous salutation for the women, the aged, and, indeed, for all human beings, with a smile for the young girls, and a caress for the children, he was the true king, not of the Louvre, Saint-Germain, Fontainebleau, or Tournelles, but the king of the streets and market stalls—a true king, a real king, since he was king of hearts!

So, at the risk of the truce of which France had so great need, when Pope Paul III.—on account of a private quarrel with the Colonna, who were rendered bold enough to take up arms against the Holy See by the support they expected to find in Philip II.—when the Pope, we say, because of this quarrel, declared that the King of Spain had forfeited the kingdom of Naples, and offered this realm to Henri II., the king had no hesitation in naming François de Guise commander-in-chief of the army he sent into Italy.

It is true that on this occasion, and perhaps for the first time, Guise and Montmorency happened to be of one mind. For, when François de Guise was outside of France, Anne de Montmorency was sure to be the first person in the realm; and, while the great captain was pursuing beyond the mountains his plans of glory, Montmorency, who believed himself a great statesman, was pursuing his plans of ambition at the court, and his most ardent ambition was, for the moment, to marry his son to Madame Diane, the legitimate daughter of the Duchesse de Valentinois, and widow of the Duke de Castro, of the House of Farnese, killed at the assault of Hesdin.

François de Guise was then at Rome, making war on the Duke of Alba.

With Duc François was the Cardinal de Lorraine, a great prince of the church, scarcely inferior to his brother in anything, and whom Pope Pius V. called the Pope beyond the mountains. "He was," says the author of the "History of Mary Stuart," "a two-edged sword as a negotiator, as proud as a Guise and as subtle as an Italian." Later on he was to conceive, mature, and put into execution that great idea of the League which placed his nephew on the steps of a throne up to the moment when both nephew and uncle fell, pierced by the swords of the Forty-five. When the six Guises were at court, the four, the Duc d'Aumale, the Grand Prior, the Marquis d'Elbeuf, and the Cardinal de Guise, never failed to come first to the levee of Cardinal Charles; then all five went to that of Duc François, who conducted them to the king.

Both, for that matter—the one as a warrior, the other as a churchman—had erected their batteries for the future: Duc François had become the master of the king, and Cardinal Charles the lover of the queen. The grave Estoille relates the fact in a manner that cannot leave the most incredulous reader in doubt: "One of my friends told me that, having slept with the valet of the cardinal in a chamber next to that of the queen-mother, he saw the cardinal, dressed only in a *robe de chambre*, going to see the said queen, and that his friend begged him not to mention it to any one, or he might lose his life."

As to the four princes of the House of Guise, to attempt their portrait would lead us too far, and, besides, the part they play in our story is almost null. Let us confine ourselves, therefore, to those we have sketched of Duc François and Cardinal Charles.

It was Cardinal Charles whom we have beheld one night, *dressed only in a robe de chambre, going to see the said queen*, that was waiting for Catherine de Médicis in her cabinet.

Catherine knew she should find him there, but she expected to find him alone.

He was, however, accompanied by a young man of from twenty-five to twenty-six years, elegantly clad, although still wearing his travelling-dress.

"Ah! it is you, M. de Nemours!" exclaimed Catherine, as soon as she perceived him. "You arrive from Italy? What news from Rome?"

"Bad!" replied the cardinal, while the Duc de Nemours saluted the queen.

"Bad! Could our dear cousin the Duc de Guise have been beaten?" asked Catherine. "Take care! Though you answered yes, I would say no, to such a degree do I hold the thing impossible!"

"No, madame," replied Nemours, "M. de Guise has not been beaten; as you say, the thing is impossible! But he has been betrayed by the Caraffa, abandoned by the Pope himself; and he has despatched me to the king to tell him that the position was no longer tenable either for his own glory or for that of France, and that he demanded reinforcements or a recall."

"And, according to our arrangements, madame," said the cardinal, "I have led M. de Nemours to you first."

"But," said Catherine, "the recall of M. de Guise is the abandonment of the King of France's claim to the kingdom of Naples, and of mine to the duchy of Tuscany."

"Yes," said the cardinal; "but you may be quite sure, madame, that we shall soon have war in France, and that then we shall not so much think of conquering Naples and Florence as of protecting Paris."

"What, Paris? You are laughing, M. le Cardinal. It seems to me that France can defend France, and Paris can protect herself without any help."

"I am afraid you are mistaken, madame," replied the cardinal. "The best of our troops, counting on the truce, have passed into Italy with my brother; and, certainly, except for the ambiguous conduct of Cardinal Caraffa and the treason of the Duke of Parma, who has forgotten what he owed to the King of France, and deserted to the Emperor, our prospects of success in Naples, and the necessity under which Philip II. would have labored of stripping himself to protect Naples, would have safeguarded us from an attack; but now that Philip II. is sure he has men enough in Italy to hold us in check, he will turn his eyes in the direction of France, and not fail to profit by its weakness. Need I add that the nephew of M. le Connétable has been guilty of a piece of folly which will give to the rupture of the truce by Philip II. an appearance of justice?"

"You mean his attack on Douai?"

"Decidedly."

"Listen," said Catherine. "You know I like the admiral as little as you do yourself; so you may do him as much harm as you can without my placing any obstacle in your way; on the contrary, I will help you all I can."

"Meanwhile, what do you decide on doing?" said the cardinal. And seeing that she hesitated, "Oh!" he said, "you can speak before M. de Nemours; he is of Savoy, it is true, but as much our friend as his cousin Emmanuel Philibert is our enemy."

"Decide yourself, my dear cardinal," casting an oblique glance at him; "I am but a woman whose weak mind has little skill in affairs of state. Decide, then."

The cardinal had understood the look of Catherine: for her there were no friends; there were only accomplices.

"No matter, madame," said Charles; "be good enough to give an opinion, and I shall take the liberty of combating it, should it happen to be in contradiction with mine."

"Well, I think," said Catherine, "that the king, being the head of the state, ought to be informed of these important things before all others. In my opinion, then, if M. de Nemours is not too tired, he ought to take a horse, join the king wherever he is, and transmit to him the intelligence which your kindness, my dear cardinal, has made me mistress of before him who should be first to hear it."

The cardinal turned to the Duke de Nemours, as if to question him.

"I am never fatigued, monseigneur," he said, "when the service of the king is in question."

"In that case," said the cardinal, "I shall order a horse for you, and also warn the secretaries that the king will hold a council on his return from the chase; come, M. de Nemours."

The young duke respectfully saluted the queen, and made ready to follow the Cardinal de Lorraine, when Catherine lightly touched the arm of the latter.

"Pass before me, M. de Nemours," said Charles de Guise.

"Monseigneur—" returned Jacques de Nemours, hesitating, "I beg of you to do so."

"And I order you, M. le Duc," said Catherine, offering him her hand.

The duke, understanding that the queen doubtless had a last word to say to the cardinal, no longer made a difficulty of obeying; and, kissing her hand, he went out first, designedly letting the hangings fall back behind him.

"What did you want to say to me, my dear queen?"

"I wanted to say to you," replied Catherine, "that the good King Louis XI., who, in exchange for five hundred thousand loaned him, gave to our ancestor Lorenzo de Médicis leave to place three *fleurs-de-lis* in our arms, was in the habit of repeating: 'If my nightcap knew my secret, I would burn it!' Meditate on this maxim of the good King Louis, my dear cardinal. You are too confiding!"

The cardinal smiled at the warning given him; he, who passed for the most distrustful statesman of the time, had met with a distrust greater than his own.

It is true he met it in the Florentine, Catherine de Médicis.

The cardinal, in turn, broke through the rampart of the tapestry hangings, and saw the prudent young man, in order not to be accused of curiosity, waiting for him ten paces further on in the corridor.

Both descended into the courtyard, where Charles de Guise ordered a page of the stables to bring him a horse, ready saddled, at once.

The page returned in five minutes, leading the horse. Nemours leaped into the saddle with the elegance of a consummate cavalier, and rode at a gallop through the main alley of the park.

The young man had been careful to ask information as to the direction taken by the chase, and was told the animal would be attacked near the road to Passy.

He, therefore, rode toward that point in the expectation that the sound of the horn would guide him to the spot where the king happened to be. But when near the road to Passy, he saw and heard nothing.

He questioned a woodcutter, who told him that the hunt was now somewhere in the direction of Conflans. He immediately turned his horse toward the point indicated.

At the end of an hour, while crossing a transverse path, he perceived, in the middle of a neighboring crossroad, a rider who was standing up in the stirrups, in order to see further, and was holding his hand to his ear in order to hear better.

This rider was a hunter, evidently trying to find his way.

However astray this hunter might be, he was more likely to have an idea of the probable situation of the king than the young duke, who had arrived from Italy hardly half an hour before. So M. de Nemours rode straight up to the hunter.

The latter, seeing a horseman approaching, and thinking he might learn something from him about the progress of the chase, also advanced some steps.

But soon both, with a similar movement, set spurs to their horses; they had recognized each other.

The strayed hunter, who tried to find his way by standing up in his stirrups in order to see, and holding his hand to his ear in order to hear, was the captain of the Scotch Guard.

The two cavaliers approached with that courteous familiarity which distinguished the young lords of the period.

Moreover, although, it is true, the Duc de Nemours was of a princely house, the Comte de Montgomery belonged to the oldest Norman nobility, a descendant of that Roger de Montgomery who helped William the Bastard to conquer England.

Now, at this period, there existed in France some old names that believed themselves the equals of the most puissant and glorious names, in spite of the inferiority of the titles they bore. It was so with the Montmorencys, whose title was only that of baron; with the Rohans, who were only seigneurs; with the Coucys, who were only sires; and with the Montgomerys, who were only counts.

As Nemours had guessed, Montgomery had lost track of the hunt, and was trying to find his way.

For that matter, the place where they found themselves was well chosen for the purpose, since it was a crossroad situated on an elevation toward which every sound must ascend, and commanding five or six paths, by one of which the animal would not fail to pass, when driven by the beaters.

The two young noblemen, who had not seen each other for more than six months, had, besides, a thousand important questions to ask: Montgomery on the subject of the army and the deeds of high emprise which M. de Guise must have naturally essayed; the other on the subject of the French court, and the fine love-adventures that must have taken place there.

They were at the liveliest part of this interesting conversation when Comte Montgomery laid his hand on the arm of the duke. He fancied he heard the baying of the pack in the distance.

Both listened. De Lorges was not deceived: at the extremity of an immense alley they saw an enormous boar pass as swiftly as an arrow; then, some fifty paces behind him, the most eager of the hounds, then the bulk of the pack, then the stragglers.

At the same moment Montgomery put his horn to his lips

and sounded the sighting of the game, in order to rally such as, like himself, had gone astray; and the number must have been great, for three persons only were on the track of the animal—a man and two women.

From the ardor with which he urged his steed, the two believed it was the king; but the distance was so great that it was impossible to tell who were the bold Amazons following him so closely. All the rest of the hunt seemed completely out of its reckoning.

Nemours and Montgomery galloped to an alley which, in view of the direction taken by the animal, allowed them to cut the chase at a right angle.

The king had, in fact, attacked the beast, which, in terms of venery, was what was called a *ragot*. It had made for one direction with the obstinacy of the older animals, and was dashing straight along on the road to Conflans. The king was at once on its track, and at the sound of his horn all the court followed the king.

But boars are bad courtiers: the one with whom, for the moment, they had to do, instead of choosing the way through the great old forest-trees and along the easy paths, had dashed into the thickest copses and closest briars; hence it resulted that, at the end of a quarter of an hour, only the most enthusiastic hunters were near the king, and that of all the ladies only three held out. These were Madame Marguerite, the king's sister, Diane de Poitiers, and Mary Stuart, the little *reinette*, as Catherine de Médicis called her.

In spite of the courage of the illustrious hunters and huntresses we have named, the difficulties of the ground, the thickness of the wood, which obliged the riders to make détours, and the height of the clumps of briars, which it was impossible to clear, soon caused them to lose sight of boar and hounds; but, at the extremity of the forest, the animal met a wall, and was forced to return on his traces.

The king, distanced for an instant, but sure of his

hounds, then halted. This gave a few hunters time to join him; the baying was soon heard again.

The portion of the forest for which the animal was now making a set was more open than the other; as a consequence, the king could resume the chase with a chance of soon having the boar at bay.

Only, the same thing happened that happened ten minutes before: each held out according as his strength and courage allowed him. Moreover, in the midst of this court, entirely composed of fair lords and gallant dames, many, perhaps, stayed behind, without being absolutely forced thereto by the slowness of their horses, by the thickness of the wood, or the inequalities of the ground; and this was clearly proved by the attitude of the groups stopping at the corners of the alleys and in the middle of the crossroads, which seemed more attentive to the conversation that was going on than to the baying of the hounds or the horns of the whippers-in.

And so it happened, when the animal came in view of Montgomery and Nemours, it was followed by only a single horseman, in whom they recognized the king, with two ladies whom they did not know.

It was, in fact, the king, who, with his usual ardor, wanted to be the first at the death, to be present at the moment when the boar would make a stand backed against some tree or rock, and would face the hounds.

The two Amazons following the horseman were Madame de Valentinois and little Queen Mary—the one the best, the other the boldest, rider in the entire court.

The boar, for that matter, was growing tired; clearly, he would have to come to a stand before long; the fiercest of the dogs were already breathing close to his hide.

For a quarter of an hour, however, he tried to escape his enemies by flight; but, feeling them nearer and nearer, he resolved to die bravely, like the courageous animal he was, and, finding a stump of a tree convenient, he planted himself there, growling and striking his immense jaws together.

No sooner had he stopped than the pack was on him, and indicated, by its redoubled baying, that the animal was making a stand.

With the baying, the sound of the horn was soon mingled. Henri arrived, following the dogs as closely as they followed the boar.

He looked around him while winding his horn in search of his arquebusier; but he had distanced even the most active whippers-in, even those whose duty it was never to lose sight of him, and saw, galloping up with all the speed of their horses, only Diane and Mary Stuart, who, as we have said, held out.

Not a ringlet of the fair duchess's head was out of place, and her velvet cap was fixed as firmly on the top as at the moment of setting out.

As for little Mary, she had lost veil and cap; and her beautiful chestnut hair, scattered to the breeze, as well as the charming flush on her cheeks, bore witness to the ardor of the chase.

At the prolonged notes the king drew from his horn, the arquebusier appeared, one arquebuse in his hand, and the other hanging from the bow of his saddle.

Behind him might be seen, through the thickness of the wood, golden broideries and the dazzling colors of robes, doublets and mantles. It was the hunters and huntresses now approaching from all sides.

The animal was doing his best; attacked at the same time by sixty dogs, he made head against all his enemies. It is true that while the sharpest teeth were blunted on his wrinkled hide, every stroke of his tusks made a deadly wound in such of his adversaries as came within its reach; but, although mortally injured, although losing all their blood, and with their entrails dragging along the ground, the *king's grays*, as they were called, were such a noble breed that they only returned the more furiously to the combat, and it could only be known that they were wounded by the stains of blood that streaked this moving carpet.

The king saw it was time to put an end to the butchery, if he were not to lose his best dogs. He threw away his horn, and made a sign for his arquebuse.

The match had been lighted; the arquebusier had but to present the weapon to the king. Henri was a good marksman, and rarely missed his aim.

With the arquebuse in his hand, he advanced to within about twenty paces of the boar, whose eyes shone like two live coals. He aimed between the eyes and fired.

The animal received the discharge in his head; but by a movement he made when the king had his hand on the trigger, the animal slightly inclined his head, and the ball glanced off the bone, killing one of the dogs.

The track of the ball could be seen between the eye and the ear of the boar by the blood that indicated its passage.

Henri remained astonished for an instant at the circumstance that the boar had not at once fallen, while his horse, all quivering, his hind legs bending under him, was beating the ground in front of him.

He handed the arquebuse to the groom, and demanded another. The other was ready, with the match lighted; the groom presented it.

The king took it, and raised the butt to his shoulder. But, before he had time to aim, the boar, doubtless unwilling to risk the chance of a second shot, scattered the dogs surrounding him by a violent thrust, opened a bloody pathway through the middle of the pack, and, quick as lightning, passed between the legs of the king's horse, which reared, giving an agonizing neigh, showed his belly, from which the blood and entrails were dropping, and suddenly fell down, with the king under him.

All this had been so instantaneous that not one of the spectators thought of rushing in front of the boar, which now turned on the king before he even had time to draw his hunting-knife.

Henri tried to reach it; it was impossible. The hunting-knife was under the king's left side, and so placed that it was useless to think of extricating it.

Brave as the king was, his mouth was already opened to cry for help—for the hideous head of the boar, its eyes of flame, its bloody jowl and teeth of steel were within a few inches of him—when suddenly he heard a voice in his ear, whose firm accents there was no mistaking, saying to him—

"Do not stir, sire; I answer for everything!"

Then he felt an arm, which raised his, and saw, like a flash of lightning, a broad, keen blade pass under his shoulder, and plunge up to the hilt in the body of the boar.

At the same moment two vigorous arms drew him back, leaving, exposed to the animal, only the new adversary who had stricken it to the heart.

He who pulled the king back was the Duc de Nemours. He who, with his knee on the ground and his arm extended, had just stricken the boar to the heart was the Comte de Montgomery.

Montgomery drew his sword from the body of the animal, wiped it on the green, grassy turf, returned it to the scabbard, and, approaching Henri II. as if nothing extraordinary had occurred—

"Sire," said he, "I have the honor to present to you M. le Duc de Nemours, who has just come from beyond the mountains, and brings news of M. le Duc de Guise and his brave army of Italy."

III

CONSTABLE AND CARDINAL

TWO hours after the scene we have described, the spectators having appeased their private or official emotion, congratulations having been tendered to Gabriel de Lorges, Comte de Montgomery, and to Jacques of Savoy, Duc de Nemours, the two saviors of the king, on the courage and address displayed by them on the occasion, and the quarry—a matter whose importance even the gravest affairs did not permit to be neglected—having been disposed of in the great court of the chateau, in the presence of the king, queen, and all the lords and ladies staying at Saint-Germain, Henri II., with a smiling countenance, as was natural in the case of one just escaped from imminent death, and who feels the fuller of life and health on account of the very greatness of the peril—Henri II., we say, entered his cabinet, where, besides his ordinary councillors, the Cardinal de Lorraine and the Connétable de Montmorency were awaiting him.

We have already mentioned the Connétable Montmorency; but we have neglected to do for him what we have done for the other heroes of our tale—that is to say, to exhume him from the tomb and make him stand up before our readers, like that great Connétable de Bourbon who was carried by his soldiers, after his death, to a painter, in order that a portrait of him might be painted standing all armed, as if he had been alive.

Anne de Montmorency was, then, the head of that old family of Christian barons of France, as they were entitled, sprung from Bouchard de Montmorency, and which has given ten constables to the realm.

He was called, and so styled himself, Anne de Montmorency—Duke, Peer, Marshal, Grand-Master, Constable, and First Baron of France; Knight of Saint-Michael and of the Garter; Captain of the king's hundred orderlies; Governor and Lieutenant-General of Languedoc; Comte de Beaumont, Dammartin, La Fère-en-Tardenois, and Chateaubriant; Vicomte de Melun and Montreuil; Baron d'Amville, Préaux, Montbron, Offemont, Mello, Chateauneuf, Rochepot, Dangu, Méru, Thoré, Savoisy, Gourville, Derval, Chanceaux, Rougé, Asprèmont, and Maintenay; Seigneur d'Ecouen, Chantilly, L'Isle-Adam, Conflans-Sainte-Honorine, Nogent, Valmondois, Compiègne, Gandelu, Marigny, and Thourout.

As may be seen from this nomenclature of titles, the

king might be king in Paris, but Montmorency was duke, count, and baron all around Paris; so that royalty itself seemed imprisoned in his duchies, counties, and baronies.

Born in 1493, he was, at the period we have reached, an old man of sixty-four who, though looking his age, had the strength and vigor of a man of thirty. Violent and brutal, he had all the rough qualities of the soldier—blind courage, ignorance of danger, insensibility to fatigue, hunger, and thirst. Full of pride, swollen with vanity, he yielded to none but the Duc de Guise, and to him only as a prince of Lorraine, for as a general he believed himself the superior of the defender of Metz and the conqueror of Renty.

In his eyes Henri II. was the *little master*; the great master had been François I., and he declined to recognize any other. An eccentric courtier and a man of tenacious ambition, he gained advantages tending to increase his wealth and power by his brutality and insolence, which another could only have obtained by suppleness and adulation. Moreover, Diane de Valentinois aided him very much in his schemes; seconding the violent old trooper with her gentle voice and look and countenance, she smoothed down all the antipathies his vehemence created, and without her help he would not have succeeded. He had been already in four great battles, and in each had done the work of a vigorous man-at-arms, but in none that of an intelligent leader. These four battles were, first, that of Ravenna; he was then sixteen years old, and followed, as an amateur and for his own pleasure, the general standard in the capacity of volunteer. The second was that of Marignano. There he commanded a company of a hundred men-at-arms, and he would have been able to boast that the most vigorous strokes were given by his sword and mace, had he not had near him, and often in front of him, his great master François I.—that hundred-handed giant, as he might be called in a certain sense, who would have conquered the world, if the world was to be conquered by him who struck the strongest and doughtiest blows. The third was that of La Bicoque, where he was colonel of the Swiss, and where he handled the pike and was left for dead. In fine, the fourth was that of Pavia. He had then become Marshal of France by the death of M. de Chatillon, his brother-in-law. Not suspecting that the battle was to take place the next day, he set out during the night to make a reconnoissance; hearing the roar of the cannon, he returned, and was taken "with the rest," says Brantome. And, in fact, at that disastrous defeat of Pavia, every one was taken, even the king.

Unlike M. de Guise, who had the strongest sympathies of the bourgeoisie and the men of the robe, he detested the bourgeois and execrated the lawyers. He let no occasion slip of giving a piece of his mind to both of them. It happened that the president of a court came to speak to him one very hot day on the subject of his office. M. de Montmorency received him with his cap in his hand, and said—

"Come, M. le President, say what you have to say at once, and in the meantime cover yourself."

But the president, believing it was to do him honor that Montmorency remained uncovered, replied—

"Monsieur, I cannot think of covering myself until you do the same."

"Why, you must be a consummate fool, monsieur!" said the constable. "Do you really fancy I have taken off my cap through love of you? No; it has been for my own ease, my friend, seeing that I am dying of the heat. Go on; I am listening."

At which the president, all confused, could do nothing but stammer. Thereupon said Montmorency to him—

"You are an idiot, M. le President! Go home and learn your lesson; then return, but not before."

And he turned on his heel.

The people of Bordeaux having revolted and killed their governor, the constable was sent against them. They, knowing he was coming and that the reprisals would be terrible, went a two days' journey to meet him, carrying the keys of the city.

But he addressed them, fully armed and on horseback: "Begone, Messieurs of Bordeaux," he said—"begone, you and your keys! I have no need of them." And, pointing to the cannons, "There are my keys; they will open your city in a different fashion from the way you open it. Ah, I'll teach you to rebel against the king and kill his governor and lieutenant! You may stake your faith, I'll have every one of you hanged!"

And he kept his word.

At Bordeaux, M. de Strozzi, who had manœuvred his troops the evening before in his presence, came to pay his respects to him, although a relation of the queen. As soon as Montmorency saw him, he exclaimed:

"Ha! good-day, Strozzi! your fellows did wonders yesterday, and they made a really fine sight; they shall have their money, therefore, to-day. I have ordered it."

"Thanks, M. le Connétable," replied Strozzi; "I cannot tell you how delighted I am to find you are satisfied with them, for I have a petition to make to you on their part."

"What is it, Strozzi? Say on!"

"They say that wood is awfully dear in this city, and the sums they are paying for it during the present severe cold are actually ruining them; they beg you to give them a ship, called the 'Montreal,' which is beached on the strand and of no further use, so that they may break it up and warm themselves."

"Why, of course I will!" said the constable; "let them set about the thing at once, break it up and warm themselves as well as they can, for it is my pleasure."

But while he was at dinner, the aldermen and councillors of the city came to him. Whether Strozzi had seen badly, or had been deceived by the report of the soldiers, or had but little acquaintance with ships old or new, the one whose demolition he asked for was still capable of making many a prosperous voyage. These worthy magistrates came, therefore, to represent to Montmorency what a pity it would be to cut up so fine a vessel, which had so far only made two or three voyages, and was registered at three hundred tons.

But the constable interrupted them in his customary tone before they were half-way:

"Good! good! And pray who are you, you idiots, to venture to prescribe to me? You must think yourselves no small people when you dare to thus utter a remonstrance in my presence. If I acted rightly—and I don't know what is keeping me from doing it—I should send and have your houses pulled to pieces instead of the ship; and if you are not out of this in a jiffy, it's just what I shall do. Go home and mind your own business; don't meddle with mine!"

And the same day the ship was broken up.

During the intervals of peace, the great anger of Montmorency was exercised on the ministers of the Reformed religion, for whom his hatred was ferocious. One of his relaxations was to go into the temples of Paris and hunt them from their pulpits; and, having one day discovered that they were holding a consistory with permission of the king, he made his way to Popincourt, entered the assembly, overturned the pulpit, broke all the benches and made a great bonfire of them; this expedition won him the surname of Captain Brûle-Bancs.

And all these brutalities were accomplished by the constable while mumbling his prayers, and especially the Lord's Prayer, which was his favorite, and which he combined in the most grotesque fashion with the barbarous orders he gave and never revoked.

Misfortune was abroad when he began in some such way as this:

"Our Father who art in heaven (*Go and hang that fellow at once!*), hallowed be Thy name (*String yon other fellow up to that tree!*). Thy kingdom come (*Let that rascal run the gantlet of the pikes!*). Thy will be done on earth (*Have those scoundrels shot immediately!*), as it is in heaven. (*Cut in pieces all those knaves who dared to hold the tower against me!*) Give us this day our daily bread (*Burn me yonder village*), and forgive us our trespasses, as we forgive those who have trespassed against us! (*Set fire to the four corners, and let not one house escape!*) And lead us not into temptation (*If the clowns cry out against it, fling them into the fire also!*), but deliver us from evil. Amen!"

This was called the *Pater-Nosters* of the constable. Such was the man Henri II. found, on entering his cabinet, seated in front of the keen, crafty, aristocratic Cardinal de Lorraine, the most courteous of high-born churchmen and the shrewdest statesman of his time.

It is easy to understand that these two natures, so absolutely contrary to each other, must constantly come in collision, and must give great trouble to the state by their ambitious rivalries.

And the more so that Montmorency's family was almost as numerous as that of Guise, the constable having had by his wife, Madame de Savoie, daughter of Messire René, bastard of Savoy and Grand-Master of France, five sons— MM. de Montmorency, d'Amville, de Méru, de Montbron, and de Thoré, and five daughters, of whom four were married to MM. de la Trémouille, de Turenne, de Ventadour and de Candale, the fifth and most beautiful of all becoming Abbess of Saint-Pierre de Rheims.

Now all these illustrious people had to be well established —a subject on which the grasping constable was meditating when the king entered.

On perceiving Henri, all rose and uncovered.

The king saluted Montmorency with a friendly and almost soldier-like gesture, while he bowed to the cardinal with every appearance of deference.

"I have summoned you, gentlemen," he said, "for the subject on which I have to consult you is grave. M. de Nemours has arrived from Italy, where affairs are turning out badly, owing to the failure of his Holiness to keep his word, and the treason of most of our allies. Everything, at first, succeeded wonderfully. M. de Strozzi captured Ostia; it is true we lost in the trenches of the city M. de Montluc

—a brave and worthy gentleman, for whose soul, gentlemen, I ask your prayers. Thereupon, the Duke of Alba, knowing the near arrival of your illustrious brother, my dear cardinal, retired to Naples. All the places in the neighborhood of Rome were, in consequence, successively occupied by us. In effect, after crossing the Milanese, the duke advanced to Reggio, where his father-in-law, the Duke of Ferrara, awaited him with six thousand infantry and eight hundred cavalry. There a counsel was held between Cardinal Caraffa and Jean de Lodève, ambassador of the king. One party was of opinion that Cremona or Pavia ought to be attacked, while Maréchal de Brissac was holding the enemy in check; the other represented that, before either could be occupied, the Duke of Alba would have doubled his army by raising levies in Tuscany and the kingdom of Naples. Cardinal Caraffa was of a different opinion: he proposed entering the march of Ancona through the Terra di Lavoro, all whose fortresses, being badly fortified, would, he said, surrender at the first summons; but the Duke of Ferrara insisted, on the other hand, that the defence of the Holy See being the principal object of the campaign, the Duc de Guise should march straight on Rome. The Duc de Guise decided for the latter course, and wished to take with him the six thousand infantry and eight hundred cavalry of the Duke of Ferrara, who refused, saying he might be attacked at any moment by the Grandduke Cosmo de Médicis or by the Duke of Parma, who had just joined the Spaniards. M. de Guise, gentlemen, was then obliged to continue his march with the few troops left him, having no hope except in the contingent which, according to Cardinal Caraffa, was to join the French army at Bologna. Arrived at Bologna with the cardinal, his nephew, the duke looked in vain for this contingent. It did not exist. Your brother, my dear cardinal, complained loudly; but Caraffa answered that he was going to look up ten thousand men lately levied in the march of Ancona. The duke tried to believe in this promise, and continued on his way through the Romagna. No reinforcement came to him; he left our army there under the command of M. d'Aumale, and proceeded to Rome directly, to learn from the Holy Father himself what he intended to do. The Pope, driven to the wall by M. de Guise, replied that he agreed, indeed, to have a contingent of twenty-four thousand men for this war, but that among these twenty-four thousand were comprised the soldiers holding the strong places of the Church; now those thus employed numbered eighteen thousand. M. de Guise saw he could only reckon on the men he had with him; but, according to the saying of the Pope, these men ought to be enough, as the French had never failed, up to this time, in their enterprises on Naples, except when they had the Sovereign Pontiff against them. Now this time, instead of being against them, the Sovereign Pontiff was with them; and, thanks to this moral and spiritual co-operation, the French were sure to succeed. M. de Guise, my dear constable, is a little like you in this respect: he never doubts of his fortune when he has his good sword by his side, and a few thousand brave men behind him. He hastened the coming of his army; and as soon as it joined him, he marched out of Rome, attacked Campli, carried it by storm, and put all, men, women and children, to the sword."

The constable received the news of this execution with the first visible sign of approbation he had given.

The cardinal remained impassive.

"After Campli," continued the king, "he laid siege to Civitella, which is, it appears, built on a craggy hill, and well supplied with fortifications. He began by battering down the citadel; but before a practicable breach could be made, our soldiers, with their usual impatience, risked an assault. Unfortunately, the place they tried to force was defended on all sides by bastions; our army was repulsed with the loss of two hundred killed and three hundred wounded."

A smile of joy broke over the lips of the constable; the invincible hero had failed before a shed.

"Meanwhile," the king went on, "the Duke of Alba had gathered his troops together at Chieti, and now marched to the succor of the besieged with an army of three thousand Spaniards, six thousand Germans, three thousand Italians, and three hundred Calabrians. It was more than double the number possessed by the Duc de Guise. This inferiority determined the duke to raise the siege and meet the enemy in the open plain between Fermo and Ascoli. He hoped the Duke of Alba would accept the battle offered him; but the Duke of Alba, sure that we should be ruined in any case, simply occupied the country, and would accept neither battle nor encounter except in positions that left us no chance of success. In this situation, without hopes of obtaining from the Pope either men or money, M. de Guise sends M. de Nemours to me to ask a considerable reinforcement, or leave to quit Italy and return. What is your opinion, gentlemen? Should we make one last effort, and send our well-beloved duke the men and money he absolutely needs, or recall him, and, by recalling him, renounce our claims to that fair kingdom of Naples, which, on the promise of his Holiness, we had intended for our son Charles?"

The constable made a gesture, as if to ask leave to speak, while at the same time indicating that he was ready to give way to the Cardinal de Lorraine; but the latter, by a slight motion of the head, gave it to be understood he might speak first.

It was, for that matter, the usual tactics of the cardinal to let his adversary speak first.

"Sire," said Montmorency, "my opinion is that we must not abandon an affair so well begun, and that your Majesty should omit no effort to support your army and your general in Italy."

"And you, M. le Cardinal?" said the king.

"As for me," said Charles de Guise, "I must ask M. de Connétable to excuse me, but my opinion is absolutely opposed to his."

"That is no surprise to me, M. le Cardinal," answered

Montmorency, bitterly. "It would have been the first time we agreed, were it otherwise. So you think, monsieur, your brother ought to return?"

"It would be, I believe, good policy to recall him."

"Alone or with his army?"

"With his army to the last man!"

"And why so? Do you think there are not enough of bandits prowling already on the highways? I happen to know there is a regular harvest of them."

"There are perhaps bandits enough prowling on the highways, M. le Connétable—there is perhaps a regular harvest of them, as you say; but we have no harvest of brave soldiers and great captains."

"You forget, M. le Cardinal, that we are in full peace, and, being in full peace, we can do without your sublime conquerors."

"I beg your Majesty to ask M. le Connétable," said the cardinal, turning to the king, "if he believes seriously in the duration of peace."

"*Morbleu!* if I believe in it," said the constable—"a nice question that!"

"Well, I am so far from believing in it," said the cardinal, "that I think if your Majesty does not wish to let the King of Spain have the glory of attacking you, you should at once attack the King of Spain."

"In spite of the truce solemnly sworn?" cried the constable, with such ardor that one would have believed in his sincerity. "But do you forget, M. le Cardinal, that it is a duty to keep one's oath? that the word of a king ought to be more inviolable than any other word, and that France has never been a recreant to her good faith, even when dealing with Turks and Saracens?"

"But then, if this is so," asked the cardinal, "why has your nephew, M. de Chatillon, instead of remaining quiet in his government of Picardy, attempted to surprise and scale the walls of Douai, in which he would have succeeded but for an old woman passing, by chance, near the place where the ladders were planted, who gave the alarm to the sentinels?"

"Why has my nephew done that?" said Montmorency, at once falling into the snare. "I am just going to tell you why he has done that."

"We are listening," said the cardinal.

Then, turning to the king, with a marked purpose in his accent, he said—

"Listen, Sire."

"Oh, his Majesty knows it as well as I do, *mordieu!*" said the constable; "for though he appears entirely taken up with his loves, have the goodness to learn, M. le Cardinal, that we do not leave him entirely ignorant of state affairs."

"We are listening, M. le Connétable," returned the cardinal, coldly; "you were about to tell the reason why M. l'Amiral made the attack on Douai."

"The reason! I could give you ten instead of one, *mordieu!*"

"Give them, M. le Connétable."

"First," replied the latter, "the attempt made by Comte Mègue, governor of Luxembourg, through the agency of his maître d'hôtel, who corrupted three soldiers of the garrison by a present of a thousand crowns in hand and promise of a pension of the same amount, for which they were to deliver up the city."

"The city which my brother has so gloriously defended; it is true," said the cardinal, "we have heard of that attempt, which, like your nephew's, has happily failed. But this makes only one excuse, and you have promised us ten, M. le Connétable."

"Oh, wait. Are you not yet aware that this Comte Mègue suborned a Provençal soldier of the garrison of Marienbourg, who, in return for the large sum given him, engaged to poison the wells of the fortress, and that the enterprise only failed because Comte Mègue did not think a single man sufficient for the job, and the others he tried to deal with discovered the conspiracy. You will not say the thing is false, M. le Cardinal, for the soldier was broken alive on the wheel."

"That would hardly be a reason for convincing me. You have, during your lifetime, M. le Connétable, broken on the wheel and hanged not a small number of people whom I consider as innocent and as much martyrs as those whom the Roman emperors named Nero, Commodus, and Domitian sent to die in their circuses."

"*Mordieu!* M. le Cardinal, would you perchance deny this enterprise of Comte Mègue on the wells of Marienbourg?"

"On the contrary, M. le Connétable, I told you I admitted it. But you promised us ten excuses for the enterprise of your nephew, and we have only two so far."

"You shall have them, *mordieu!* you shall have them! Are you ignorant, for example, that Comte Berlaimont, intendant of the finances of Flanders, made a plot with two Gascon soldiers and got them to pledge themselves, with the help of Sieur de Vèze, captain of a company of foot in the king's service, to deliver the city of Bordeaux to the King of Spain, provided they were seconded by five or six hundred men? You just say no to this fresh plot of the Catholic king, and I shall answer that one of these two soldiers, arrested near Saint-Quentin by the governor of the place, confessed everything, and acknowledged that he had even received the reward promised in the presence of Antoine Perrenot, Bishop of Arras. Come now, M. le Cardinal, say no! *mordieu*, say no!"

"I have not the slightest intention of doing so," replied the cardinal, smiling, "seeing that it is the truth beyond doubt, M. le Connétable, and I do not care to expose my soul to peril by such a lie. But this only makes three infractions of the treaty of Vaucelles by his Majesty the King of Spain, and you have promised us ten."

"Oh, I can easily furnish you ten, or a dozen if you want them! For instance, has not Maitre Jacques de Flèche, one of King Philip's best engineers, been caught sounding the fords of the Oise, and conducted to La Fère, where he confessed that Emmanuel Philibert, Duke of Savoy, had ordered M. de Berlaimont to pay him money for drawing the plans of Montreuil, Roye, Doullens, Saint-Quentin, and Mézières—places the Spaniards want to seize—in order to control Boulogne and Ardres and prevent the revictualling of Marienbourg?"

"All this is perfectly correct, M. le Connétable, but we are not yet near the ten."

"Eh, *mordieu!* do we require ten in order to see that the truce has, in reality, been broken by the Spaniards, and that if my nephew, M. l'Amiral, has made an attempt on Douai, he had a perfect right to do so?"

"And I have no intention of asking you to say anything further, M. le Connétable; those four proofs are enough to show me that the truce has been broken by Philip II. Now, the truce being broken, not once, but four times, it is the King of Spain who violates his word by breaking the truce, and not the King of France who will violate his by recalling from Italy his army and general and preparing for war."

The constable bit his white mustaches; the crafty spirit of his adversary had just made him confess the opposite of what he had meant to say.

But the cardinal had hardly ceased speaking, and the constable biting his mustaches, when the sound of a trumpet playing a foreign air was heard in the courtyard of the chateau of Saint-Germain.

"Oh, oh!" said the king, "what mischievous page is that, lacerating my ears with an English air? Go and find out, M. de l'Aubespine, and let the little rascal have a sound whipping for his merry pranks."

M. de l'Aubespine went out to execute the orders of the king.

Five minutes after, he returned.

"Sire," said he, "it is neither page, equerry, nor whipper-in who has played the air in question; it is an

English trumpeter accompanying a herald sent you by Queen Mary."

Scarcely had M. de l'Aubespine finished these words, when the trumpet sounded again, this time playing a Spanish air.

"Ah!" said the king, "after the wife, the husband, it would seem."

Then, with that majesty which all those old kings of France knew how to assume so well when the occasion needed—

"Messieurs," he said, "to the throne-room! Warn our officers, as I shall the court. Whatever be the message our cousin Mary and our cousin Philip may send us, it is necessary to do honor to their messengers."

IV

WAR

THE sounds from the English and Spanish trumpets had re-echoed, not only in the hall of council, but throughout the entire palace, being, as they were, a sort of double echo from the North and from the South.

The king found, therefore, that the court was already pretty well informed of the condition of things; all the ladies were at the windows, and eyes were fixed curiously on the two heralds and their suite. At the council door, the constable was met by a young officer sent him by his nephew Coligny—the same Coligny we saw entering the room of Charles V. on the evening of his abdication.

The admiral was, as we have already said, governor of Picardy; he would therefore, in case of invasion, be the one first exposed to attack.

"Ah, it is you, Théligny!"[1] said the constable, in a low voice.

---
[1] This Théligny was no relation of the kinsman of Coligny of the same name killed in the massacre of Saint-Bartholomew.

"Yes, monseigneur," replied the young officer.

"And you bring news of the admiral?"

"Yes, monseigneur."

"Have you seen or spoken to any one on the subject, so far?"

"The news is for the king, monseigneur," answered the young officer; "but I have been directed to communicate it to you first."

"Very well," said the constable; "follow me."

And just as the Cardinal de Lorraine had led the Duc de Nemours to the apartments of Catherine de Médicis, so the constable led M. de Théligny to those of Madame de Valentinois.

But, in the meantime, the reception was being held.

At the end of a quarter of an hour, the king—having the queen on his right, all the great officers on the steps of the throne; around him, seated in armchairs, Madame Marguerite and Madame Elisabeth of France, Mary Stuart, the Duchesse de Valentinois, the four Marys; in fine, the entire brilliant court of the Valois—the king gave orders for the English herald to be introduced.

Long before he made his appearance, the jingling of his spurs and of those of the men-at-arms forming his escort was heard in the antechambers. At last he crossed the threshold, clad in the tabard with the English arms embroidered on it, and advanced with his head covered, stopping within ten steps of the throne. There he uncovered, and, putting one knee to the ground, said in a loud voice:

"Mary, Queen of England, Ireland, and France, to Henri, King of France, greeting! Because you have given aid and comfort to the English Protestants, enemies of our person, religion and state, and because you have promised them succor and protection against the just prosecutions of which they are now the object, we, William Norry, declare war against you on land and sea, and as a sign of defiance, we throw here the glove of battle."

And the herald flung at the feet of the king his iron gauntlet, which resounded harshly on the floor.

"It is well," replied the king, without rising. "I accept this declaration of war; but I wish the whole world to know that I have kept the good faith due to our mutual good friendship; and, since it is her pleasure to attack France for so unjust a cause, I hope, through the favor of God, that she will gain no more by her action than her predecessors have done when they have attacked mine. For that matter, I speak to you mildly and civilly, because it is a queen who sends you; if it were a king, I would speak to you in a different tone."

And, turning to Mary Stuart—

"My gentle Queen of Scotland," he said, "as this war concerns you not less than me, and as you have quite as many rights to the crown of England as my sister has to that of France, if not more, pick up, I pray you, that glove, and make a gift to the brave Sir William Norry of the gold chain around your neck, which the Duchesse de Valentinois will be good enough to replace by the chain of pearls she has on hers. I, in turn, shall replace in such manner that she shall not suffer too much loss thereby. Go! To pick up a woman's glove, a woman's hands are needed!"

Mary Stuart rose, and, with all her exquisite grace, unfastened the chain from her neck and flung it round that of the herald; then, with that lofty air that so well became her countenance—

"I pick up this glove," she said, "not only in the name of France, but also in the name of Scotland! Herald, tell my sister Mary what I have said."

The herald stood up, bent his head slightly, and, stepping back to the left of the throne, said—

"It shall be done according to the desires of King Henri of France and Queen Mary of Scotland."

"Introduce the herald of our brother Philip II.," said the king.

The same jingling of spurs was heard, announcing the

approach of the Spanish herald, who entered still more haughtily than had his colleague; and, all the time twisting his Castilian mustaches, he approached within ten steps of the king, and said, without bending the knee, contenting himself with a slight inclination of the head—

. "Philip, by divine clemency, King of Castile, Leon, Granada, Navarre, Aragon, Naples, Sicily, Majorca, Sardinia, the isles, Indias, and lands of the ocean; Archduke of Austria; Duke of Burgundy, Lothier, Brabant, Limbourg, Luxembourg, and Guelders; Count of Flanders and Artois; Marquis of the Holy Empire; Seigneur of Friesland, Salins, Malines, the cities and countries of Utrecht, Overyssel, and Groeningen; Sovereign in Asia and Africa; to you, Henri of France, we make known that because of the assault made on the city of Douai, and the pillage of the city of Sens, both having been by the orders and under the direction of your governor of Picardy, and because we regard the truce sworn between you and us at Vaucelles as broken, we declare war against you on land and sea; as gage of which defiance, in the name of my said king, prince and lord, I, Guzman d'Avila, herald of Castile, Leon, Granada, Navarre, and Aragon, fling here my glove of battle."

And, ungloving his right hand, he flung the glove insolently at the feet of the king.

Then the deeply tanned and manly face of Henri II. became pale, and in a somewhat altered tone he replied:

"Our brother Philip II. anticipates us, and therefore we have some reason to reproach him; but he would have done better, since he has so many personal grievances against us, to have made of this quarrel a personal quarrel. We would have very willingly answered for our acts face to face and body to body, and the Lord God would then have judged between us. Tell him, however, Don Guzman, that we accept with the utmost confidence the war which he declares against us; but I should be far more pleased still, if he were to arrange a meeting between me and him instead of one between our two armies."

And as the constable touched his arm meaningly—

"And you will add," continued Henri, "that when I made this proposal, my good friend, M. de Montmorency, touched my arm, because he knows there is a prophecy that I shall die in a duel. Well, at the risk of the fulfilment of that prophecy, I persist in the proposal, although I have no doubt that this prediction will give sufficient confidence to my brother to induce him to accept. M. de Montmorency, I pray you, as Constable of France, to pick up the glove of King Philip."

Then to the herald—

"Stay, my friend," he said, taking a bag placed behind him for the purpose, and full of gold, "it is far from here to Valladolid; and as you have come hither to bring us such good news, it is not fitting that you should spend your master's money or your own on the route. Take, therefore, these hundred crowns of gold to defray the expenses of your journey."

"Sire," replied the herald, "my master and I belong to a country where gold grows, and we have only to stoop to pick it up."

And, saluting the king, he took a step backward—

"Ah, proud as a Castilian!" murmured Henri. "M. de Montgomery, take that sack and make largess of what it contains through the window."

Montgomery took the sack, opened the window, and threw the gold to the lackeys in the court, who received it with joyous hurrahs.

"Gentlemen," continued Henri, rising, "there is always high festival at the court of France when a neighboring sovereign declares war on its king; there shall be double festival this evening, since we have received declarations of war at the same time from a king and a queen."

Then, turning to the two heralds who were standing, the one on his left, the other on his right—

"Sir William Norry, Don Guzman d'Avila," said the king, "seeing that you are the causes of the festival, you are, as representing King Philip, my brother, and Queen Mary, my sister, invited to it of right."

"Sire," whispered the constable to Henri, "would it please you to hear the fresh news from Picardy, brought from my nephew by a lieutenant of the dauphin's regiment named Théligny?"

"Yes, indeed," said the king. "Bring him to me; he shall be welcome."

Five minutes afterward, the young man was led into the chamber of arms, and, bowing respectfully before the king, waited until the latter should address him.

"Well, monsieur," said the king, "what news do you bring of the health of M. l'Amiral?"

"As far as that goes, excellent, sire; never has M. l'Amiral been stronger."

"Then may God keep him so, and all will be well! Where did you leave him?"

"At La Fère, sire."

"And what news did he charge you to transmit to me?"

"Sire, he has charged me to tell your Majesty to prepare for a serious war. The enemy has assembled more than fifty thousand men, and M. l'Amiral believes that all his preceding attempts have been only a false demonstration to conceal his real plans."

"And what has the enemy been doing up to now?" asked the king.

"The Duke of Savoy, who is commander-in-chief," replied the young lieutenant, "has advanced as far as Givet, accompanied by Count Mansfield, Count Egmont, the Duke of Aerschott, and the principal officers of his army, where the general rendezvous of the hostile forces was established."

"I have learned as much through the Duc de Nevers, governor of Champagne," said the king; "he even added, in his despatches on the subject, that he believed Emmanuel Philibert aimed principally at Rocroy and Mézières; and, believing Rocroy, which has been only lately fortified, was in bad condition to sustain a siege, I recommended the Duc de Nevers to see if it would not be better to abandon it. Since that time I have had no news of him."

"I bring some to your Majesty," said Théligny. "Sure of the strength of the place, M. de Nevers shut himself up in it, and, sheltered behind its walls, has so well received the enemy that after several skirmishes, in which he lost a few hundred men, he has forced him to retire across the ford of Houssu, between the village of Nismes and Hauteroche; from thence the enemy took his way by Chimay, Glayon, and Montreuil-aux-Dames; passed by La Chapelle, which he pillaged, and Vervins, which he reduced to ashes; in fine, he has advanced as far as Guise, and M. l'Amiral has no doubt it is his intention to besiege that place, in which M. de Vassé has shut himself up."

"What troops does the Duke of Savoy command?" asked the king.

"Flemish, Spanish, and German troops, sire; very nearly forty thousand foot and fifteen thousand horse."

"And how many can M. de Chatillon and M. de Nevers dispose of?"

"Sire, were they to unite all their forces, they could hardly dispose of eighteen thousand infantry, and from five to six thousand cavalry; without reckoning that, among the latter, are fifteen hundred or two thousand Englishmen, whom it would be necessary to distrust, in case of war with Queen Mary."

"So that, considering the number of men we shall be forced to leave as garrisons in the cities, twelve or fourteen thousand men are the most we shall be able to give you, my dear constable," said Henri, turning to Montmorency.

"Well, be it so, sire; with the few you give me I shall do my best. I have heard that a famous general of antiquity, named Xenophon, had only ten thousand soldiers under his orders when he accomplished a magnificent retreat of a hundred and fifty leagues; and that Leonidas, King of Sparta, commanded at most a thousand men when he arrested for eight days, at Thermopylæ, the army of King Xerxes, which was, however, far more numerous than that of the Duke of Savoy."

"So you are not discouraged, my dear constable?" said the king.

"Quite the contrary, sire! And, *mordieu!* I have never been so joyous and of such good hope. I only want to find a man who can give me some information as to the state of Saint-Quentin."

"Why so, constable?" asked the king.

"Because with the keys of Saint-Quentin the gates of Paris are opened, sire; it is an old proverb. Do you know Saint-Quentin, M. de Théligny?"

"No, monseigneur; but if I dared—"

"Dare then! dare, *mordieu!* the king permits you."

"Well, then, M. le Connétable, I have with me a kind of groom given me by M. l'Amiral, who, if he wishes, can, I fancy, give you some information on the state of the city."

"What! if he wishes!" cried the constable. "He shall wish, you may be certain."

"Without doubt," said Théligny, "he will not dare to refuse answering the questions of M. le Connétable, only, as he is a very shrewd rascal, he may answer them after his own fashion."

"After his own fashion? You'll find his own fashion will be after mine, M. le Lieutenant."

"Ah! that is just the point on which I would beg you not to make any mistake. He will answer after his own fashion, and not after yours; seeing that as you, monseigneur, do not know Saint-Quentin, you cannot tell whether he is speaking the truth or not."

"If he does not speak the truth, I shall have him hanged."

"Yes; it is a means of punishing him, but not of utilizing him. Believe me, M. le Connétable, he is an adroit, cunning fellow, very brave when he wishes—"

"How, when he wishes? He is not brave at all times, then?" interrupted Montmorency.

"He is brave when others are looking on, and when they are not looking on, if it is his interest to fight. One can't expect anything more of an adventurer."

"My good constable," said the king, "he who wishes the end wishes the means. This man may render us some services. M. de Théligny knows him; let M. de Théligny conduct the inquiry."

"Be it so," said the constable; "but I assure you, sire, I have a way of talking to people—"

"Yes, monseigneur," replied Théligny, smiling, "we know your way, and it has its good side; but with Master Yvonnet, it would have the effect of sending him to the side of the enemy on the first opportunity; and he could render them all the services against us which he can now render us against them."

"To the side of the enemy, *morbleu!* to the side of the enemy, *sacrebleu!*" shouted the constable. "Why, in that case, he ought to be hanged at once. He is a cutthroat, a bandit, a traitor then, this groom of yours, M. de Théligny."

"He is an adventurer quite simply, monseigneur."

"Oh, oh! and my nephew makes use of such rascals?"

"War is war, monseigneur," rejoined Théligny, laughing.

Then, turning to the king—

"I place my poor Yvonnet under the safeguard of your Majesty, and ask that, whatever he may say or do, I may bring him back with me as safe and sound as I have brought him hither."

"You have my word," said the king; "go and fetch your groom."

"If the king permit," replied Théligny, "I shall content myself with making a sign to him, and he will come up."

"Do so."

Théligny opened a window looking on the park, and beckoned to some one.

Five minutes afterward, Master Yvonnet appeared at the

threshold of the door, clad in the same cuirass of buffalo, the same maroon-velvet jacket, the same boots, in which we have already presented him to the reader.

He held in his hand the same cap adorned with the same plume.

Only everything was two years older than then. A copper chain, which was once gilt, was hanging from his neck and playing sportively on his breast.

The young man only needed a glance to show him with whom he had to deal, and doubtless he recognized M. le Connétable or the king, or perhaps both, for he kept himself respectfully near the door.

"Come forward, Yvonnet; come forward, my friend," said the lieutenant, "and know you are in presence of his Majesty Henri II. and of M. le Connétable, who, on account of the way I have extolled your merits, have desired to see you."

To the great stupefaction of the constable, Master Yvonnet did not appear the least astonished in the world at his merits gaining him such an honor.

"I thank you, lieutenant," said Yvonnet, taking three steps and then halting, half through distrust, half through respect; "my merits, small though they be, are at the feet of his Majesty and at the service of M. le Connétable."

The king noticed the difference the young man placed between the homage rendered to the royal majesty and the obedience offered to M. de Montmorency.

Without doubt, this difference also struck the constable.

"All right!" he said; "no phrases, my fine fellow! Answer squarely, or if not—"

Yvonnet darted a glance at Théligny which meant, "Do I run any danger, or is it an honor they are doing me?"

But, strong in the king's promise, Théligny took hold of the interrogatory.

"My dear Yvonnet, the king knows you are a gallant cavalier," he said; "very much admired by the ladies, and that you devote to your toilet all the revenues your intelligence and courage can procure. Now, as the king desires to put your intelligence to the test at once, and your courage later on, he charges me to offer you ten golden crowns if you consent to give him, as well as to M. le Connétable, some positive information respecting the city of Saint-Quentin."

"Would you have the goodness to tell the king, lieutenant, that I am a member of an association of honest persons who have all sworn to distribute among the members half their several gains, whether acquired by dint of intelligence or of force; so that of the ten crowns offered me, five would belong to me only, the other five being the property of the association."

"And what hinders you from keeping the ten, idiot," retorted the constable, "and saying nothing of the good fortune that falls to your share?"

"My word, M. le Connétable. We are too small people, we are, to venture on breaking it."

"Sire," said the constable, "I distrust strongly those people who do things only for money."

Yvonnet bent low before the king.

"I ask your Majesty's leave to say two words."

"Well, upon my word! This rascal has—"

"Constable," said the king, "I beg you—"

Then smiling—

"Speak, my friend," said he to Yvonnet.

The constable shrugged his shoulders, took three steps backward, and began to walk backward and forward, like a man who does not care to take part in the conversation.

"Sire," said Yvonnet, with a respect and grace that would have done honor to a refined courtier, "I beg your Majesty to remember that I have not fixed any price on the services which I can and ought to render to you as your humble and obedient subject; it was my lieutenant, M. de Théligny, who spoke of ten crowns of gold. Your Majesty being unaware most certainly of the association existing between me and my eight comrades, all equally in the service of M. l'Amiral, I thought it my duty to mention that, while thinking you were giving me ten crowns of gold, you were giving me five only, the other five being for the association. Now that your Majesty deigns to question me, I am ready to answer, and that without there being any question of five or ten or twenty crowns of gold; but purely and simply on account of the respect, obedience, and devotion I owe my king."

And the adventurer bowed before the king with as much dignity as if he had been the ambassador of an Italian prince or a count of the Holy Empire.

"Nothing could be better!" said the king; "you are quite right, Master Yvonnet. Let us not reckon beforehand and you will find yourself not the worse for it."

Yvonnet smiled in a fashion which meant, "Oh, I know with whom I am dealing."

But as all these little delays irritated the impatient temper of the constable, he turned again to the young man, and, tapping the floor with his foot, said—

"Look here now, as all your conditions are arranged, will you be so kind as to tell me what you know of Saint-Quentin, you scoundrel?"

Yvonnet looked at the constable, and, with a roguish expression belonging only to the Parisian, said—

"Saint-Quentin, monseigneur? Saint-Quentin is a city situated on the river Somme, six leagues from Fère, thirteen from Laon, and thirty-four from Paris; it has twenty thousand inhabitants, a corporation composed of twenty-five municipal officers—namely, a mayor in office, a mayor who has just held office, eleven aldermen, and twelve councillors; these magistrates elect and appoint their own successors, which they select among the bourgeois, in virtue of a decree of the parliament dated the 16th of December, 1335, and of a charter of King Charles VI. dated 1412."

"Ta, ta, ta!" cried the constable, "what the devil is that imp of misfortune dinning us with? I ask you what you know of Saint-Quentin, beast?"

"Well, I have told you what I know, and I can guarantee to you the correctness of my information; I have it from my friend Maldent, who is a native of Noyon, and spent three years in Saint-Quentin as attorney's clerk."

"Hold, sire," said the constable, "believe me, we shall get nothing out of this knave, until we have him on a good wooden horse, with four balls of twelve pounds tied to each leg."

Yvonnet remained impassive.

"I am not precisely of your opinion, constable. I believe we shall get nothing out of him, as long as we try to force him to speak; but I believe we shall learn all we want to know by leaving him to M. de Théligny. If he knows what he has told us—just the things he could not be expected to know—you may be sure he knows something else besides. Is it not true, Master Yvonnet, that you have studied not only the population, geography, and constitution of the city of Saint-Quentin, but that you are also acquainted with the condition of its ramparts and the disposition of its inhabitants?"

"Should my lieutenant wish to interrogate me, or should the king do me the honor to address me the questions to which he desires an answer, I shall do my best to satisfy my lieutenant and to obey the king."

"The rascal is all honey now!" murmured the constable.

"Come now, my dear Yvonnet," said Théligny, "prove to his Majesty that I have not deceived him when I praised your intelligence so highly, and describe to him, as well as to M. le Connétable, the condition of the ramparts at the present moment."

Yvonnet shook his head.

"Would not one imagine that the knave knows all about it!" growled the constable.

"Sire," replied Yvonnet, without paying any attention to the sneer of Montmorency, "I have the honor to tell your Majesty that the city of Saint-Quentin, ignorant that it runs any danger whatever, and consequently not having prepared any means of defence, is hardly secure from a sudden assault."

"But then," asked the king, "has it not ramparts?"

"Yes, undoubtedly," answered Yvonnet—"ramparts strengthened by round and square towers connected by curtains with two bastions, one of which defends the suburb of l'Isle; but the boulevard has not even parapets, and is protected only by a fosse dug in front. Its ground-plan, which does not rise above the surrounding lands, is commanded in many places by hills in the neighborhood, and even by houses situated on the border of the exterior fosse; and on the right of the Guise highway and the gate of l'Isle, the old wall—it is the name of the rampart at that point—is so low that a man, be he ever so inactive, could easily scale it."

"But, you scoundrel!" cried the constable, "if you are an engineer, you should say so at once!"

"I am not an engineer, M. le Connétable."

"What are you, then?"

Yvonnet lowered his eyes with affected modesty.

"Yvonnet is in love, monseigneur," said Théligny; "and to reach the fair enslaver who dwells in the Faubourg d'Isle, he has been obliged to study the strong and weak points of the walls."

"Ah," murmured the constable, "a nice reason that, indeed!"

"Well, then, continue," said the king, "and I shall give you a fine gold cross as a present for your mistress the first time you see her on your return."

"And never cross of gold will have shone on a lovelier neck than Gudule's. I may say so with confidence, sire."

"And now this base villain is actually making the portrait of his mistress for us!" said the constable.

"And why not, if she is pretty, my cousin? You shall have the cross, Yvonnet."

"Thanks, sire."

"And now is there a garrison, at least, in the city of Saint-Quentin?"

"No, M. le Connétable."

"No!" cried Montmorency, "and how is that?"

"Because the city is, by its charter, exempt from military occupation, and its defence is confided to the bourgeois themselves—a right they hold to extremely."

"The bourgeoisie and their rights indeed! Sire, believe me, things can never go well as long as the bourgeoisie and the communes claim rights nobody knows of what kind, derived from nobody knows whom!"

"From whom? I am going to tell you, my cousin, from the kings, my predecessors."

"Well, if your Majesty will only intrust me with the task of taking back all these rights from the bourgeoisie, you may rely on it, the things shall be done quickly enough."

"We shall take thought of this later on, my dear constable. The Spaniards require all our attention at present. We should have a good garrison in Saint-Quentin."

"The admiral was negotiating for that very purpose at the time I left," said Théligny.

"And he must have succeeded by this time," said Yvonnet, "considering that he had Maitre Jean Pauquet on his side."

"Who is Maitre Jean Pauquet?" demanded the king.

"Gudule's uncle, sire," replied Yvonnet, with an accent that was not exempt from a certain imbecility.

"What, you knave!" cried the constable, "do you make love to a magistrate's niece?"

"Jean Pauquet is not a magistrate, M. le Connétable," replied Yvonnet.

"And what, then, is this Jean Pauquet of yours?"

"The syndic of all the weavers."

"Jesus!" exclaimed Montmorency, "what in the world are we coming to! Compelled to negotiate with a syndic of weavers, when it is the king's good pleasure to place a garrison in one of his cities. You will tell your Jean Pauquet that I intend to have him hanged if he does not open, not only the gates of the city, but the doors of the houses as well, to whatever men-at-arms I choose to send there."

"I think it would be quite as well if you let M. l'Amiral manage the business, M. le Connétable," said Yvonnet, shaking his head; "he knows better than you, monseigneur, the way to talk to people like Jean Pauquet."

"I really think you are arguing with me," said Montmorency, with a threatening gesture.

"Cousin, cousin," said Henri, "let us, pray, finish the business we have begun with this brave fellow. You will have it in your power to judge of the truth of his statements, since the army will be under your command, and you are to join it as soon as possible."

"Oh!" said Montmorency, "not later than to-morrow! I am in a hurry to bring all these bourgeois to their senses. A syndic of weavers, *mordieu!* a fine personage to negotiate with an admiral! Peuh!"

And he went to the embrasure of one of the windows and began gnawing his nails.

"Now," asked the king, "are the approaches to the city easy?"

"On three sides, yes, sire; on the Faubourg d'Isle side, the Rémicourt side, and the chapel of Epargnemaille side; but on the Tourival side it is necessary to cross the Grosnard marshes, which are full of places where you have no chance once you sink."

The constable had approached to listen to this detail, which interested him.

"In case of need, would you undertake," he said, "to guide across the marsh a body of troops that could enter or leave the city?"

"Doubtless; but I have already told M. le Connétable that Maldent, one of our associates, would do his business better, having lived three years in Saint-Quentin, while

I have gone there only at night, and then by the speediest route."

"And why speediest?"

"Because when I am alone at night, I am afraid."

"How!" cried Montmorency, "you are afraid?"

"Certainly, I am afraid."

"And you confess it, you rascal?"

"Why not, since it is true?"

"And what are you afraid of?"

"I am afraid of the will-o'-the-wisps, the ghosts, and the *loups-garoux.*"

The constable burst out laughing.

"Ah, you are afraid of the will-o'-the-wisps, the ghosts, and the *loups-garoux?*"

"Oh, yes, I am horribly nervous!"

And the young man shivered.

"Ah, my dear Théligny," said Montmorency, "I compliment you on your squire! I am warned; I don't care to have him for a night guide."

"In fact, it would be better to employ me by day."

"And leave you the night to see your Gudule, eh?"

"You see, monseigneur, that my visits have not been useless, and the king thinks as much, since he has graciously promised me a cross."

"M. de Montmorency, let forty gold crowns be given to this young man for the excellent information he has afforded us and the service he has offered to render. You will add ten crowns besides to buy a cross for Mademoiselle Gudule."

The constable shrugged his shoulders.

"Forty crowns!" he grumbled; "forty lashes of a whip! forty strokes of a cane! forty blows of the butt-end of a halberd on his shoulders!"

"You hear me, cousin; my word is pledged. Do not make me break my word."

Then to Théligny—

"M. de Théligny," continued the king, "the constable will give orders to have you supplied with horses from my stables at the Louvre and Compiègne, so that you may march as quickly as possible. Do not be afraid of laming them, and try to reach La Fère before to-morrow. M. de Chatillon cannot be warned too soon that war is declared. A good journey, monsieur, and good luck!"

The lieutenant and his squire saluted the king respectfully and followed the constable.

Ten minutes afterward they were galloping on the road from Paris, and the constable went back to the king, who had not left his cabinet.

V

IN WHICH THE READER FINDS HIMSELF AGAIN IN A COUNTRY HE KNOWS SOMETHING OF

HENRI II. was waiting for the constable, in order to give orders of the highest importance without any delay.

M. de Montgomery, who had, some years before, led French troops to the aid of the regent of Scotland, was sent to Edinburgh to ask that, in pursuance of the treaty signed between that kingdom and France, the Scotch should declare war on England, and that the lords composing the council of the regency should send to France ambassadors empowered to conclude the marriage between the young Queen Mary and the dauphin.

At the same time an instrument was drawn up with the consent of the Guises, by which Mary Stuart transmitted to the King of France her realm of Scotland and all the rights she had or might have over that of England, in case she died without male heir.

As soon as the marriage was celebrated, Mary Stuart was to take the title of Queen of France, Scotland, and England. Meanwhile, the triple arms of France, Scotland,

and England were engraved on the plate of the young sovereign.

In the evening, as the king had said, there was a splendid fete in the chateau of Saint-Germain, and the two heralds on their return to their respective princes might tell in what joyous fashion declarations of war were received at the court of France.

But before the first window of the chateau was illuminated, two cavaliers, mounted on magnificent steeds, were galloping out of the courts of the Louvre, and, after gaining the Barrière de la Villette, dashed along the La Fère highway.

At Louvres, they stopped a moment to breathe their horses, which they changed at Compiègne, as had been agreed on; after which, in spite of the advanced hour of the night and their want of rest, they resumed their journey and started at a gallop for La Fère, which they entered at eight in the morning.

Nothing fresh had occurred since the departure of Théligny and Yvonnet.

Short as was the time the latter had spent at Paris, he had found an opportunity to renew his wardrobe at the shop of a ready-made clothier of his acquaintance, who did business in the Rue Pretres Saint-Germain l'Auxerrois. The jacket and maroon breeches had then given place to doublet and hose of green velvet embroidered with gold, and a cherry-colored cap adorned with a white plume. A sash of the same color as the cap was wrapped round him, with the ends stuffed into boots that were almost irreproachable, armed with gigantic copper spurs. If his new garb was not quite fresh, it had at least been so little worn and by so careful an owner that only persons of very bad taste would make any uncalled for remarks on it or perceive that it came from a ready-made outfitter's, and not from a tailor's workshop. As to the chain, Yvonnet concluded, after deep thought, it had still enough gilding on it to deceive those looking at it from a distance of a few yards.

It was his lookout to see that they had no nearer view.

Let us hasten to add that the gold cross had been conscientiously purchased; only no one ever knew whether Yvonnet had employed equally conscientiously the whole of the ten crowns given him by Henri II. for that purpose, in making the purchase for the niece of Jean Pauquet.

Our belief is that Yvonnet had clipped enough from that cross to provide himself, not only with the doublet and green velvet breeches, the cherry-colored cap and white plume, the buffalo-leather boots and copper spurs, but also with an elegant cuirass placed in a portmanteau on the croup of his horse, and which rattled in quite a warlike fashion with every motion of the horse.

But it must be said that, as all this had for aim to defend or adorn his person, and as his person belonged to Mademoiselle Gudule, the fact that Yvonnet thus used the clippings of his mistress's cross would by no means show that the money of King Henri II. had been turned from its destination.

For that matter, he no sooner cleared the gate of La Fère than he was able to judge of the effect produced by his new outfit. Franz and Heinrich Scharfenstein were, in their capacity as purveyors of the association, busy leading to the camp an ox they had just acquired; and with that instinct of self-preservation which makes animals object to being butchered, the ox was refusing to proceed—as far as in him lay; for Heinrich Scharfenstein was dragging him by a horn, while Franz was pushing him behind.

At the noise of the horse's hoofs on the pavement, Heinrich raised his head, and recognizing our squire—

"Oh, Franz!" he cried, "only look at Meinherr Yvonnet; isn't he beautiful?"

And in his admiration, he let go the horn of the ox, which, profiting by his liberty, swung round, and would have regained his stall, if Franz, who, as we have said, was stationed in the neighborhood of the tail, had not seized that member, and, stiffening all his sinews, brought the animal to a sudden stand by his herculean strength.

Yvonnet sent him a protecting salute with his hand, and passed on.

They arrived at Coligny's quarters.

The young lieutenant was recognized, and entered the cabinet of the admiral at once, followed by Yvonnet, who, with his habitual tact and in spite of the change wrought in his exterior, remained respectfully at the door.

M. de Chatillon, leaning over one of those imperfect maps made at that period, was trying to complete it by the information a man in front of him, with cunning features, pointed nose, and intelligent eyes, was giving him.

This man was our friend the Picard Maldent, who, as Yvonnet had said, having been an attorney's clerk in Saint-Quentin for three years, knew the city and its environs as well as his writing-desk.

Coligny, at the noise made by Théligny on entering, raised his head, and recognized his messenger.

Maldent gently turned his eyes toward the door, and recognized Yvonnet.

The admiral offered his hand to Théligny; Maldent exchanged a look with Yvonnet, who drew the strings of the upper orifice of a purse from his pocket to indicate that his journey had not been wholly unprofitable.

Théligny gave an account to Coligny in a few words of his interview with the king and M. le Connétable, and handed to the governor of Picardy the letters of his uncle.

"Yes," said Coligny, reading, "my opinion has been the same as his: Saint-Quentin is, in fact, the city to be guarded above all. So your company, my dear Théligny, has gone there yesterday. You will join to-day even, and announce my speedy arrival."

And, absorbed in the information given him by Maldent, he bent anew over the map, and continued his annotations.

Théligny knew the admiral—a man of deep and serious thought, who must be let do what he was doing; and as, according to all probability, when his notes were finished, Coligny would have further orders to give him with respect to Saint-Quentin, the lieutenant approached Yvonnet.

"Go and wait for me in the camp," he whispered, "I will take you up on my way, when I have received the final instructions of M. l'Amiral."

Yvonnet bowed silently and went out. He found his horse at the door, and in an instant was outside the city.

The camp of Coligny, placed first at Pierrepont near Marle, had been afterward transported near La Fère. Too weak to hold his ground in an open country with the fifteen or eighteen hundred men he commanded, the admiral, fearing a surprise, had gained the neighborhood of a fortified city, believing that, small as his army was, it could make a stand behind good walls.

The line of the camp passed, Yvonnet stood up on his spurs to try if he could recognize any of his companions, and find out where they had fixed their quarters.

Soon his gaze was attracted by a group, in the middle of which was a man who looked like Procope, seated on a stone and writing on one knee.

Procope had utilized his clerical knowledge; from the moment it became certain that the enemy would be soon encountered, he was busy drawing up wills at five sous each.

Yvonnet understood that the quondam usher was like M. de Coligny, and did not fancy being disturbed in his grave occupation.

He cast another look around him, and perceived Franz and Heinrich Scharfenstein, who, having given up the design of leading their ox to the camp, had tied its legs together, and were carrying it thither, with the help of the pole of a carriage, the extremities of which rested on each of their shoulders.

A man who was no other than Pilletrousse was making signs to them at the door of a tent in rather good condition.

Yvonnet recognized the domicile in which he had the right to a ninth part, and in a few seconds was beside Pilletrousse, who, before giving any sign of welcome to his companion, walked round him once, then twice, then for the third time, Yvonnet, like the cavalier of an equestrian statue, looking on with a smile of satisfaction as his companion accomplished this circumambulation.

After the third turn, Pilletrousse halted, and with a clacking of the tongue to denote his admiration—

"*Peste!*" said he, "that is a pretty horse, and well worth forty gold crowns. Where the devil did you steal it?"

"Hush!" said Yvonnet, "speak with respect of the animal; he comes from his Majesty's stables, and only belongs to me as a loan."

"That's rather annoying," said Pilletrousse.

"And why so?"

"Because I had a purchaser."

"Ah!" returned Yvonnet, "and who was your purchaser?"

"I," said a voice behind Yvonnet.

Yvonnet turned round and cast a quick glance upon the person presenting himself with this haughty monosyllable, which was to make the success of the tragedy of "Medea," a hundred years later.

The bidder for the horse was a young man of from twenty-three to twenty-four years, half armed, half unarmed, as was the fashion with men of war when in camp.

Yvonnet needed only to let his eyes fall on those square shoulders, on that head framed in a red beard and red hair, on those clear blue eyes full of obstinacy and ferocity, to recognize the speaker.

"You have just heard my answer," he replied. "The horse, in reality, belongs to his Majesty the King of France, who has had the goodness to lend it to me for my return to the camp; if he claims it, I must of course give it back to him; if he leaves it with me, it is at your disposal, the price, it is unnecessary to say, being discussed and arranged beforehand between us."

"I admit the justice of what you say," replied the gentleman; "keep it for me, then. I am rich and disposed to be liberal."

Yvonnet saluted.

"Besides," continued the gentleman, "it is not the only affair concerning which I should wish to treat with you."

Yvonnet and Pilletrousse saluted together.

"What is the number of your band?"

"Of our troop, you mean, monsieur," retorted Yvonnet, a little hurt by the epithet.

"Of your troop, if you like it better."

"Unless in my absence some of my comrades have been unfortunate," answered Yvonnet, with a questioning glance at Pilletrousse, "there ought to be nine."

A look of Pilletrousse reassured Yvonnet, even supposing that he was really anxious on the subject.

"And all brave?" asked the gentleman.

Yvonnet smiled; Pilletrousse shrugged his shoulders.

"The fact is, you have a pretty sample there," said the gentleman, pointing to Franz and Heinrich, "if these two are members of your troop."

"They are," replied Pilletrousse, laconically.

"Then we can treat—"

"Pardon," said Yvonnet; "but we belong to M. l'Amiral."

"Except on two days of the week, when we can work on our own account," observed Pilletrousse. "Procope, foreseeing the two cases, introduced these clauses into the agreement: first, when we have some enterprise to undertake on our own behalf; second, when some honorable gentleman makes us a proposal of the kind the gentleman here present seems disposed to make."

"I only want you for a single day or for a single night; so nothing could be better. Now, in case of need, where shall I find you?"

"At Saint-Quentin, probably," said Yvonnet; "I know that I shall be there in person this very day."

"And two of us," continued Procope, "Lactance and Malemort, are there already. As to the rest of the troop—"

"As to the rest of the troop," interrupted Yvonnet, "they are sure to follow us there, as, from what I heard M. l'Amiral say, he will be there himself in two or three days."

"Well," said the gentleman, "at Saint-Quentin, my braves!"

"At Saint-Quentin, monsieur."

The latter made a slight motion of the head and retired.

Yvonnet followed him with his eyes until he was lost in the crowd; then, calling a vagabond who attended to the wants of the associates, and received therefor his temporal and spiritual nourishment, he threw him the reins of his horse.

The first intention of Yvonnet had been to approach Pilletrousse, and make him a confidant of his reminiscences in connection with the unknown; but, doubtless considering him of too material an organization for the reception of a secret of such importance, he drove back the words which were already on the tip of his tongue, and appeared to be giving his attention wholly to the work Franz and Heinrich were accomplishing.

Heinrich and Franz, after having, as we have said, with the help of the carriage-pole, which they had passed between the four legs, brought their recalcitrant ox up to the middle of the camp even, had deposited him in front of their tent.

Then Heinrich entered the tent to fetch his mace, which he had some difficulty in finding, Fracasso, seized with a fit of poetic inspiration, having thrown himself on a mattress, in order to dream at his ease, and having made of this mace a pillow to support his head.

This mace, simple in form and humble in material, was merely a ball twelve pounds in weight fitted to an iron bar; it was, with a gigantic two-handed sword, the usual weapon of the two Scharfensteins.

Heinrich at last found it, and, in spite of the groans of

Fracasso, whom he came on in the full fire of composition, he dragged it from under his head, and returned to join Franz, who was waiting for him.

Hardly had Franz untied the forelegs of the ox, when the animal made a sudden effort and half rose. This was Heinrich's opportunity; he raised the iron mace until, bending backward, it touched his loins, and, with all his strength, struck it between the two horns of the ox.

The animal, which had begun to bellow, stopped, and fell as if thunderstruck.

Pilletrousse, who, with flaming eyes and like a dog in leash, was only awaiting the moment, rushed upon the prostrate animal and opened the artery of the neck. After which, he clove him from the lower lip to the opposite extremity, and proceeded to cut him up.

Pilletrousse was the butcher of the association; Heinrich and Franz, the purveyors, bought and killed the animal, whatever it might be. Pilletrousse flayed it, divided it, and laid apart the best pieces for the association; in a sort of stall at some distance from the common tent, adorned with all the art of which he was a master, the different pieces of which he wished to get rid. Now, Pilletrousse was so adroit a carver, and so clever a merchant, that it rarely happened but, during the two or three days of the sale, he drew from this part of the animal a few crowns more than it cost.

All this was to the profit of the association, which, as may be seen, could not fare badly as long as it was seconded by each of its members as it was by such of its members as we have passed in review.

The cutting up was over, and the public sale was commencing, when a cavalier made his appearance in the midst of the crowd which thronged around the stall of Maitre Pilletrousse, and which was buying—each according to his means—everything from the fillet to the tripes.

This cavalier was Théligny, who, having been furnished with letters from the admiral for the mayor, the governor

of the city, and Jean Pauquet, syndic of the weavers, was
come in search of his squire Yvonnet.

He also brought news that as soon as M. de Coligny had
assembled the troops expected by him, and had spoken with
his uncle, M. le Connétable, he would set out with five or
six hundred men for Saint-Quentin.

Maldent, Procope, Fracasso, Pilletrousse, and the two
Scharfensteins would form part of the garrison, and would
join Malemort and Lactance in the city, who were there
already, and Yvonnet, who, as he would start with M. de
Théligny, would be there in two or three hours.

The adieus were short, Fracasso not having yet finished
his sonnet, and seeking a rhyme for the verb *perdre*, which
he could not find; the two Scharfensteins, while very fond
of Yvonnet, being of a very undemonstrative nature; and,
in fine, Pilletrousse contenting himself with saying to the
young man, with a grasp of the hand, so busy was he with
his sale—

"Try to keep the horse!"

VI

SAINT-QUENTIN

AS YVONNET had said to M. le Connétable, it is six
leagues from La Fère to Saint-Quentin.

The horses had already made a long journey the
night before, and that without any other halt than an hour
spent at Noyon.

They had now had a rest of two hours, it is true; still,
as there was no occasion to hurry, except the desire of
Yvonnet to see Gudule again, they spent nearly three hours
in making the six leagues that separated them from the
term of their ride.

At last, after clearing the exterior boulevard, after leaving on the right the Guise highway, which bifurcates a

hundred yards from the old wall, after making themselves known at the gate and plunging under the vault beneath the rampart, the two cavaliers found themselves in the Faubourg d'Isle.

"Monsieur, will you be kind enough to give me leave for ten minutes," asked Yvonnet, "or would you like, by turning aside a few steps, to get some news of what is passing in the city?"

"Ah, ah!" laughed Théligny, "it would appear we are in the neighborhood of Mademoiselle Gudule's dwelling?"

"You are right, monsieur," said Yvonnet.

"Is there any indiscretion in—?" asked Théligny.

"Not the least in the world," answered Yvonnet. "In the daytime, I am a mere acquaintance of Mademoiselle Gudule, exchanging a word and a salute with her. It has always been my principle not to do anything to injure the future prospects of fair young girls."

And turning to the right, he advanced into a little lane, bordered on one side by a long garden wall, and on the other by several houses, one of which was pierced by a window entirely framed in creeping plants.

Rising on his spurs, Yvonnet reached exactly to the window, beneath which stood a pillar, calculated to give pedestrians the same advantage, for love or business, which Yvonnet derived from being on horseback.

The moment he arrived, the window was opened as if by magic, and a charming face, all rosy with delight, appeared in the midst of the flowers.

"Ah, it is you, Gudule!" said Yvonnet; "how did you guess my arrival?"

"I did not guess it; I was at my other window that looks upon the road to La Fère. I saw two horsemen in the distance, and although it never occurred to me that you might be one of them, I could not keep my eyes off these travellers. When you came to a certain point I recognized you. Then I ran here, all trembling with fear, for I dreaded you might pass without stopping—first, because you were not alone, and next, because you are so handsome I feared you might have reached such fortune that you would think of me no longer."

"The person I have the honor to accompany, my dear Gudule, and who has given me permission to converse with you a moment, is M. de Théligny, my lieutenant; he will soon have some questions to put to you, as well as I, on the state of the city."

Gudule cast a timid glance upon the lieutenant, who made a gentle inclination to her, to which the young girl replied by a "God preserve you, monseigneur!" uttered with much emotion.

"As to the costume in which you see me, Gudule," continued Yvonnet, "it is the result of the king's liberality, who has even, on learning that I had the happiness to know you, deigned to charge me to present you, in his name, with this fine gold cross."

And, at the same time, he drew the cross from his pocket, and offered it to Gudule, who, hesitating to accept it, cried—

"What are you talking about, Yvonnet? and why do you make sport of a poor girl?"

"I do not make sport of you in any way, Gudule, and here is my lieutenant, who will tell you that what I affirm is the truth."

"In fact," said Théligny, "I was present, my fair child, when the king charged Yvonnet to make this present."

"You are acquainted with the king, then?" asked Gudule, quite astounded.

"Since yesterday, and since yesterday the king is acquainted with you, Gudule, as well as with your worthy uncle, Jean Pauquet, for whom my lieutenant has a letter from M. l'Amiral."

The lieutenant made a further sign of assent; and Gudule, who, as we have said, at first hesitated, now passed her trembling hand through the flowers—a hand which Yvonnet kissed as he placed the cross in it.

Théligny, approaching, then said—

"And now, my dear M. Yvonnet, will you please ask Gudule where her uncle is, and in what disposition we are likely to find him?"

"My uncle is at the Town Hall, monseigneur," said Gudule, who could hardly keep her eyes away from the cross, "and I think well disposed to defend the city."

"Thanks, my fair child. Come away, Yvonnet."

Gudule made a little sign of entreaty, and blushing up to the whites of her eyes—

"Then, monseigneur," said she, "if my father asks me where this cross came from—"

"You may tell him it comes from his Majesty," returned the young officer, smiling, who understood the alarm of Gudule; "that it has been given by the king in recognition of the good services which your uncle Jean and your father Guillaume have rendered him and are still likely to render him. In fine, if you do not wish—as is very possible—to name M. Yvonnet, you will add that it is I, Théligny, lieutenant in the company of the dauphin, who have brought you this cross."

"Oh, thanks, thanks!" all joyous, and clapping her hands together; "but for this, I would never dare to wear it."

Then in quick low tones to Yvonnet—

"When shall I see you again?" she asked.

"When I was three or four leagues from you, Gudule, you saw me every night," replied Yvonnet; "judge how often you must see me when I am living in the same city."

"Hush!" said Gudule.

Then lower still—

"Come early," she said; "I think my father will pass the whole night at the Town Hall."

She withdrew her head, and disappeared behind the curtain of verdure and flowers.

The young men followed the causeway between the Somme and the fountain La Ferrée. Half-way on the route, they turned from the abbey and church of Saint-Quentin-en-Isle, and crossed the first bridge, which led to the chapel in which the relics of the holy martyr were to be discovered, then a second bridge, which brought them to the strait of Saint-Pierre, and at last a third bridge which, after it was cleared, placed them in front of the two towers flanking the gate of Isle.

The gate was guarded by a soldier of Théligny's regiment and by a bourgeois of the city.

This time Théligny had no trouble in getting himself recognized; it was the soldier who came to him to ask him for news. People were saying that the enemy was very near; and this little company of a hundred and fifty men found itself somewhat isolated in the midst of all these bourgeois who were running right and left, frightened out of their wits, and who were losing their time in discussions at the meetings in the Town Hall—meetings at which there was indeed much discussion, but very little action.

Besides this, Saint-Quentin seemed to be a prey to frightful disorder. The principal artery—which cuts the city for two-thirds of its length, and into which, like the affluents of a great river, ran, on the right, the Rue Wager, the Rue des Cordeliers, the Rue d'Issenghien, the Rue des Ligniers, and on the left, the Rue des Corbeaux, the Rue de la Truie-qui-file and the Rue des Brebis—was thronged with people; and this multitude, become denser still on the Rue de la Sellerie, was packed so close on the great square that, as far as our cavaliers were concerned, it was like a wall almost impossible to break through.

Still, when Yvonnet placed his cap on the end of his sword, and standing in his stirrups, shouted, "Make way! make way for the people of M. l'Amiral!" the crowd, hoping they were coming to announce a reinforcement, made such violent efforts to open a path that at last the two cavaliers were able to start from the church of Saint-Jacques and reach the steps of the Town Hall, at the top of which was the mayor, Messire Varlet de Gibercourt.

THE PAGE OF THE DUKE OF SAVOY 269

They had arrived at an opportune moment. A meeting had just been held; and, thanks to the patriotism of the inhabitants, roused to fury by the eloquence of Maitre Jean Pauquet and his brother Guillaume, it had been unanimously resolved that the city of Saint-Quentin, faithful to its king and relying on its holy patron, would defend itself to the last extremity.

The news brought by Théligny, that the admiral was approaching with a reinforcement, raised the enthusiasm to the very highest pitch.

The citizens, at the very moment and without leaving the spot, organized themselves into companies which named their own leaders. Each company contained fifty men.

The mayor opened the arsenal of the Town Hall; unfortunately it was very poorly furnished. Only fifteen cannon were found in it, some in a very bad condition, and fifteen ordinary arquebuses and twenty-one arquebuses *à croc*; but there was quite an abundance of halberds and pikes.

Jean Pauquet was named captain of one of those companies, and Guillaume, his brother, lieutenant in another. So we see that honors were raining on this family, but these honors were dangerous.

The sum total of the troops consisted then of a hundred and twenty or a hundred and thirty men of the Dauphin's Company, commanded by Théligny; a hundred men or thereabout, of the company of M. de Breuil, governor of Saint-Quentin, which arrived eight days ago from Abbeville, and two hundred bourgeois organized into four companies of fifty men each. Three of these companies were composed of arbalétriers, pikemen, and halberdiers; the fourth was armed with arquebuses.

Suddenly a fifth was seen to appear, which was not expected, and, because of its unexpected appearance and the elements forming it, created boundless enthusiasm.

It arrived by the Rue Croix-Belle-Porte, and consisted of a hundred Jacobin monks, all carrying pikes or halberds.

A man, covered with a robe, under which might be seen a coat of mail, led them, with a naked sword in his hand.

Hearing the shouts raised as they passed, Yvonnet turned round, and, looking attentively at their captain, "May the devil burn me," he said, "if it is not Lactance!"

In fact, it was Lactance. Foreseeing that a tough struggle was in prospect, he had retired among the Jacobins of the Rue des Rosiers, in order to do penance, and put himself, as far as possible, in a state of grace. The good fathers received him with open arms, and Lactance, although wholly devoted to the task of confessing and communicating, still remarked their patriotism, and thought it would not be a bad thing to utilize it. As a result of his cogitations, he imparted to them, as an inspiration from heaven, the idea that came to him of forming them into a military company; the proposal was favorably received. The prior consented to take an hour from Matins, and half an hour from Vespers, and devote the time to drilling; and, at the end of three days, Lactance, judging the monks sufficiently practiced in military manœuvres, had drawn them from the convent, and, as we have said, had led them to the square of the Town Hall, amid the acclamations of the multitude.

Saint-Quentin could therefore reckon, for the moment, on a hundred and twenty men of the Dauphin's Company, on a hundred men of the company of the governor of the city, on two hundred bourgeois, and a hundred Jacobin monks—in all, five hundred and twenty combatants.

Hardly had the mayor, governor, and the other magistrates of the city inspected their forces, when loud cries rose from the ramparts, and people were seen arriving along the Rue de l'Orfèverie and the Rue Saint-André, who were lifting their arms to heaven in a despairing fashion.

After numberless inquiries and questions, it was learned that an immense number of peasants had been seen running along the plain which stretches from Homblières to Mesnil-Saint-Laurent, pushing through the harvest fields, and exhibiting, as far as could be judged at the distance they were still from the city, undoubted evidences of terror.

That very moment the gates were ordered to be closed, and the ramparts manned.

Lactance, who, in the thick of dangers, always preserved the coolness of a true Christian, immediately ordered his Jacobins to harness themselves to the cannon, and plant eight of them on the wall extending from the gate of lsle to the tower of Dameuse, two on the wall of the Vieux-Marché, three on the wall between the Grosse Tour and the postern of the Petit Pont, and two on the old wall at the Faubourg d'Isle.

Théligny and Yvonnet, who were on horseback, and who felt that, in spite of their terrible ride of the evening before, their steeds were still sound in wind and limb, issued forth through the Rémicourt gate, forded the river, and dashed across the plain to learn what was the cause of the flight of all these people.

The first individual they met was supporting his nose and a part of his cheek with his right hand, trying, as well as he could, to keep these two precious objects in their place, and, at the same time, making eager signs with his right to Yvonnet.

Yvonnet rode toward him, and recognized Malemort.

"Ah!" howled the latter, with all the strength of his lungs, "to arms! to arms!"

Yvonnet redoubled his pace, and, seeing his comrade streaming with blood, he jumped to the ground, and examined his wound.

It would have been terrible from the ravages it would have made on a virgin countenance; but the face of Malemort had been so terribly carved already that a gash more or less did not count.

Yvonnet made four folds of his handkerchief, with a hole in the centre to give passage to the nose of Malemort; then, having laid the patient on the ground and placed the wounded head on his knee, he bandaged the face so lightly and so adroitly that the ablest surgeon could not have done better.

During this time Théligny was picking up information. This is what had happened:

In the morning the enemy appeared in sight of Origny-Sainte-Benoite. Malemort, who happened to be there, having, with his usual instinct, scented that there would be a good many blows struck in that quarter, had excited the inhabitants to resistance. They had consequently retired into the castle with all the arms and war supplies they could gather. There they held out for nearly four hours. But the castle, being attacked by the whole van of the Spanish army, was carried by assault. Malemort did wonders; however, it became at last necessary to retreat. Pressed too closely by three or four Spaniards, he stabbed one, knocked down another; but while he was attacking the third, the fourth struck at his face sidewise, making an awful gash a little below the eyes. Malemort, understanding how impossible it was to defend himself with a wound that blinded him, gave a loud cry, and fell backward, as if he had been suddenly killed. The Spaniards searched him, and took three or four sous parisis, which he happened to have about him, and went back to their companions, who were engaged in a more profitable kind of plundering. Thereupon Malemort rose, set back his nose and cheek in their natural places, did his best to keep them there with his hand, and directed his course to the city to give the alarm.

And this was why Malemort, ordinarily the first to attack and the last to retreat, found himself this time, contrary to all his habits, at the head of the fugitives.

Théligny and Yvonnet had learned all they wanted to learn. Yvonnet took Malemort up behind him, and all three entered the city, crying, "To arms!"

The entire city was awaiting their return. In an instant it was known that the enemy was only four or five leagues distant; but such was the resolution of the inhabitants that this news, so far from depressing, stimulated them.

Luckily, among the men brought by M. de Breuil were found fifty gunners; to them were assigned the fifteen cannon drawn by the Jacobin brothers to the ramparts. Three attendants were required for each; the monks offered to complete the batteries, and were accepted. After an hour's practice, a spectator would have fancied they had never done anything else in their lives.

It was time, for at the end of an hour the first Spanish columns came in sight.

The Town Council resolved to send a courier to the admiral to warn him of the situation; but no one wished to leave the city at the moment of danger.

Yvonnet proposed Malemort.

Malemort uttered loud cries: since his wound was attended to, he felt, he said, much livelier than ever before; it was fifteen months since he had a real good fight. The blood was choking him, and the little he had lost was a great relief to him.

But Yvonnet observed to him that he would have a horse; that he would be allowed to keep this horse; that in two or three days he would return in the suite of Coligny, and that, thanks to this horse, he would be able, during the sorties that would take place, to advance further than if he was on foot.

This last consideration decided Malemort.

We may add that, in addition to this, Yvonnet had that influence over Malemort which weak, nervous natures always have over powerful ones.

Malemort mounted horse, and galloped in the direction of La Fère.

Those who remained behind might be tranquil; at the gait the adventurer rode at, the admiral would be warned in less than an hour and a half.

Meanwhile, the gates were thrown open to receive the poor inhabitants of Origny-Sainte-Benoite, and all in the city were eager in their offers of hospitality. Then persons were sent into all the surrounding villages—Harly, Rémicourt, La Chapelle, Rocourt, and Abbiette—to requisition all the flour and grain that could be found in them.

The enemy advanced on an immense line, and on a depth that led the garrison to fancy it would have to deal with the entire Spanish, German and Walloon army; that is to say, with fifty or sixty thousand men.

Just as when the lava descends from the crater of Etna or Vesuvius, the houses crumble, and the trees are on fire before the torrent of flame reaches them, so, in front of all this black line which was advancing, houses might be seen disappearing in a blaze, and villages in a state of conflagration.

The entire population gazed on this spectacle from the height of the rampart of Rémicourt, from the galleries of the collegial church, which commands the city, from the summit of the tower of Saint-Jean, from the Red Tower, and the tower of L'Eau; and at every fresh blaze a concert of curses arose, and seemed, like to a cloud of ill-omened birds, to take flight and settle down upon the enemy.

But the enemy was advancing for all that, chasing away the people before them, as the wind was chasing the smoke of the conflagrations. During some time the gates of the city continued to receive the fugitives; but they were soon obliged to shut them, the enemy being so near.

And then the poor peasants belonging to the burning villages might be seen trying to pass by the city, to find a refuge at Vermand, Pontru and Caulaincourt.

Soon the drums beat again.

It was a signal for all non-combatants to quit the ramparts and the towers.

At last none remained along the entire line but the combatants, silent and taciturn, as men always are when gathered together to meet a danger.

The vanguard could now be perfectly distinguished. It was composed of pistoliers, who, having crossed the Somme between Rouvroy and Harly, spread swiftly over all the circumference of the city, occupying the approaches to the gates of Rémicourt, Saint-Jean and Ponthoille.

Behind the pistoliers, three or four thousand men, who might be recognized from the regularity of their march as belonging to those old Spanish bands reputed to be the best troops in the world, passed the Somme in their turn, and marched in the direction of the Faubourg d'Isle.

"I have every reason to believe, my dear Yvonnet," said Théligny, "that the music will begin on the side of the house of your charmer. If you like to see how the tune is played, come with me."

"Very willingly, lieutenant," said Yvonnet, who felt those nervous shudders passing through his body which, in his case, was always the sign of an approaching battle.

And, with lips closely pressed and cheeks slightly pale, he proceeded toward the gate of Isle, where Théligny was leading nearly the half of his men, leaving the rest to support the citizens and, at need, show them an example.

We shall see later on that it was the citizens who showed the soldiers the example, instead of receiving it from them.

They arrived at the Faubourg d'Isle. Yvonnet got a hundred steps in front, and had time to tap at the window of Gudule, who ran up all in a tremble, and to advise the young girl to descend into the lower apartments, seeing that it was not unlikely the balls would play at shuttlecock with the chimneys of the houses. He had not finished, when, as if to support his words, a ball passed swiftly with a hiss, and overturned a gable whose pieces fell like a shower of aerolites around the young man.

Yvonnet leaped from the street on the post in front of the house, clung with both hands to the sill of the window, and, seeking amid the flowers for the trembling lips of the young girl, imprinted a very tender kiss on them, and then fell back into the street.

"Should any misfortune happen to me, do not forget me too quick," said he; "and if you forget me, don't let it be for a Spaniard or a German or an Englishman!"

And, without waiting for the assurance the young girl was about to give that she would love him always, he took his way to the old wall and found himself behind the parapet, a few steps from the spot he was accustomed to scale during his nocturnal rambles.

As had been foreseen by Théligny, who did not, in fact, arrive on the scene of battle until after his squire, it was there the music was beginning.

The music was noisy, and made the heads that heard it bend more than once; but gradually the bourgeois, who had at first supplied food for laughter to the soldiers, grew accustomed to it, and then became more furious than the others.

However, the Spaniards came on in such increasing numbers that the bourgeois were forced to abandon the exterior boulevard, which they had at first attempted to defend, but which, without a parapet, and commanded by the neighboring heights, soon became no longer tenable. Protected by the two pieces of cannon, and by the arquebusiers of the old wall, they accomplished their retreat in good order, leaving three killed, but carrying off their wounded.

Yvonnet was dragging along a Spaniard, through whose body he had passed his sword, and whose arquebuse he had taken; but as he had not had leisure to take, at the same time, the cartridges hanging from the baldrick of the dead man, he was drawing him aside, hoping that his trouble would not be lost, and that the pockets might be as well furnished as the baldrick.

This confidence was rewarded: besides their three months' pay, distributed to the Spaniards the evening before to give them courage, each of them had appropriated a fair share of plunder during the five or six days they held the country. We cannot say whether Yvonnet's Spaniard had appropriated more or less than the others; but, after visiting his pockets, Yvonnet appeared very well satisfied with what he found there.

Behind the soldiers of Théligny and the bourgeois of the

city, the two Spanish leaders, named Julian Romeron and Carondelet, took possession of the exterior boulevard, as well as of all the houses lining the causeway of Guise and of La Fère. These formed what was called the Haut Faubourg; but when they tried to clear the space between the exterior boulevard and the old wall, they were received with such a well-directed fire that they had to regain the houses, from the windows of which they continued firing until the darkness of night put an end to the encounter.

It was only then that Yvonnet judged it proper to turn round his head. Then, ten paces in his rear, he saw the pale face of a charming young girl, who, under the pretence of making sure that her father was there, had, in spite of the prohibition, encroached on the ground of the combatants.

His eyes glanced from the young girl to his lieutenant.

"My dear M. Yvonnet," said the latter, "you have been fighting or riding now two days; you must be tired. Leave to others, then, the task of watching on the ramparts, and try to get a good, pleasant rest until to-morrow. You will find me where there is firing."

Yvonnet did not need to be told twice. He saluted his lieutenant, gave a meaning glance at Gudule, and then started for the causeway, as if intending to go into the city.

But, mistaking his way, doubtless on account of the darkness, he strayed into the suburbs; for, ten minutes later, he was in that little lane, in front of that little window, and with one foot on that post from the top of which so many things could be done.

What Yvonnet did was to cling to two little white hands, which had quickly passed through that little window, and drew him so skilfully and adroitly inside that it was easy to see it was not the first time they were employed in this exercise.

The things we have just related occurred on the 2d of August, 1557.

VII

THE ADMIRAL KEEPS HIS WORD

AS MIGHT easily be foreseen, Malemort made quickly the six leagues that separated Saint-Quentin from the camp of La Fère.

Before an hour and a half had elapsed, he was at the door of M. l'Amiral.

Although any one who witnessed the arrival of this man, after such a headlong gallop, his clothes covered with blood, his face with bandages, would have found it impossible to recognize Malemort under a mask that concealed everything but the eyes and mouth, yet it was easy to recognize in him a messenger of bad news.

He was, therefore, on the very instant introduced to Coligny.

The admiral was with his uncle; the constable had just arrived.

Malemort related the capture of Origny-Sainte-Benoite, the massacre of those who tried to defend the castle, the burning of all the villages on the line of march of the Spanish army, whose passage left a track of fire and smoke behind it.

On the instant the uncle and nephew arranged their two courses of action.

Coligny, with five or six hundred men, would set out at once for Saint-Quentin, would shut himself up in the city, and hold out to the last extremity.

The constable, with the rest of the soldiers in the camp, would join the army of the Duc de Nevers, whose force amounted to only eight or nine thousand men, and who was too weak, consequently, to attack the Spanish army, amounting to more than fifty thousand, but would watch and harass it, and be always ready to profit by its mistakes.

This little troop manœuvred on the confines of the Lyonnais and the Thiérache.

The admiral immediately ordered the signal to saddle to be sounded, and the drums to beat the departure; but, in accordance with the advice of Maldent, he decided to take the road to Ham, instead of following the direct line. From all he had learned, he gathered that the Spaniards would attack Saint-Quentin by Rémicourt and the Faubourgs Saint-Jean and d'Isle.

Consequently, on these three sides Coligny would find an obstacle to his project.

The only road that, according to Maldent, would still have a chance of being free was that from Ham to Saint-Quentin, passing through marshes that were impracticable, except for those knowing the paths through them.

Coligny took with him three bands of foot-soldiers. These bands were commanded by Captains Saint-André, Rambouillet, and Louis Poy. But the third, which had arrived from Gascony that very day, was so exhausted that it had to stop on the road between Ham and La Fère.

Soon after the constable and the admiral left La Fère, they found sitting on his haunches, in the middle of the road, a huge black dog, which began howling with all his might. When they chased him, he ran before them about a hundred paces, sat down in the same fashion, and howled more horribly than ever. Chased again, he acted in a similar way, his howls becoming stronger and more desperate than before.

Then the constable, looking at M. de Coligny—

"What the devil do you think of this, nephew?" he asked.

"Faith, I think the music is in no way pleasant, monsieur, *and I believe we are likely to play the comedy.*"

"Yes, *and perhaps the tragedy as well,*" replied the constable.[1]

At this prediction both of them embraced, the admiral continuing his way to Ham, the constable returning to La Fère, which he left the same evening.

But another omen awaited the latter when he quitted the city.

He had scarcely gone a league on the road to Laon, when a kind of pilgrim, with a long beard and dressed in a long robe, seized the reins of his horse, crying—

"Montmorency! Montmorency! I announce to thee that in three days all thy glory shall be in the dust!"

"Be it so," said the constable; "but I announce to thee that before that thine shall be in the gutter!"

And he gave him so rough a blow with his fist that the poor prophet fell unconscious on the roadside, and had his jaw broken.[2]

The constable went on his way, as did the admiral, each carrying with him his fatal omen.

Coligny reached Ham about five in the evening. His resolution was not to stop any time until he reached Saint-Quentin. Therefore, after allowing his soldiers an hour's rest, he resumed his march with his gendarmes and two companies of infantry only.

At Ham, MM. de Jarnac and de Luzarches did all they could to retain him, pointing out the services he could do in the open country, and offering to go and shut themselves up there in his stead; but he answered—

"I would rather lose everything I possess than not bring to those brave people, who have shown such a good disposition to defend their city, the aid I promised them!"

And, as we have said, he set out, without a minute's delay, at the hour he had appointed.

At the gates of Ham he met the Abbot of Saint-Prix. He was a very noble prelate, named Jacques de la Motte;

---

[1] "Mémoires de Mergey," folio 250.   [2] "Mémoires de Melvil."

was at the same time canon of Saint-Quentin, Chartres, Paris, and Le Mans; he possessed, besides, two priories, and when he died, he had been canon under five kings, beginning with François I.

Coligny, suspecting that the illustrious traveller came from Saint-Quentin, went up to him; the warrior and the churchman recognized each other.

When the first shots were fired at the gate of Isle, the abbot quitted the city by the Faubourg de Ponthoille, and was going with all speed to inform the king of the position of Saint-Quentin, and ask for succor. So, as the admiral had foreseen, the last road left open was the one he followed.

"M. l'Abbé," said the admiral to the prelate, "since you are about to see the king, do me the favor to tell his Majesty that you have this night met me at the head of a good troop, and that I reckon, with God's help, to enter Saint-Quentin, where I hope to do him good service."

And, having saluted the abbot, he continued on his way.

A league further on he began to perceive the fugitives of Origny-Sainte-Benoite and other villages nearer Saint-Quentin, who, not finding a refuge in the city, had been forced to fly beyond it. The poor creatures were worn out with fatigue—some still limping along, still others lying at the foot of trees, and dying of hunger and exhaustion.

The admiral distributed some help among them, and then resumed his march.

Two leagues from Saint-Quentin, night overtook him; but Maldent was there. He answered for the safety of those who wished to follow him; and, hoping there would be a liberal reward at the end of the journey, he offered, as a proof of his good faith, to march in front of the admiral's horse with a rope about his neck.

The band of Captain Rambouillet agreed to take a path pointed out to it; but Captain Saint-André declared he had a good guide of his own, and asked to follow him.

No obstacle presented itself on the road to Saint-Quentin. The city had not been entirely invested; one of its sides, that of the Faubourg de Ponthoille, had been reserved for the English army, which was likely to arrive at any moment, and it was exactly this side that the admiral was approaching.

As a precaution, a view had been taken of the situation of the city and of its besiegers from the height of Savy, and it was perceived that the fires of the enemy extended only from the chapel of Epargnemaille to within some distance of Gaillard; it almost looked as if a path had been expressly opened for the little troop of the admiral.

This was the very point that troubled him; he was afraid of an ambuscade.

Procope, who, from his frequent conferences with Maldent, had become familiar with the Picard dialect, offered to reconnoitre.

The admiral accepted, and called a halt.

At the end of three-quarters of an hour the adventurer returned; the road was perfectly free, and he was able to approach so close to the rampart that he saw the sentinel who was patrolling between the gate of Ponthoille and the tower facing the Pré aux Oisons.

Then Procope whistled to the sentinel across the little rivulet which at that period ran along the foot of the wall; the sentinel stopped, and tried to penetrate the darkness.

Procope whistled a second time, and, sure that he had been seen, announced the approach of the admiral.

In this way the post at the gate of Ponthoille would be warned, and the admiral introduced into the city immediately on his arrival.

Coligny praised highly the intelligence of Procope, approved of all he had done, and now resumed his march with more confidence, guided still by Maldent.

At thirty yards from the gate a man rose from a fosse; he held a pistol in his hand, ready to be fired, if, instead of a friendly troop, the troop approaching was a hostile one.

Suddenly a long thick mass of shadow was noticed on the ramparts; it was a hundred men, who had been summoned to this point in case the news given by Procope to the sentinel might be a deception to conceal a surprise.

The man with the pistol, who had started up from the fosse, was Lieutenant Théligny.

He advanced, saying—

"France and Théligny!"

"France and Coligny!" replied the admiral.

The recognition was instantaneous; and the promised reinforcement having arrived, the gates were thrown open.

The admiral and his hundred and twenty men entered.

At the same moment the report of his arrival spread through the city; the inhabitants left their houses, half-clad, shouting with joy. Many wished to illuminate; some had already begun.

The admiral ordered the shouts to cease and the lights to be extinguished. He feared the enemy might be more on the alert on account of this, and redouble their watchfulness. Besides, Saint-André and his troop had not yet arrived.

At three o'clock in the morning there was no news of them yet.

Then, as it was near daybreak, and it was of the utmost importance that they should not fall in with any Spanish troops, Lactance advanced with six or eight of his Jacobins.

The good fathers, whom their habit protected from all suspicion, offered to scatter about the country for a radius of one or two leagues, and bring back the strayed company.

Their offer was accepted, and they set out, some by the gate of Ponthoille, others by the Sainte-Catherine postern.

Between four and five in the morning a troop of sixty men, led by two Jacobin fathers, made its appearance.

Then, toward six, a second troop of from fifty-five to sixty arrived, also led by a monk.

Captain Saint-André was with this second troop. The guide had gone astray, and led the others astray with him.

The rest of the fathers arrived, one after another; and

God, who protected them, permitted that for this time no misfortune should happen to any of them.

As soon as the last man had entered the city, Coligny ordered the roll-call.

It was found that, thanks to him, the garrison was reinforced by two hundred and fifty men. It was, numerically, a very weak relief; but the presence of its leader, by restoring courage to the most timid, had produced an immense moral effect.

Théligny, the mayor, and governor of the city, gave an exact account of what took place the evening before. Convinced more than ever that it was necessary to defend the Faubourg d'Isle to the last extremity, Coligny proceeded toward this point first. At the top of the old wall, in the midst of the balls that whistled around him, he decided that in the evening, at nightfall, a sortie should be made, with the object of burning the neighboring houses, from the interior of which the Spaniards were constantly harassing the soldiers guarding the ramparts. If they succeeded in this, and took from the besiegers the boulevard they had seized the evening before, a trench might then be dug in front of the old wall, in order to cover it by a mask, and save the curtains from the fire of the besiegers.[1]

Meanwhile, to concentrate on this point all the means of defence possible, Coligny ordered an embrasure to be opened at each flank of the rampart, on which two pieces of cannon were placed.

Then, these first urgent dispositions made, he thought it time to examine the quality and quantity of the enemies with whom he would have to deal.

It was easy enough, for that matter, to recognize by the banners over their tents to what nation belonged the soldiers and the princes commanding them.

From the place where he was—that is to say, from the

---

[1] See, on the siege of Saint-Quentin, the excellent work of M. Charles Gomart.

most advanced angle of the old wall—the admiral perceived three camps perfectly distinct, each placed on a hill.

The furthest was that of Count Schwartzburg. The intermediate one was that of Counts Egmont and Horn—those two inseparables, not to be separated even in death. The nearest camp was that of Emmanuel Philibert.

Facing the admiral were the Spanish troops, who had taken part in the fight of the evening before, commanded by Julian Romeron and Carondelet.

In fine, on his left extended the extreme point of the principal camp.

This camp, which covered nearly half a league of ground, and in which the Duke of Savoy pitched his tents later on, was almost entirely surrounded by the river Somme. This stream forms a semicircle from the place where it rises to where it passes between Saint-Quentin and the Faubourg d'Isle.

It stretched along an entire side of the wall, from the river to the Faubourg Saint-Jean.

In this camp were the quarters of Field-Marshal Benincourt, the Margrave of Berg, the Duke of Saimona, Count Schwartzburg, Count Mansfeld, Bernard de Mendoza, Ferdinand Gonzague, the Bishop of Arras, Count Feria, Count Rinago, Marshal Carcheris, Duke Ernest of Brunswick, Don Juan Manrique, Messire de Bossu, Messire de Berlaimont, Comte de Mègue, and Sieur Lazori de Schwendy—in fine, the quarters of the heavy cavalry and the halberdiers.

From Tour Saint-Jean to the big tower—that is to say, at the point diametrically opposite the Faubourg d'Isle—stretched the Flemish camp, where a battery stood from which the firing was so terrible that from that day to this the line occupied by that battery has been called Hell Street.

In fine, there remained that face of the city extending from Ponthoille to Tourival, which, as we have said, was completely unoccupied by the enemy so far, being the position reserved for the English army.

This sort of preparatory review having been gone

through, the admiral descended to the Town Hall. There he ordered that he should be given a list of all men fit to bear arms; that search be made for all the arms that might still be in the city; that the names of all the workmen and workwomen be taken down who could be employed at the earthworks; that a perquisition should be made with the view of gathering together all the tools, spades, shovels, baskets, pickaxes, and such like; that an account should be drawn up of all grain, flour, wines, cattle, provisions of every sort contained in the public magazines as well as in private houses, for the purpose of establishing some order in the consumption and avoiding pillage. In fine, he demanded an exact account, not only of the artillery, but also of the quantity of powder and balls, as well as the number of men serving the cannon.

During the tour he had just made the admiral had seen only two mills: a windmill situated at the end of the Rue du Billon, near the Red Tower, and a water-mill on the Somme, at the foot of the Faubourg d'Isle. These two mills were not enough for grinding the corn necessary for the consumption of a city of twenty thousand inhabitants.

He expressed his fears on this point. But the aldermen at once reassured him, declaring there were fifteen or sixteen hand-mills in the city which could be worked by horses, and which, if kept going constantly, would suffice for the nourishment of the city and garrison.

Then Coligny saw to the billeting of the soldiers, adopting the division of the city into four quarters, but subdividing those quarters into sixteen parts, for the surveillance of which he appointed sixteen citizens and sixteen officers, all whose decisions were to be in concert. The troops were assigned to the guard of the walls, conjointly with the bourgeois militia, each body having to protect its respective quarter. The Town Council was to sit permanently, in order to be able to answer without delay to all the requisitions addressed to it.

In fine, the admiral presented to the corporation the gentlemen forming what to-day we should call his staff, who were to act as intermediaries between him and the magistrates.

In addition to these officers Captain Languetot was named superintendent of artillery, having at his disposal ten men-at-arms to whom was assigned the mission of verifying the quantity of powder employed by the cannoneers each day, and who were particularly charged to watch that this precious powder should be sheltered from all danger.

While going along the ramparts, Coligny remarked, near the gate Saint-Jean, at hardly a hundred paces from the wall, a large number of gardens filled with fruit-trees and surrounded by lofty and dense hedges. These trees and hedges offered to the enemy a cover that allowed him to approach the ramparts.

As these gardens belonged to the chief persons of the city, the admiral asked the council's consent to clear them: this consent was given without any difficulty; and all the carpenters of the city were at once set to work cutting down the hedges and fruit-trees. Their branches were destined for fascines.

Then, seeing the assembly of the same mind and same spirit, nobles, bourgeois, and soldiers animated, if not with the same enthusiasm, at least with the same energy, Coligny retired to the house of the governor, where he had appointed a meeting of the officers of all the companies.

This house was situated in the Rue de la Monnaie, between the Templerie and the Jacobins.

The officers were informed of what had just been done. The admiral spoke of the good spirit of the inhabitants, and their resolution to defend themselves to the last extremity; he urged them, by softening, as much as possible, the hardships of the situation, to maintain cordial union between those two powers so rarely in accord—the army and the bourgeoisie.

Each captain had, besides, to furnish, on the spot, a

statement of the condition of his company, in order that the admiral might know exactly the number of men he could dispose of, and figure up how many military mouths had to be fed.

Then, going up with an engineer to the gallery of the Collegiate, he pointed out, from that elevated point, where a view of the entire circumvallation of the city could be embraced, the excavations that had to be filled up and the elevations that had to be levelled down.

These orders having been given, and being alone with the officer whom he intended sending to the constable to obtain a reinforcement of troops, while it was still possible to revictual the place, he decided that the Savy road, all covered with vines and debouching through a chain of little hills, was the most favorite route for such troops as might try to enter the city.

Captain Saint-André had, in fact, entered from this quarter in full daylight, and without being seen.

Then, these orders being given, and these dispositions arranged, Coligny at last remembered that he was a man, and returned to snatch a few hours' repose.

VIII

THE TENT OF THE ADVENTURERS

WHILE all these measures for the public safety were being taken by Coligny, on whom rested the entire responsibility of the defence of the city, and while the admiral, a little reassured, as we have said, by the ardor of the soldiers and the courage of the citizens, had retired to the governor's palace to take a little repose, our adventurers, ready, also, to fight for the city—because Coligny had taken them into his pay, after certain reservations had been made by Procope—our adventurers, taking everything carelessly, waiting for the first signal of the trumpet and the drum, had pitched their tent a hundred paces from the gate of Isle, and established their domicile on a vacant piece of ground extending, in front of the Cordeliers, from the extremity of the Ruè Wager to the talus of the wall.

As a result of the entrance of Coligny into Saint-Quentin they were all united again. They were settling accounts.

Yvonnet, standing, had just faithfully poured into the common treasury the half of the sum he owed to the liberality of King Henri II.; Procope, half the fees he had received as notary; Maldent, half of the wages he earned as guide; Malemort, half of the gratuity given him for going to warn Coligny, all wounded though he was, of the arrival of the Spaniards; Pilletrousse, in fine, half of the amount he had gained by selling what was left of the ox of the two Scharfensteins.

As to the latter, as there had been no fight, they had nothing to contribute to the pile, and were busy roasting the remains of the quarter of the ox left after the distribution of the other three-quarters by Pilletrousse, not at all concerning themselves about the future scarcity of provisions likely to result from the blockade.

Lactance brought two large sacks of wheat and a sack of beans, which he offered to the community instead of money; it was a present to our adventurers from the convent of the Jacobins, whose monks had, as we know, been organized into a regiment and had chosen Lactance as captain.

Fracasso was all absorbed in his search for a rhyme to *perdre*, which he did not find.

Under a kind of shed, hastily built, the two horses of Yvonnet and Malemort were munching their hay and enjoying their oats.

A portable mill was established under the shed, not to have it near the horses, but to have it under cover; the duty of turning it was intrusted to Heinrich and Franz.

The pecuniary affairs of the association were in a good condition; and forty golden crowns, carefully counted by

Procope, counted over again by Maldent, and arranged in a line in piles by Pilletrousse, were ready to enter the common chest.

Should the association continue equally prosperous for a whole year, it was the intention of Procope to purchase a notary's or an attorney's business in some village; Maldent's to purchase a little farm on the road to La Fère—a farm he knew of old, for he was, as we have said, from that country; Yvonnet's to marry some rich heiress, to whose hand his elegance and fortune would give him a double title; Pilletrousse's to found some great butchery either in Paris or in a provincial town; Fracasso's to have his poems printed after the manner of M. Ronsard and M. Jodelle; in fine, Malemort's to fight for his own hand, and this as long as he liked—a stipulation that would save him from being bothered by the warnings of his comrades and those into whose service he entered, that he was taking too little care of his personal safety.

As to the two Scharfensteins, having no idea, they had no project.

At the moment when Maldent was counting the last crown, and Pilletrousse was building up the last pile, a kind of shadow fell upon the adventurers, indicating that some opaque body had interposed between them and the light.

Instinctively Procope stretched forth his hands toward the gold; Maldent, quicker still, covered it with his cap.

Yvonnet turned round. The same young man who had tried to buy his horse in the camp of La Fère was standing at the entrance to the tent.

Quick as Maldent had been in covering the money with his cap, the unknown had seen it; and, with the prompt glance of a man to whom such reckonings are familiar, he had calculated that the sum they were so anxious to hide from his eyes amounted to some fifty crowns of gold.

"Ah, ah!" said he, "it would seem the harvest has not been bad! An unseasonable moment to propose doing a little business with you; you are sure to be hard as the devil, my masters!"

"That depends on the gravity of the business," said Procope.

"There are several kinds of business," said Maldent.

"Does this business lead to anything further than the benefit to be gained from the business itself?" asked Pilletrousse.

"If there are blows to be given, I'm your man," said Malemort.

"Provided it be not an expedition against any church or convent, it might be arranged," said Lactance.

"Particularly if it occur by moonlight," said Fracasso. "I am in favor of nocturnal expeditions; they alone are poetic and picturesque."

Yvonnet said nothing; he was gazing at the stranger.

The two Scharfensteins were entirely occupied in roasting their piece of beef.

All these observations, each of which painted the character of the speaker, issued almost simultaneously from the lips of the adventurers.

The young man smiled. He replied, at the same time, to all the questions, regarding, successively, the person to whom was addressed the fraction of his answer.

"Yes," he said, "the affair is grave; no graver could be imagined. And, although there are advantages to be gained outside the business itself, as there are a good share of blows to be given and taken, I reckon on offering you a reasonable sum, and one that must satisfy the most difficult. Moreover, religious minds need not be alarmed," he added; "there is no question of church or convent; and it is probable that, for greater security, we shall act by night; I must say, however, that I should prefer a dark night to a night lighted up by moon and stars."

"Well, well," said Procope, who usually took charge of the discussion of the interests of the society, "develop your proposal, and we shall see if it be acceptable."

"My proposal is," replied the young man, "to hire you for a nocturnal expedition, or a skirmish, or combat, or battle in open day."

"And what shall we have to do in this nocturnal expedition, or skirmish, or combat, or battle?"

"You will have to attack him whom I attack, to surround and strike him until he dies."

"And if he surrenders?"

"I warn you beforehand that he shall have no quarter from me."

"*Peste!*" said Procope; "it is war to the death, then?"

"To the death! you are right, my friend!"

"Good!" growled Malemort, rubbing his hands; "that's the way to talk!"

"But still," said Maldent, "if the ransom was good, it seems to me it would be better to hold to ransom than to kill."

"Consequently, I shall treat of the ransom and the death at the same time, in order that these two cases be provided for."

"That is to say," returned Procope, "that you buy the man, living or dead?"

"At the same price."

"Good!" said Maldent; "it seems to me, however, that a live man is worth more than a dead one."

"No, for I would buy the live man from you only to make him a dead one; that's all."

"Let us see," said Procope; "how much do you give?"

"A moment, Procope!" said Yvonnet; "it is right that M. Waldeck should tell us who the man is."

The young man made a bound backward.

"You have pronounced a name—" said he.

"Which is yours, monsieur," returned Yvonnet, while the adventurers looked at one another, beginning to suspect that it was to Yvonnet they should leave the care of their interests.

The young man scowled with his thick red eyebrows.

"And since when have you recognized me?" he asked.

"Do you wish me to tell you?" answered Yvonnet.

Waldeck hesitated.

"Do you remember the Chateau du Parcq?" continued the adventurer.

Waldeck turned pale.

"Do you remember the forest of Saint-Pol-sur-Ternoise?"

"It is just because I remember it that I am here, and making the proposal you are discussing."

"Then it is Duke Emmanuel Philibert that you are proposing to us to kill," said Yvonnet, quietly.

"*Peste!*" cried Procope, "the Duke of Savoy!"

"You see it was good to have an explanation," said Yvonnet, casting a side glance at his companions.

"And why should one not kill the Duke of Savoy?" exclaimed Malemort.

"I do not say that the Duke of Savoy may not be killed," retorted Procope.

"Nor I!" said Malemort; "the Duke of Savoy is our enemy, since we have taken service with the admiral, and I do not see why he should not be killed like another!"

Maldent made a sign of assent.

"It should cost dearer!" he said.

"Not to say that it would endanger our souls!" said Lactance.

"Bah!" said Waldeck, with his evil smile; "do you believe that, if he is not in hell for something else, Benvenuto Cellini has been damned for slaying the Connétable de Bourbon?"

"The Connétable de Bourbon was a rebel, *distinguo*," said Procope.

"And, moreover, as he was fighting against Pope Clement VII., it was a pious work to kill him," added Lactance.

"Oh! and of course your Duke of Savoy is such a friend of Pope Paul IV.!" returned Waldeck, shrugging his shoulders.

"Well, well, that is not the question at all," said Pilletrousse; "the question is the price."

"Good!" returned Waldeck; "that is called returning to the question. What do you say to five hundred gold crowns—a hundred as earnest-money, and four hundred when the thing is done?"

Procope shook his head. "I say that we are still far from the sum required."

"I am sorry," said Waldeck, "for, not to lose time, this is my last offer. I have five hundred gold crowns, and not a carolus more; if you refuse, I shall have to look elsewhere."

The adventurers sought one another's eyes; five out of the seven shook their heads. Malemort alone was of opinion that they should accept, because he saw there were blows to be given and taken. Fracasso had fallen back into his poetic reveries.

"For that matter," said Waldeck, "there's no hurry; you will reflect. I know you; you know me. We dwell in the same city; we can easily find each other again."

And, saluting the adventurers with a slight nod, he turned on his heel, and was gone.

"Ought we to call him back?" said Procope.

"Faith!" said Maldent, "five hundred crowns are not found under every hedge!"

"And then," said Yvonnet, "it is all he has; the loveliest girl in the world cannot give more than that."

"My brethren," said Lactance, "the lives of the princes of the earth are under the direct guardianship of Heaven; one risks one's soul by touching them. We must touch them, then, only for a sum that will allow each one of us to purchase the indulgences of which he shall have need, whether we succeed or no. The intention, my brethren— the worthy prior of the Jacobins told me so yesterday—the intention, my brethren, is taken for the deed."

"There is no doubt," said Procope, "that the deed itself would gain us more than the sum mentioned in the proposal. What if we did it on our own account, eh?"

"Yes," said Malemort; "let us do the job."

"Gentlemen," said Procope, "the idea is M. Waldeck's. To take from a man his idea, especially when he has confided it to us, would be robbery. You know my principles in matters of law."

"Well," said Yvonnet, "if the idea is his, and he has a property in it, I think it would be as well to accept the five hundred crowns."

"Yes; let us accept and have a fight!" cried Malemort.

"Oh, there's no hurry," said Maldent.

"And if he treats with others?" asked Yvonnet.

"Yes, if he treats with others?" repeated Procope.

"Let us accept and have a fight!" howled Malemort.

"Yes! yes! let us accept!" cried all, with one voice.

"Let us accept!" cried the two Scharfensteins, who entered at the moment, bearing on a plank their piece of roast beef, and, without knowing what it was all about, ranged themselves on the side of the majority, giving a fresh proof of good disposition.

"Then let some one run after him and call him back," said Procope.

"Let me!" said Malemort. And he rushed out.

But no sooner had he done so than he heard some shots in the direction of the Faubourg d'Isle, which suddenly increased to a lively fusillade.

"A fight! a fight!" cried Malemort, drawing his sword, and running toward the sound, which came from a point directly opposite to that made for by the bastard of Waldeck, who was going toward the tower of L'Eau.

"Oh, oh! there is fighting at the Faubourg d'Isle!" exclaimed Yvonnet; "I must see what has become of Gudule!"

"But the business?" cried Procope.

"Finish it as you like," said Yvonnet; "whatever you do will be well done—I give you my proxy."

He rushed after Malemort, who had already passed the first bridge, and had his foot on the island forming the strait of Saint-Pierre.

Let us follow, in our turn, Malemort and Yvonnet, in order to find out what was taking place at the Faubourg d'Isle.

IX

A FIGHT

IT WILL be recollected that, on entering the government palace, Coligny had given orders, toward the evening, for a sortie, having for object to burn the houses lining the exterior boulevard, under cover of which the Spaniards were able to fire on the defenders of the city, who, stationed on an interior plateau, had no shelter from it.

These orders had been given to MM. Théligny, Jarnac, and Luzarches.

Consequently, at six in the evening, the three officers collected a hundred men from their companies and a hundred and twenty citizens of good will, led by Guillaume and Jean Pauquet.

These two hundred and twenty men were to attack two thousand.

Hardly thirty paces from the old wall the road bifurcates, as we have already stated.

One of these branches leads to Guise, the other to La Fère.

The houses to be destroyed lay on each side of this road, and on each of its branches.

The little troop, once out of the city, had therefore to divide itself into two bands: one attacking on the right, the other on the left, and setting fire to the houses at the same time.

Guillaume and Jean Pauquet, who knew the localities, took charge of these two bands.

At half-past six the gate of the Faubourg d'Isle was opened, and the little troop marched out at double quick.

But secret as had been the gathering, quick as had been the sortie, the gathering had been signalled by the sentries, and the sortie anticipated by Carondelet and Julian Romeron.

The result was that at the opening of each street the French found a platoon of Spaniards double their number, and that from each window there was a hail of death upon them.

But still, such was the impetuosity of their shock that the platoons of Spaniards defending the two streets were broken, and, in spite of the fire from the windows, five or six houses were invaded.

No need of saying that Malemort, shouting, howling, cursing, and, above all, striking, had managed to make his way to the head of the two columns, and to be the first to enter one of the houses.

Once in the house, it is useless to say that Malemort forgot he was there to burn it; and, rushing up the staircase, he gained the upper story.

On the other hand, those who came with him forgot that he had entered before them, and, remembering only their orders, piled up fagots in the lower rooms, and especially at the foot of the staircase.

They then set fire to them.

The same happened to two or three houses lining the boulevard.

The Spaniards had at first supposed the attack to be an ordinary sortie; but they soon guessed the aim of the French from the clouds of smoke escaping from the ground-floors.

Then they united all their efforts, and, being ten times superior to the little troop, they repulsed it.

But the latter had at least been partially successful: flames were beginning to issue from the roofs of two or three houses.

It will be remembered that Yvonnet, not having been one of those selected for the sortie, had had the idea of utilizing his time by visiting Mademoiselle Gudule, whose terrors he calmed; these terrors were great, for, as we have said, the father and uncle of the young girl acted as guides on this occasion.

For a moment the cries, shouts, noise of the fusillade

were so loud that Yvonnet himself was anxious to learn what was passing, and crept into the garret, accompanied by the young girl, who followed him like his shadow, a little through fear, but much through love.

Then, through a dormer window, he could form some idea of what was going on.

The firing from the arquebuses never ceased; and, at the same time, the clash of steel against steel showed that there was a hand-to-hand conflict in the streets.

This was not all. As we have said, the smoke issued through the roofs of four or five houses, and in the midst of the smoke human beings were seen going and coming quite scared.

These were the Spaniards, surprised by the conflagration, and who, as the stairs were burning, could not descend from the upper stories of the houses.

It was easily seen that the Spaniards in the houses were in great fear; but, in one case, this fear rose to absolute dismay.

It was where Malemort was operating, who, paying no attention at all to the conflagration, was attacking, smiting, fighting, in the midst of the smoke.

At the moment Yvonnet put his nose out of the window the scene was passing on the first story.

Such of the Spaniards as preserved some coolness while defending this first story, having to wrestle at once with the flames and with a man who seemed to be a demon, at last jumped out of the window.

The others instinctively retreated to the second story.

Malemort did not trouble himself about those who leaped from the windows; but he pursued those who fled to the second story, howling his favorite cry, "A fight!"

During all this time the devouring element was doing its office, Malemort was pursuing the Spaniards, and the fire was pursuing Malemort.

Doubtless the adventurer owed his by no means usual invulnerability this time to the powerful ally marching behind him, to whom he evidently paid no attention.

Soon the smoke obscured the second story, as it had the first, and the fire darted its tongues of flame through the floor.

One or two Spaniards, braving the danger of the fall, jumped through the windows of the second story just as their comrades had jumped through those of the first. Others tried to escape by the roof.

Two men and the half of a third man succeeded in getting through a dormer window; we say *the half of a third man*, because the latter seemed to have been brought to a halt, and showed unmistakably by the expression of his countenance that things were happening to that part of his body remaining behind which were very disagreeable.

Malemort was, in fact, dealing that inactive portion of the human frame fearful blows with his sword.

The Spaniard, after making vain attempts to join his companions running along the roofs, fell back, and, in spite of a final effort to hang on to the sill of the window, disappeared at last entirely.

Five minutes after it was the face of Malemort that appeared at the dormer window, instead of that of the Spaniard. The new face was easily recognizable by its linen mask—a souvenir of the last battle of the owner, which appeared at the window instead of that of the Spaniard.

He saw his two enemies flying, and was setting out in pursuit.

Malemort might have been taken for a tiler or a rope-dancer, so steadily did he tread the narrow path.

If he had been a Mussulman his shadow would undoubtedly have crossed, without the aid of a balancing pole, that bridge of Mahomet's Paradise which leads from earth to heaven, and is not broader than the edge of a razor.

The two fugitives soon saw the danger that menaced them.

One of them came to a decision immediately: at the risk of breaking his legs, he slid down the slope of the roof, seized the border of the window, and slipped through into the room below.

This house, though placed between two fires, had so far escaped.

Malemort did not bother himself about the Spaniard who had so far succeeded in his perilous slide, and continued his pursuit of the one who remained.

From their observatory Yvonnet and Gudule followed the course of these aerial gymnastics—Yvonnet with all the interest such a spectacle would naturally produce in a man, Gudule with all the terror it must excite in a woman.

In this fashion the two acrobats, going from house to house, gained the last roof, which, like many of our old buildings, seemed to lean forward in order to admire itself in the river.

This house was of wood, and was burning on all sides.

Arrived at the extremity of the roof, and, seeing that he could not go further, except Saint-James, the patron of Spain, lent him wings, the fugitive, who doubtless did not know how to swim, turned back, resolved to sell his life dearly.

The struggle began; but at the moment it reached its highest degree of fury the roof cracked to give exit to the smoke first, and the flames afterward; then it tottered, then sank, burying both combatants in its frightful crater.

One of them disappeared entirely. The other hung on to a rafter that, though burning, was still solid, recovered his centre of gravity, made his way, all on fire, to the extremity of the rafter, and then, launching himself from the top of a second story, threw himself into the Somme.

Gudule uttered a loud cry; Yvonnet almost flung himself out of the window; for a moment both hardly breathed. Was the bold plunger engulfed forever, or was he going to reappear?

Then, the second question, was it the Spaniard, or was it Malemort?

Soon the surface of the water bubbled, and a head was seen to appear, then arms, then a torso, which swam, according to the flow of the water, evidently with the design of landing behind the old wall.

The moment the swimmer took this direction, it was pretty certain it was Malemort.

Yvonnet and Gudule descended rapidly, and ran to the point where the swimmer, in all probability, was going to land. And, in fact, they arrived just in time to drag out of the water, half burned, half drowned, the furious fighter, who, utterly exhausted, fainted in their arms, and brandished his sword, shouting, "Battle! battle!"

Bad as was Malemort's case, every one did not get off as well as he did.

Repulsed, as we have said, by the old Spanish band of Carondelet and Don Julian, the soldiers and bourgeois, after succeeding in burning two or three houses, not having been able to retreat in as orderly a manner as was desirable, were huddled together at the old wall in a manner that gave the Spaniards a chance of having their revenge.

Thirty soldiers and twenty townsmen remained on the square; and for a time it looked as if the Spaniards would enter pell-mell with those they were pursuing. Yvonnet heard the cries of the Spaniards, who were already howling, "The city is taken!" He ran to the tent of the adventurers, all the time shouting, "To arms!" and returned with a reinforcement of a hundred men—one part of whom scattered along the ramparts, while the other rushed upon the enemy, already under the vault.

But at the head of those who rushed to the aid of the faubourg were the two Scharfensteins, armed, the one with his club, the other with his two-handed sword. The blows fell upon the Spaniards thick as those of the flail upon the threshing-floor, and all had to recoil before the two giants.

Once the Spaniards were driven out of the vault, the question was to close the gates. Now, this was not a thing easily done, for the enemy opposed it with all their might— some holding the doors back with their hands, others with the butts of their muskets. But the two Scharfensteins managed to get between the combatants and the wall; and, stiffening themselves against it, they gradually, but irresistibly, succeeded in bringing the folds of the door together, and shot the bolts across them.

This task accomplished, they breathed noisily and in such perfect unison that it almost looked as if these two bodies had but a single pair of lungs.

But the two giants had hardly regained their normal condition, when a cry of terror resounded, "To the walls! to the walls!"

Two breaches had, in fact, been made in the wall, one on each side of the gate, with the object of transporting from that quarter the earth needed for constructing certain platforms for artillery; these breaches had been closed up with bales of wool, etc.

Now, when the besiegers were driven from the gate, they bethought themselves of the breaches, and hoped to carry the city by making a sudden dash on them.

The two Scharfensteins, on rushing out of the vault, had only to cast a glance round them to judge of the imminence of the peril. In spite of their usual custom of fighting together, a division of their strength was, in the circumstances, so urgent that, after exchanging a few words with their usual laconic sobriety, the uncle ran to the breach on the right, the nephew to the breach on the left.

The enemy, being supplied with those long pikes which, at the time, formed the regular weapon of the Spanish infantry, were mounting to the assault of both breaches, driving citizens and soldiers before that forest of steel.

Heinrich Scharfenstein, for the moment proprietor of the mace, saw that this short heavy weapon would be almost useless against the Spanish pikes ten feet long; he hung his mace to his belt, and, without ever slackening his course, picked up a huge block of stone lying on the rampart, and ran with this enormous mass to the breach, crying, "Look out!"

It was the breach at which Yvonnet was fighting.

The latter saw him, and divined his intention. With a sweep of his sword he kept back his comrades, and gave free course to the Spaniards who were mounting the breach; but, the moment they were half-way up on the wall, the German giant made his appearance on the top of the breach, raised above his head the block he had until now carried on his shoulder, and, combining all the impetus of his strength with the natural weight of the projectile, he launched it on the first ranks of the Spaniards with a violence that no catapult ever constructed could surpass.

The rock descended, bounding through the dense column, breaking, crushing, pulverizing everything it met on its way.

Then, through the road opened for him, Heinrich rushed with his terrible mace, and, striking right and left, soon made an end of those whom the gigantic block had spared or had only half reached.

In less than ten minutes this breach was cleared of the besiegers.

Franz had also wrought deeds equally marvellous.

He, too, had cried to the soldiers and citizens to look out, and at his voice their ranks had opened; then with his great two-handed sword he began to mow down that harvest of lances, with every stroke cutting off five or six pikeheads, as easily as Tarquin, in the garden of Gabiæ, hewed off the heads of the poppies in presence of his son's messenger. Then, when he had now before him men armed with sticks only, he flung himself into the Spanish ranks, and began mowing down men with the same fury he had until now shown in mowing down lances.

Consequently, the Spaniards were baffled at this point also.

But an unforeseen incident was very nearly making Franz lose all the fruit of the glorious succor he had just brought to the people of Saint-Quentin.

A man, more ardent even than himself after the human quarry, slipped under his arm, shouting, "Battle!" and rushed in pursuit of the Spaniards.

It was Malemort, who, after regaining consciousness, had swallowed a bottle of wine given him by Gudule, and at once returned to the charge.

Unfortunately, two or three of those he was pursuing, seeing that they were followed by only a single man, turned round, and although, as the heads of their pikes had been lopped off, their only weapons were a sort of stick, one of them with a blow of his stick knocked down and utterly stunned Malemort.

Citizens and soldiers uttered a cry of regret; they believed the brave adventurer dead. Luckily Franz had made certain observations on the thickness of his comrade's skull. He ran up to him, with one stroke of his formidable sword split the head of the Spaniard, who was about to finish Malemort with his dagger, took his companion by the foot, and hurried with him to the breach, where he flung him. Then Malemort began to open his eyes, murmuring, "Battle!" in the arms of Lactance, who ran up with his Jacobins.

Behind the monks came the admiral, at the head of a small band of select arquebusiers; these opened such a well-directed fire on the exterior boulevard and on such houses as still remained standing, that the Spaniards were forced to get under cover, and for some time kept very quiet.

The admiral then investigated the condition of affairs: the loss had been very great, and the Faubourg d'Isle escaped being carried by storm only by a very narrow chance. Many captains did their best to persuade the admiral to abandon this point, the defence of which had so far cost the garrison and the citizens combined a loss of over threescore men; but Coligny was firm: he was convinced that the prolongation of the siege, perhaps the safety of the city, depended on the occupation of this suburb.

He gave orders that every effort should be made during the approaching night to repair the two breaches and do whatever else could be done for the safety of the quarter.

The Jacobins, whose sombre monastic habits rendered

them less noticeable in the darkness, were assigned to this duty, which they performed with the impassive courage of monastic devotion.

As a nocturnal attack was feared, the arquebusiers watched on the rampart; while, to give the alarm, in case the enemy might think of turning the old wall, sentries were stationed at intervals of twenty yards along the entire line of the marshes of the Somme.

It was a terrible night for the city of Saint-Quentin, this night of the 3d and 4th of August—a night when it had to bewail the loss of its first dead!

So every one watched over his house and quarter with the same zeal with which the sentries watched over the Faubourg d'Isle.

The poor inhabitants of the faubourg, understanding that the hottest part of the attack and defence would be there, were quitting their houses, dragging after them in carts or hand-barrows their most valuable possessions. Among the emigrants who abandoned the faubourg for the city was Guillaume Pauquet, whose brother Jean offered him the hospitality of his house, situated at the angle made by the Rue du Vieux-Marché and the Rue des Arbalétriers.

His daughter Gudule, still stunned by the events of the day, entered the city, leaning on his arm; she turned her head from time to time, saying to herself it was from her sorrow at seeing abandoned to certain destruction the house in which she was born, but in reality to make sure that the handsome Yvonnet was not losing sight of her.

In fact, Yvonnet was following, at a reasonable distance, the bourgeois, his daughter, and the weavers whom Jean Pauquet had lent his brother to help him in transporting his furniture, and who were conscientiously acquitting themselves of their duty.

It was, then, a great consolation for poor Gudule to see the young man crossing Saint-Quentin through its entire length, bisecting the square of the Hotel de Ville, following the Rue Sainte-Marguerite, the Rue du Vieux-Marché, and, at the corner of the Rue aux Pourceaux, saw him enter her uncle's house, known by its sign of the *Navette couronnée*.

Under pretence of great fatigue—and the pretence was plausible after such a day—Gudule asked leave to retire at once to her room, and she was permitted to do so without further remark.

Gudule really began to believe that there was a special providence for lovers when she saw that the lodging intended by her uncle for her and her father was a kind of little pavilion, forming the angle of the garden, and opening on the road running along the rampart.

So as soon as she found herself alone in her new domicile, her first care was to extinguish the lamp, as if she had gone to bed, and open the window, in order to explore the neighborhood, and see what facility this window could offer to a nimble climber.

The facility was great: this portion of the rampart, which extended between the gate of the Vieux-Marché and the tower Dameuse, was certainly the most deserted in the city. A rope-ladder eight or ten feet high would perform for the pavilion of the Rue des Arbalétriers the same office performed by the post at the house in the Faubourg d'Isle.

It is true the partitions separating the room of Gudule from the room of Guillaume were very slight, and the slightest noise in her chamber would be likely to arouse paternal suspicion; but, the ladder of ropes once suitably fixed, what should hinder Gudule from descending on the rampart instead of Yvonnet mounting to her chamber?

By this arrangement either the lovers would have very bad luck, or the chamber, remaining solitary, would be necessarily noiseless and voiceless.

Gudule was plunged into all these strategetical combinations which for the moment, made of her a tactician almost as able as the admiral himself, when she saw a shadow glide along the garden wall.

Yvonnet was also engaged in a tour of explorations, and reconnoitring the new field of battle on which he was to manœuvre. It was not a siege difficult to make, was this of Maitre Pauquet's house, particularly for a man who, like our adventurer, had a spy in the place.

Consequently, everything was arranged for the following night without any difficulty.

Then, as the footsteps of Guillaume Pauquet were heard on the staircase, falling a little heavy on account of the fatigue of the day, Gudule closed her window, and Yvonnet disappeared through the Rue Saint-Jean.

X

M. DE THÉLIGNY

DAYBREAK found the admiral on the rampart. Far from being cast down by the check of the evening before, Gaspard de Coligny decided that a fresh attempt should be made.

In his opinion, the enemy was aware that the city had received a reinforcement, but was utterly ignorant of its extent. They must try to convince the Spaniards that this reinforcement was much larger than it was in reality.

Emmanuel Philibert might thus be led to undertake a regular siege, if he were forced to believe that the city could not be taken by a surprise; now a regular siege was a respite for ten days, for a fortnight, perhaps for a month, and during that period the constable would make an attempt to relieve them, or the king would have leisure to adopt the measures required by the circumstances.

He therefore summoned M. de Théligny, the young lieutenant of the Dauphin's Company.

This officer presented himself immediately. He had done wonders the preceding evening at the Faubourg d'Isle, and yet had escaped without a wound; so that the soldiers, seeing him emerge without a scratch from a fusillade of balls, from the midst of swords and lances, had baptized him *the Invulnerable.*

He approached the admiral, gay and smiling, like a man who has just done his duty, and is ready to do it again. The admiral led him behind the parapet of one of the towers.

"M. de Théligny," he said, "do you see yon Spanish post well from here?"

Théligny made a sign that he saw it perfectly.

"Well, it seems to me it could be easily surprised with thirty or forty troopers. Order out thirty or forty men of your company, put a safe man at their head, and carry that post for me."

"But, M. de Coligny," asked Théligny, smiling, "why should I not be that safe man myself who is to command the sortie? I confess I believe every one of my officers to be a safe man; but I am also pretty certain, for very different reasons, that I am a safe man myself."

The admiral laid a hand on his shoulder.

"My dear Théligny," he said, "men of your character are rare; they ought not, therefore, to be exposed to the risk of falling in a mere skirmish. Give me your word of honor that you will not command this sortie, or I remain on the rampart, half dead with fatigue though I am."

"If that is the case, M. l'Amiral," said Théligny, bowing, "retire, take some repose, and allow me to conduct this enterprise: I pledge you my word not to leave the city gate."

"I count on your word, monsieur," said Coligny, gravely.

Then, as if he wished to have it understood that the gravity of his voice and face was only due to this recommendation not to leave the city—

"As for myself, my dear Théligny," he added, "I do not intend returning to the governor's palace, as it is too far from here; I shall go to M. Jarnac's, throw myself on a bed, and sleep for an hour or two. You'll find me there."

"Rest easy, M. l'Amiral," replied Théligny; "I watch."

The admiral descended the rampart in front of the tower of Guise, and entered into the second house of the Rue de Rémicourt, which was the one inhabited by M. de Jarnac.

Théligny followed him with his eyes; then, turning toward an ensign—

"Thirty or forty men of goodwill of the Company of the Dauphin!" he said.

"You shall have them on the instant, lieutenant!" replied the ensign.

"How can that be? I did not give any order until now."

"It is true; but M. de Coligny's words were caught on the wing by a person who happened to be near you. This person at once ran to the barracks, shouting, 'Dauphins! Dauphins! to battle!'"

"And what sort of a man is this who has so well executed my orders before they were given?"

"By my faith," replied the ensign, laughing, "he looks much more like a devil than a man: the half of his face is covered with a bloody bandage, his hair is burned down to the skull, his cuirass is full of holes before and behind, and his clothes are in rags!"

"Ah! very well," said Théligny; "I know the fellow. You are right; he is not a man, he is a devil!"

"And look, lieutenant, there he is," said the ensign.

And he pointed to a horseman coming at full gallop from the gate of Isle.

It was Malemort, half burned, half drowned, half stunned in the sortie of the evening before, and who, feeling only the better for it all, was insisting on a new sortie.

At the same time, from the opposite side—that is to say, debouching on the Rue du Billon, at the extremity of which was a barracks—a little band of forty horsemen was advancing.

With the activity which distinguished him when there was question of giving or receiving blows, Malemort had found time to run to the quarter, make known the intentions of the admiral, gain the gate of Isle, saddle his horse, and return to the gate of Rémicourt, where he arrived, as we see, at the same time as the horsemen of the Dauphin's Company.

All the return he asked for the zeal and activity he had just displayed was the favor of being allowed to form part of the expedition, and this was granted him.

Moreover, he had declared that if he were not allowed to join the principal sortie, he would make one on his own account; and if the gates were not opened for him, he would jump down from the rampart.

Only Théligny, who knew what he was from having seen him at work the evening before, advised him not to separate from the principal body and to charge in the ranks.

Malemort promised all he was asked to do.

The gate was opened, and the little troop issued forth.

But no sooner was Malemort outside of the gate than he rode in a straight line across the country at a furious gallop, and shouting "Battle!" being carried away by the fury which possessed him, and not being able to restrict himself to the road followed by his companions, which, under cover of trees and from the favorable lay of the ground, was to bring the forty horsemen quite close to the Spanish post.

During this time the admiral, as he had expressed his intention of doing, had retired to the house of M. de Jarnac, and thrown himself on a bed; but, harassed by a sort of presentiment; and, in spite of his fatigue, not being able to sleep, he got up at the end of half an hour, and, thinking he heard cries from the rampart, he seized his sword and scabbard and went out hastily.

He had scarcely taken twenty steps in the Rue de Rémicourt when he saw MM. de Luzarches and de Jarnac running toward him. It was easy guessing from their alarmed appearance that something serious had occurred.

"Ah!" said M. de Jarnac, "you know already?"

"Know what?" asked Coligny.

The two officers looked at each other.

"You did not know," said M. de Luzarches; "why, then, did you come out?"

"I could not sleep; I felt a kind of presentiment. When I heard cries I rose, and so here I am."

"Come, then!"

And the two officers rapidly ascended the rampart with the admiral.

The rampart was thronged with spectators.

This is what had taken place.

The premature attack of Malemort had given the alarm. The Spanish post was more numerous than had been imagined; the soldiers and officers of the Dauphin's Company, who thought they were going to surprise the enemy, found the enemy on horseback, and double their number. At this sight the charge slackened; some horsemen turned rein, the cowardly abandoning the brave. The latter were engaged with forces so superior in numbers that without reinforcements they must give way. Théligny forgot his word pledged to the admiral: with no weapon but his sword, he jumped on the first horse within his reach, dashed through the gate, and called on those who had turned rein not to desert their companions; some of them rallied to him, and with nine or ten men he threw himself into the middle of the Spaniards, hoping to make a diversion.

An instant after, all that was left of the forty troopers was flying toward the city.

Their number was diminished by a third, and M. de Théligny was not with them.

It was then MM. de Jarnac and de Luzarches, judging it necessary to inform the admiral of this new check, had run to the house in which he was supposed to be taking a little rest, and had met him half-way from it.

All three were now on the rampart commanding the theatre of the catastrophe.

Coligny questioned the fugitives; they told him what we have just related.

They could tell nothing certain about M. de Théligny; they had seen him fall on the Spaniards like a thunderbolt, and strike the Spanish officer on the face with his sword; but he was then at once surrounded, and as he did not carry any offensive weapon, he fell at the end of a few seconds, pierced with wounds.

But one soldier insisted that, all weaponless and wounded as M. de Théligny was, that brave officer was still alive, because he saw him make a movement as if to call for help at the moment he was galloping by him.

Although his hope was a feeble one, the admiral ordered the officers of the Dauphin's Company to make an effort, at any risk, to bring back M. de Théligny, dead or alive.

The officers wanted nothing better than the chance of avenging their comrade; they were already making for the barracks, when a sort of Goliath issued from the crowd, and, bearing his hand to his helmet, said—

"Excuse me, Meinherr Admiral; there is no need of a company to find the poor lieutenant. If you like, Meinherr Admiral, I and my nephew Franz will go in search of him, and are sure to bring him back, dead or alive!"

The admiral turned toward the author of this worthy proposal: he was one of those adventurers he had taken into his service without reckoning too much on them, but who, in the few encounters he witnessed them in, had certainly done noble service.

He recognized Heinrich Scharfenstein; four paces behind him Franz was standing, like his shadow, in the same attitude.

He had seen both the evening before, each defending one of the breaches of the Faubourg d'Isle; a glance had been enough to enable him to judge of their value.

"Yes, my brave fellow, I accept. What do you ask for this?"

"I ask a horse for myself, and another for my nephew Franz."

"But that is not what I mean."

"Well, let us see. Yes, I want two men to ride behind us."

"Be it so; what next?"

"Next? That's all. Except it would be well to have the horses fat and the men lean."

"Well, you can choose the men and horses yourself."

"Good!" said Heinrich.

"But I meant about the reward."

"Oh! as for the money part, that's Procope's affair."

"Procope has nothing to do with this," said the admiral. "I promise for Théligny alive, a gratuity of fifty crowns, and for Théligny dead, a gratuity of twenty-five."

"Oh, oh!" said Heinrich, laughing with his big laugh, "I'll search as long as you like at such a price as that!"

"Well, then, go," said the admiral, "and lose no time!"

"At once, Meinherr Admiral! at once!"

And, in fact, Heinrich began at once to select the horses. The ones he preferred were the heavy cavalry animals, stoutly built, vigorous, and solid on their limbs.

Then he began the inspection of men.

Suddenly he uttered an exclamation of joy; he had just perceived Lactance on one side, and Fracasso on the other. A pentient and a poet were the two leanest things Heinrich knew in the world.

The admiral did not know what to think of all these preparations; but he felt he might rely, if not on the intelligence, at least on the instinct of the two giants. The four adventurers descended the talus of the rampart, disappeared under the vault of the gate of Rémicourt; then, a moment after, the gate being opened for them, they reappeared, two on each horse, but taking all the precautions as to shade and shelter possible—advantages neglected by Malemort.

Then they were lost behind a little eminence rising to the right of the mill of La Couture.

It would be impossible to express the interest that attached to this expedition of four men going to dispute a dead body with a whole army, for the opinion of the least pessimistic was now that Théligny must be really dead.

So that the silence observed by the three or four hundred persons packed on the rampart as long as the four adventurers were in sight continued after they disappeared behind the hill.

It almost looked as if this crowd feared, by a word, by a breath, by a movement, to awaken the watchfulness of the enemy.

At the end of an instant a volley was heard from eight or ten arquebuses.

Every heart gave a bound.

Almost at the same moment Franz Scharfenstein reappeared, carrying, not a man, but two men, in his arms.

Behind him the cavalry and infantry of the expedition was defending the retreat.

The cavalry was composed only of a horse and a man; doubtless, one of the two horses had been slain by the discharge they had just heard.

The infantry consisted of Fracasso and Lactance, each armed with an arquebuse.

Eight or ten Spanish troopers harassed the retreat. But when the infantry was too closely pressed, Heinrich made a charge and saved it by the terrible blows he dealt with his club; on the other hand, if it was the cavalry that was too closely pressed, two shots fired from two arquebuses with remarkable symmetry and unity, laid two Spaniards low, and gave Heinrich time to breathe.

However, Franz was gaining ground, and in a few seconds, thanks to his enormous strides, he found himself beyond the reach of all pursuit.

There was a cry of joy and admiration when he began climbing the talus, bearing in his arms these two bodies, living men or corpses, as a nurse would have borne two children.

He laid one half of his burden at the feet of the admiral.

"That is yours," he said; "he is not quite dead."

"And the other?" he said, pointing to the second wounded man.

"Oh, the other," said Franz, "doesn't matter. It's Malemort. He'll be himself in a minute. He is the devil himself; nothing can kill him."

And he laughed that laugh peculiar to uncle and nephew, which might have been called the laugh of the Scharfensteins.

At this moment, the three other adventurers, cavalry and infantry, amid wild cheering, entered the city.

Théligny, as Franz Scharfenstein said, was not yet dead, although pierced by seven sword-thrusts and three balls. His condition was easily seen, the Spaniards having stripped him to his shirt and left him where he fell, being quite certain he would never rise again.

He was carried immediately to M. de Jarnac's, and laid on the bed, where the admiral an hour before had not been able to rest, being disturbed by a presentiment of what had happened.

There, as if the wounded man had only waited for this moment, he opened his eyes, looked around him, and recognized the admiral.

"A doctor! a doctor!" cried Coligny, quickly, grasping at a hope which he had entirely given up until now; but Théligny stretched out his hand to him—

"Thanks, M. l'Amiral," he said; "God permits me to open my eyes once more and recover my voice in order to ask you very humbly to pardon me for having disobeyed you."

The admiral stopped him.

"Ah, my dear Théligny," said he, "it is not for you to ask my pardon, for if you have disobeyed me, it has been through excessive zeal for the king's service; but if you are as bad as you think, and if you have anything to ask, ask it of God."

"Oh, monsieur!" said Théligny, "I have happily to ask pardon of God only for those faults which a gentleman may confess; while by disobeying you I have committed a grave offence against discipline. Forgive me then, M. l'Amiral, so that I may die tranquil."

M. de Coligny, a warm appreciator of all true courage, felt the tears coming to his eyes on hearing this young officer, who was on the point of abandoning a life so full of fair promise, apparently only troubled by a moment's forgetfulness of the orders of his general.

"Since you insist on it," he said, "I pardon you a fault of which every brave soldier ought to be proud, and if this alone disturbs your last hour, die tranquilly and in peace, as died the Chevalier Bayard, the model of us all!"

And he bent down to imprint a kiss on the pale brow of the dying young soldier.

The latter made an effort, and rose.

The lips of the admiral touched the forehead of the young officer, who murmured—

"Thanks!"

And he fell back, breathing a sigh.

It was his last.

"Gentlemen," said Coligny, wiping away a tear, and addressing those who surrounded him, "there is a brave soldier the less in the world. May God grant us all such a death!"

XI

THE AWAKING OF M. LE CONNÉTABLE

GLORIOUS as had been the two checks encountered by the admiral, they were not the less checks, and showed him the absolute necessity of being promptly reinforced in face of such a numerous army and such active vigilance.

Consequently he took advantage of the fact that the absence of the English army still left one entire side of the city free to send messengers to his uncle, the constable, in order to obtain the largest reinforcements possible. For this purpose he summoned Maldent and Yvonnet to his presence—Yvonnet, who had been the guide of poor Théligny, and Maldent, who had been his own guide.

The constable must be either at Ham or at La Fère; one of the two messengers would therefore go to Ham, the other to La Fère, to carry news to the constable and point out the best means of succoring Saint-Quentin.

This means, which the absence of the English army rendered easy, consisted simply in despatching a strong column by the Savy highway, which terminates at the Faubourg Ponthoille; while as soon as it made its appearance, Coligny would make a sortie from the opposite side of the city and keep the attention of the enemy engaged until the advancing column made its way safely into Saint-Quentin.

The two messengers started the same evening, bearing each a pressing request, the one on the part of Malemort, the other on that of the despairing Gudule.

Malemort had received a sword-thrust in his side; luckily it had passed through an old scar—a thing which almost always happened to him, for there was hardly a part of his body that did not show a cicatrice. Malemort entreated his comrade to bring back with him certain herbs absolutely necessary for the renewal of that famous balm of Ferragus, of which he consumed such awful quantities.

Gudule, who had received through the heart a thrust in a certain sense more painful and deadly than that of Malemort, recommended Yvonnet to watch with the greatest care over a life with which hers was bound up. While waiting for the return of her beloved Yvonnet, she would pass all her nights at her window looking out upon the rampart of the Vieux-Marché.

Our two adventurers left through the gate of Ponthoille; then, when they had travelled together nearly half a league on the road to Ham, Yvonnet struck across the country to reach the road to La Fère, while Maldent continued on that of Ham.

Yvonnet passed the Somme between Gauchy and Gruois, and got on the La Fère route at Cérisy.

As it is at La Fère the constable is staying, we shall follow Yvonnet rather than Maldent.

At three in the morning, Yvonnet knocked at the gate of the city, which refused obstinately to open; however, the porter, learning that a night visitor had arrived from Saint-Quentin, at last drew it back sufficiently to let him slip through.

The order had been given by the constable to admit without delay any messenger coming from his nephew, and bring him before him, whatever the hour might be.

At half-past three in the morning, the constable was roused from slumber.

The old soldier was lying in a bed—a luxury he rarely allowed himself during a campaign; but he had under the pillow his constable's sword, and on a chair close to the bed, his armor and helmet; which indicated that on the slightest alarm he would be able to attack an enemy or defend himself.

Those who served under him were, moreover, accustomed to be summoned at all hours of the day or night, either to give their opinion or to receive his orders.

Yvonnet was received into the chamber of the indefatigable old man, who, knowing a messenger had arrived, was waiting for this messenger, half raised up and leaning on his elbow.

Hardly did he hear the footsteps of Yvonnet than, with his ordinary brutality, he said—

"Come forward here at once, rascal!"

It was not a time for the display of tender sensibilities. Yvonnet came forward.

"Closer, closer," said the constable, "until I see the whites of your eyes, knave! I like to look at those I am speaking to."

Yvonnet advanced to the side of the bed.

"Here I am, monseigneur," said he.

"Ah! there you are; how fortunate!"

He took his lamp and gazed on the adventurer with an expression that did not show the inspection was favorable.

"I have seen that sharper's face somewhere already," said the constable, speaking to himself.

Then to Yvonnet—

"Are you going to give me the trouble of finding out where I have met you, rascal? Come, tell me at once; you must remember."

"And why should I remember better than you, monseigneur?" not being able to resist the temptation of addressing a question in his turn to the constable.

"Because," replied the old soldier, "you see a constable of France by chance once in your life, while I see every day a heap of rogues like you."

"You are correct, monseigneur," replied Yvonnet. "Well, you saw me in presence of the king."

"What!" said the constable; "in presence of the king? You visit the king, then, villain?"

"I have done so at least on the day I had the honor of seeing you there, M. le Connétable," answered Yvonnet, with the most exquisite politeness.

"Hum!" muttered the constable. "In fact, I remember; you were with a young officer whom my nephew sent to the king."

"With M. de Théligny."

"That's so," said the constable. "And are things going on all right yonder?"

"On the contrary, M. le Connétable, things are going all wrong."

"How all wrong? Take care of what you say, rascal!"

"I am about to say the truth, monseigneur. The day before yesterday we had, after a sortie at the Faubourg d'Isle, about sixty men placed *hors de combat.* Yesterday, in trying to carry a Spanish position in front of the Rémicourt gate, we lost fifteen troopers of the Dauphin's Company and their lieutenant, M. de Théligny—"

"Théligny!" interrupted the constable, who believed himself invulnerable, after surviving so many engagements, battles and skirmishes. "Théligny let himself be killed? The fool! What next?"

"The next, M. le Connétable, is a letter from M. l'Amiral, asking speedy succor."

"You should have begun with that, knave!" said the constable, tearing the letter out of the hand of the adventurer.

And he read it, all the time interrupting himself to give orders, as was his habit—

" 'I shall hold the Faubourg d'Isle as long as I can—'

"And he will do well, *mordieu!* Some one send me M. Dandelot!

" '— for from the heights of the faubourg a battery of artillery can sweep the Rémicourt rampart its entire length, from the Tower à l'Eau to the Red Tower.'

"Tell Maréchal de Saint-André to come here!

" 'But in order to defend the Faubourg d'Isle and the other points threatened, I shall need a reinforcement of two thousand men at least, having in reality but five or six hundred under my orders.'

"*Corbleu!* he must have four thousand! I wish to see the Duc d'Enghien at once! By what right do these gentlemen sleep when I am awake? M. d'Enghien immediately! Let us see what my nephew has to say further!

" 'I have only sixteen pieces of cannon and forty cannoniers; I have only fifty or sixty arquebuses; finally, I have only ammunition for a fortnight and provisions for three weeks.'

"How! is all this true?" cried the constable.

"The exact truth every word, monseigneur," replied Yvonnet, graciously.

"Indeed! I should like to see a scoundrel of your kind give the lie to my nephew. Hum!"

And the constable glared ferociously on Yvonnet.

Yvonnet bowed and took a step backward.

"Why do you step back?" asked the constable.

"Because I think monseigneur has no more questions to ask me."

"You are mistaken. Come here!"

Yvonnet resumed his place.

"How do the bourgeois conduct themselves?" asked the constable.

"Most excellently, monseigneur."

"The rascals! I should like to see them do otherwise!"

"Even the very monks have taken up arms."

"The hypocrites! And you say they fight?"

"Like lions. And as to the women, monseigneur—"

"They whine and weep and tremble, eh? It is all the jades are good for."

"On the contrary, monseigneur, they encourage the combatants, nurse the wounded, and bury the dead."

"The trollops!"

At this moment the door opened, and a gentleman all armed, except his head, which was covered with a velvet cap, made his appearance on the threshold.

"Ah, come here, M. Dandelot!" said the constable. "Here is your brother making such an outcry in his city of Saint-Quentin that one would think somebody was going to cut his throat."

"Monseigneur," said M. Dandelot, laughing, "if your nephew, my brother, is making such an outcry, you know him well enough to be sure it is not from fear."

"Oh, yes, *morbleu!* I know something is wrong, and that's what annoys me. So I have summoned you and M. le Maréchal de Saint-André."

"Here I am, monseigneur," interrupted the marshal, appearing in turn at the entrance to the room.

"Good, good, marshal; but M. d'Enghien is apparently not coming."

"Excuse me, monseigneur," said the duke, entering; "here I am."

"*Tripes et boyaux*, messieurs!" said the constable, hurling his rough oath the more violently at them because, as all seemed to be performing their duty, he had no excuse for gratifying the habitual ill-humor that formed the basis of his character; "*tripes et boyaux*, gentlemen, we are not in Capua, to sleep as if nothing was the matter!"

"The accusation does not touch me," said the marshal, "for I have been up already."

"And I," said the Duc d'Enghien, "have not yet been to bed."

"No; I was speaking of M. Dandelot."

"Of me!" said Dandelot; "pardon me, monseigneur; I have been making the rounds, and have been here before these gentlemen. I was on horseback when I met them, and have come here on horseback."

"Then I suppose I must be speaking of myself," said Montmorency. "It seems I am now old and good for nothing, since I am the only one who has been in bed. *Tête et sang!*"

"But, constable," returned Dandelot, laughing, "who the devil has said such a thing?"

"No one, I hope; for I would break his jaw, as I broke the jaw of that ill-omened prophet I met on the highway the other day. But we have something else to attend to. We have to see how we can help this poor Coligny who has fifty thousand men pegging away at him. Fifty thousand men! What do you say to it? In my opinion, my nephew is afraid and sees double."

The three officers smiled at the same time and with the same expression.

"If my brother says fifty thousand men," said Dandelot, "there are fifty thousand men, monseigneur."

"And more likely sixty thousand than fifty thousand," said the marshal.

"And what do you think, M. d'Enghien?"

"Of course the same as those gentlemen do, M. le Connétable."

"Then you are as usual of an opinion directly opposed to mine?"

"No, monseigneur," replied Dandelot; "but we are of the opinion that the admiral tells the truth."

"Well, are you ready to run some risk to help the admiral?"

"I am ready to risk my life," answered Dandelot.

"And we also," replied the Maréchal de Saint-André and the Duc d'Enghien in the same tone.

"Then all is well," said the constable.

After this, turning round toward the antechamber, in which there was a great noise—

"*Corbleu!*" he exclaimed, "where does all that racket come from?"

"Monseigneur," said one of the sub-officers of the guard, "it is a man who has just been arrested at the gate of Ham."

"Off with him to prison, then!"

"It is thought he is a soldier disguised as a peasant."

"Have him hanged!"

"But he appeals to M. l'Amiral, and says he has come from him."

"Has he a letter or safe-conduct?"

"No, and that is why we thought he might be a spy."

"Let him be broken on the wheel!"

"An instant!" cried a voice in the antechamber; "even M. le Connétable cannot break people on the wheel in that fashion."

And after some clamor and a noise indicating there had been a struggle, a man rushed from the antechamber into the room.

"Ah!" cried Yvonnet, "take care of what you do, monseigneur; it is Maldent."

"Maldent; what has that to do with it?" asked the constable.

"It is the second messenger sent by M. l'Amiral, and who, having set out from Saint-Quentin at the same time as I, arrives naturally two hours after me, having come by Ham."

And in fact it was Maldent, who, not finding the constable at Ham, had taken a horse and galloped to La Fère, fearing that some obstacle might have stopped Yvonnet on the road.

Now how was it that Maldent, who had started dressed as a soldier, and with a letter from the admiral, arrived dressed as a peasant and without a letter? It is a problem which our readers, with their customary perspicacity, will be able to solve in one of the following chapters.

XII

THE ESCALADE

LET our readers not be surprised at seeing us follow, with a minuteness belonging to the historian rather than to the romancer, all the details, every point in the attack and defence, of that glorious siege of Saint-Quentin — a siege equally glorious for besieger and besieged.

Moreover, in our opinion, the glory of a country is made up of its defeats quite as much as of its victories; the glory of our triumphs is enhanced by that of our reverses.

What people, in fact, would not have succumbed after Crécy, Poitiers, Agincourt, Pavia, Saint-Quentin, or Waterloo? But the hand of God was over France, and after each fall France rose greater than she was before.

It was after bending eight times under his cross that Jesus saved the world.

France, under this relation, may be considered, if we are permitted to say so, the Christ of nations.

Saint-Quentin is nevertheless one of the stations on her way of the cross.

Her cross was the monarchy.

Happily behind the monarchy was the people.

This time again, behind the fallen monarchy, we are about to see the people standing.

During the night following the departure of Yvonnet and Maldent, the admiral was warned that the sentinels mounting guard at the Faubourg d'Isle believed they heard the sound of sappers at work.

Coligny rose and ran to the threatened point.

The admiral was an experienced captain. He leaped from his horse, lay down on the rampart, placed his ear to the ground, and listened.

Then, rising—

"It is not," he said, "the noise of sappers; it is the rolling of cannon. The enemy is about to erect a battery against us."

The officers looked at one another.

Then Jarnac advanced and said—

"You know, M. l'Amiral, that it is the opinion of every one the place is not tenable?"

The admiral smiled.

"It is mine also, gentlemen," said he; "and yet, you see, we have held it for the last five days. If, when urged by you, I had retreated, the Faubourg d'Isle would have been in the hands of the Spaniards for the last five days, and all their preparations for attacking the city on this side completed. Now let us not forget this, gentlemen: every day gained is as useful to us as are the last breathing spells to the stag pursued by the hunters."

"Then your opinion is, monseigneur?"

"My opinion is that we have done on this side all that it is humanly possible to do, and that we must carry in another direction our energy, devotion, and vigilance."

The officers acquiesced with a bow.

"At daybreak," continued Coligny, "the Spanish cannon will be formed in battery, and the firing will begin; at daybreak, therefore, all the artillery we have here, as well as all the ammunition, balls, bales of wool, carts, handbarrows, pickaxes, and pioneers' tools, must be in the city.

One part of our men will attend to this; another will pile up fagots and fascines in the houses, and set them on fire; I shall myself protect the retreat of our soldiers and cut the bridges behind them."

Then when he saw around him the poor unfortunates to whom these houses belonged, and who were listening to him with an expression of despair—

"My friends," said he, "if your houses were spared by us, they would be demolished by the Spaniards, who would use the wood and stone for constructing masks and digging their trenches; sacrifice them, therefore, in the name of your king and country. I assign to you the task of setting them on fire."

The inhabitants of the Faubourg d'Isle looked at one another, exchanged some words in a low tone, and one of them, advancing, said—

"M. l'Amiral, my name is Guillaume Pauquet; you see my house from here. It is the largest in the quarter. I shall set fire to it with my own hands; and my neighbors and friends, here present, are prepared to do to theirs what I am about to do to mine."

"Is this true, my children?" said the admiral, with tears in his eyes.

"Is what you demand for the good of the king and country, M. l'Amiral?"

"If we can only hold out for a fortnight, my friends, France is saved!" said Coligny.

"And to hold out even for ten days, must we burn our houses?"

"I believe, my friends, it is necessary."

"Then, if the houses are burned, you promise to hold out for ten days?"

"I promise, my friends, to do all that a gentleman devoted to my king and country can do," said the admiral. "Whoever speaks of surrender shall be thrown over the walls by me; and if I speak of surrender, do the same to me."

"It is well, M. l'Amiral," said one of the inhabitants of the faubourg; "since you order us to burn our houses, we are going to set them on fire."

"But," said a voice, "I hope the abbey of Saint-Quentin-en-Isle may be spared."

The admiral turned in the direction of the voice, and recognized Lactance.

"Saint-Quentin-en-Isle less than all the rest," answered the admiral. "The rampart of Rémicourt is commanded from the platform of Saint-Quentin-en-Isle; and a battery of cannon established there would render the defence of the rampart impossible."

Lactance raised his eyes to heaven, and heaved a profound sigh.

"Besides," continued the admiral, smiling. "Saint-Quentin is, above all, guardian of the city, and he will not take umbrage at our ruining his abbey to save his clients."

Then, taking advantage of this moment of goodwill which seemed to inspire all and each with the same devotion, he ordered the cannon to be drawn to the city, as well as the different objects mentioned by him, and everything to be done in the greatest possible silence.

This work was begun with as much zeal, it must be said, as was displayed by those carrying fascines into their houses; men harnessed themselves cheerfully and courageously to the cannon and carts, and set to work hauling them into the city.

At two in the morning all was finished; and there remained behind the old wall only the number of arquebusiers necessary to deceive the enemy into the belief that it was still defended, and the men who, with torch in hand, were ready to set fire to their houses.

At daybreak, as the admiral had foreseen, the enemy fired the first volley. A breaching battery had been established during the night, and it was the noise made by the men forming it the admiral had heard.

This first volley was the signal agreed on for setting fire to the houses. Not one of the inhabitants hesitated; each applied his torch, and in a moment a curtain of smoke rose in the sky, soon to be succeeded by a curtain of flame.

The faubourg was burning from the church of Saint-Eloi to the church of Saint-Pierre-au-Canal; but in the midst of this immense furnace, the abbey of Saint-Quentin remained intact, as if some superhuman power had turned the conflagration aside from it.

Three times did citizens and soldiers and workmen, through fire, and over the flying bridges—for the others had been cut down—renew the attempt to destroy it, and three times did the attempt fail.

The admiral from the top of the gate of Isle was watching the progress of the flames, when Jean Pauquet, separating from those around him and approaching the admiral with his woollen cap in his hand, said—

"Monseigneur, an old man of the city says he has heard his father tell of a storehouse of powder existing in one of the two towers flanking the gate of Isle, if not in both."

"Good!" said the admiral, "we must see to this. Where are the keys?"

"Ah, the keys!" said Jean Pauquet, "who can know anything about them? The doors have not been opened for the last hundred years, perhaps."

"Then we must get levers and crowbars to open them."

"They are not needed," said a voice; "let me drive against the door, and the door will open."

And Heinrich Scharfenstein, followed by his nephew Franz, advanced three steps toward Coligny.

"Ah, it is you, my brave giant?" said the admiral.

"Yes, I and my nephew Franz."

"Well, push, my friend! push!" And the two Scharfensteins approached each a folding-door, buttressed himself against it, and with the same mechanical action and the same movement, counted:

"*Ein! zwei! drei!*"

And at the word *drei*, each, making a mighty effort, drove in the leaf he was planted against, and so successfully that each fell with it.

Only as the resistance offered by the doors was different, Franz fell headlong his whole length, while Heinrich was lucky enough to fall on his hips.

But both rose up with their customary gravity, saying—"Now!"

They entered the towers.

One of them, as Jean Pauquet had stated, did in fact contain two or three thousand pounds of powder; but, as he had also said, this powder had been there so long that when the kegs were lifted they fell into dust.

The admiral then ordered sheets to be brought and the powder to be transported to the arsenal.

As soon as he saw the order was being executed, he returned to breakfast and to get a little rest, having been on his feet since midnight, and eaten nothing since the evening before.

He had just sat down to table when it was announced that one of the messengers sent by him to the constable had returned and asked to speak to him without delay.

It was Yvonnet.

Yvonnet announced that the succors demanded by him would arrive the next day, under the command of M. Dandelot, Maréchal de Saint-André and the Duc d'Enghien.

They were to consist of four thousand foot-soldiers, who would follow the Savy route, as the admiral suggested, and enter by the Faubourg de Ponthoille.

Maldent had remained at La Fère to act as guide to M. Dandelot.

Yvonnet was at this stage of his recital and had raised a glass of wine poured out for him to drink to the health of the admiral, when all at once the earth trembled, the walls shook, the glass of the windows flew in pieces, and a roar was heard like that of a hundred pieces of cannon discharged at the same time.

The admiral rose; Yvonnet, seized with one of his nervous movements, rested his glass, still full, on the table.

At the same time a cloud passed over the city, borne by the west wind, and a strong stench of sulphur spread into the room through the broken glass.

"Oh, the unhappy men!" cried the admiral; "they did not take the proper precautions, and the powder has blown up!"

Immediately, without waiting for news, he left the house and ran to the gate of Isle.

All the population was hurrying to the same quarter; it was useless for Coligny to make inquiries; these people were hurrying in the direction of the noise, but were ignorant of its cause.

Coligny was not mistaken; the interior of the tower was gutted and smoking like the crater of a volcano. A spark from the immense conflagration in the neighborhood had entered through an embrasure, and set fire to the terrible combustible.

Forty or fifty persons had perished; five officers had disappeared.

The tower offered a breach to the enemy by which twenty-five assailants could mount in a line.

Fortunately, the veil of smoke and flame between the faubourg and city concealed this breach from the Spaniards. The devotion of the inhabitants, who had set fire to their houses, had then saved the city.

Coligny understood the danger: he appealed to the good-will of all; but the bourgeois alone responded. The soldiers who had been withdrawn from the faubourg had gone away to rest and refresh themselves.

Among those who had done so were the two Scharfensteins; but as their tent was only about fifty yards from the theatre of the event, they were among the first to answer the appeal of the admiral.

Two precious auxiliaries were uncle Heinrich and nephew Franz under the circumstances; their herculean strength, their gigantic stature, made them fit for everything. They took off their jackets, turned up their sleeves, and became masons.

Three hours after, whether it were that the enemy knew nothing of what had occurred or was preparing another enterprise, the tower was repaired without any opposition and rendered almost as solid as before.

All that day—it was the 7th of August—passed without the enemy making the slightest demonstration; he seemed to confine himself to a simple blockade. Without doubt, he was awaiting the arrival of the English army.

During the evening, the sentinels noticed some movement in the direction of the Faubourg d'Isle.

The Spaniards of Carondelet and Julian Romeron, taking advantage of the dying out of the conflagration, were beginning to appear in the faubourg and draw near the city.

Thereupon all the watchfulness of the besieged was exercised on that side.

In the evening at ten, the admiral called a council of the chief officers of the garrison; he announced that the expected reinforcement would, in all probability, arrive that night. The wall must be secretly manned from Tourival to the gate of Ponthoille, in order to hold themselves in readiness to bring aid, if necessary, to Dandelot and his men.

Yvonnet, who, in his capacity as messenger, had been initiated into all these arrangements, was delighted with them, and as far as lay in his power—for his peculiar knowledge of certain localities gave him considerable influence—he pushed his nocturnal investigations in the direction of the Rémicourt, Isle and Ponthoille gates.

This new disposition, in fact, left the rampart of the Vieux-Marché entirely free from troops, except a few sentinels; and it was there, as the reader will recall, that the house of Jean Pauquet was situated, and especially the little pavilion inhabited by Mademoiselle Gudule.

Consequently, about eleven, on one of those gloomy nights so esteemed and blessed by lovers on the way to their mistresses, and by warriors preparing a surprise, our adventurer, followed by Heinrich and Franz, armed, like him, to the teeth, was advancing cautiously through the Rue des Rosiers, de la Fosse, and de Saint-Jean, which latter connects—at about a hundred yards from the tower Dameuse—with the rampart of the Vieux-Marché.

The three adventurers followed this road because they knew all the space extending between the tower Dameuse and the gate of the Vieux-Marché was free from sentinels, the enemy not having yet made any demonstration on this side.

The boulevard was therefore gloomy and deserted.

Why was this band, which, in spite of its formidable appearance, had not any hostile appearance, composed of Heinrich and Franz on the one side and of Yvonnet on the other?

By that natural law which decrees that in this world weakness must seek strength, and strength must love weakness.

With whom, among his eight companions, was Yvonnet most closely united? With Heinrich and Franz. Why? Because they were the strongest, and he was the weakest.

As soon as the two Scharfensteins had a moment to themselves, whose society did they run to seek?

Yvonnet's.

Consequently, when Yvonnet needed help, whose help did he seek?

That of the two Scharfensteins.

Under his garb, always so carefully attended to, always so elegant and dainty, and contrasting so strangely with the rough, soldierly dress of the two giants, Yvonnet, when followed by them, resembled some aristocratic child holding two mastiffs in leash.

It was, as we have said, because of this attraction of weakness for strength, and this sympathy of strength for weakness, that on this very evening, Yvonnet asked the two Scharfensteins to come along with him, and that the latter, as usual, answered, as they rose and armed themselves—

"Very willingly, Meinherr Yvonnet."

For the two Scharfensteins addressed Yvonnet as *Meinherr*—a distinction they did not grant to any other of their companions.

It was because their affection for Yvonnet was mingled with a profound respect.

Never did uncle or nephew presume to speak first in the presence of the young adventurer; no, they heard him talk of fine women, fine arms, fine dress, satisfied to give a nod of assent, or breaking into one of their big laughs, when an evident witticism claimed such attention.

Where Yvonnet was going when Yvonnet said, "Come with me!" concerned them little; he said, "Come!" that was enough, and they followed this charming star of their fancy as satellites follow a planet.

This evening, Yvonnet was going to his mistress; he had said to the two Scharfensteins, "Come!" and, as we see, they came.

But with what object, since the presence of a third party at such a rendezvous is always annoying, did Yvonnet ask for the company of the two giants?

In the first place, let us hasten to say that the brave Germans were not troublesome witnesses. They closed one eye, they closed two, they closed three, they closed four, on a word, a sign, a gesture from their comrade, and kept them religiously closed until a word, a sign, or a gesture of their comrade allowed them to open them.

Yvonnet brought them with him because, it will be remembered, to reach the window of Gudule's pavilion he needed a ladder; and, instead of taking a ladder, he found it simpler to take the two Scharfensteins, which absolutely amounted to the same thing.

The young man had, as may be imagined, a collection of signals, sounds and cries, by the aid of which he announced his arrival to his mistress; but this evening he needed not signal nor sound nor cry—Gudule was at her window, expecting him.

Nevertheless, when she saw three men coming instead of one, she prudently retreated.

But when Yvonnet separated from his companions, he was recognized; and the young girl, still trembling, but no longer frightened, came back to the window.

Yvonnet explained in two words the danger a soldier ran in a besieged city walking with a ladder on his back; a patrol might believe he carried the ladder with the view of communicating with the besiegers. Once such a belief settled in the mind of the patrol, it would be necessary to have explanations with the patrol's officer, with the captain, perhaps with the governor, and account for the destination of the ladder; now, however delicately these explanations might be managed, the honor of Mademoiselle Gudule would be compromised.

It was better, then, to bring two sure friends, on whose discretion he could rely, like his two comrades.

But how would these friends take the place of a ladder? This Mademoiselle Gudule had some trouble in understanding.

Yvonnet resolved to lose no time in developing his theory, but to proceed at once to a demonstration. With this object, he called the two Scharfensteins, who, opening the immense compass of their legs, were beside him in three strides.

Then he backed up the uncle against the wall, and made a sign to the nephew.

In less time than it takes to relate it, Franz placed one foot between the joined hands of his uncle and another on his shoulder; then, having reached the top of the window, he took Mademoiselle Gudule by the waist, she regarding him with much curiosity all the time; and before she could make a motion to defend herself—a motion she would perhaps not have made, even if she had time for it—she found herself borne from her chamber and placed on the boulevard beside Yvonnet.

"There," said Franz, laughing, "there you have the young woman you asked for."

"Thanks," said Yvonnet.

And, drawing the arm of the young woman within his own, he led her to the obscurest part of the rampart.

This was the circular summit of one of the towers, and protected by a parapet three feet high.

The two Scharfensteins sat down on a stone bench lying along the curtain.

It is not our intention to relate here the conversation of Mademoiselle Gudule and Yvonnet. They were young, and in love; they had not met for three nights and three days, and had so much to say that a report of their quarter of an hour's discourse would certainly exceed the limits of this chapter.

We say a quarter of an hour's, because at the end of a quarter of an hour, notwithstanding the animation of the dialogue, Yvonnet suddenly stopped, placed his hand on the pretty mouth of the young girl, leaned forward, and listened.

A sound like that made by the steady tramp of a great number of feet on the turf seemed to come to his ear as he listened.

Looking forward, he thought he saw an immense black serpent creeping up to the wall.

But the night was so dark and the noise so imperceptible that all this might be an illusion as well as a reality, especially as the sound and movement suddenly stopped.

Yvonnet looked and listened, but neither saw nor heard anything more.

Yet while holding the young girl clasped to his breast, he kept his eyes eagerly fixed on the point to which they were first directed, and stretched his neck out between the battlements.

Soon he thought he saw the gigantic serpent raise its head against the gray wall, and rise along this wall, as if to reach the parapet of the curtain.

Then, like a hydra-headed monster, the serpent darted out a second head near the first, and a third near the second.

Upon this all became clear to Yvonnet; without losing a minute, he took Gudule in his arms, and, recommending her to be silent, passed her to Franz, who, with the aid of his uncle, restored her to her chamber in the same manner in which she had been carried out of it.

Then, running to the nearest ladder, the young man reached it just as the first Spaniard stood upon the parapet of the curtain.

Great as was the darkness, a gleam of light could be seen through the shadow; next a cry was heard, and the Spaniard, pierced by the slender sword of Yvonnet, fell backward from the wall.

The noise of his fall was lost in a frightful crash; it was the second ladder laden with men, which, hurled back by the sinewy arm of Heinrich, tore along the wall with a hoarse, grating sound.

On his side, Franz discovered an abandoned beam in his path; and, raising it above his head, he let it fall on the very centre of the third ladder.

The ladder was broken at a place above two-thirds of its height from the ground; and men, ladder, and beam were pitched pellmell into the fosse.

Meanwhile Yvonnet, while striking with all his might, was at the same time shouting as loudly as he could—

"To arms! to arms!"

The two Scharfensteins ran to his aid, at the very moment two or three Spaniards had set foot on the rampart and were pressing him closely.

One of the assailants fell cloven by the enormous sword of Heinrich; another rolled senseless under the mace of Franz; the other, as he was making ready to strike Yvonnet, was seized by the waist by one of the two giants, and hurled over the wall.

At the same moment Jean and Guillaume Pauquet appeared at the extremity of the Rue du Vieux-Marché, attracted by the cries of the three adventurers, and bearing each a torch in one hand and an axe in the other.

From that moment the surprise was a failure; and in response to the united cries of the bourgeois and the adventurers, succors arrived both from the Saint-Jean tower and the big tower bordering on the Faubourg Ponthoille.

Then at the same time, and as if all these attacks had been part of one general movement, and arranged to break out together, the detonation of a thousand arquebuses was heard half a league away in the plain, in the direction of Savy, behind the chapel of Epargnemaille; and between the earth and the sky arose that reddish cloud which hovers above a lively fusillade.

The two enterprises—that of the Spaniards to surprise the city, and that of Dandelot to succor it—had both failed.

We have seen how chance caused the failure of that of the Spaniards; we must now tell how this same chance caused the failure of that of the French.

"THE PAGE OF THE DUKE OF SAVOY"
END OF PART ONE

www.ingramcontent.com/pod-product-compliance
Lightning Source LLC
Chambersburg PA
CBHW031250230426
43670CB00005B/114